Eat Your Heart Out, Ho Chi Minh

Or
Things You Won't Learn at Yale

Tony   Thomson

ISBN: 146638901X
ISBN 13: 9781466389014

Memoir: "A record of events, a history treating of matters from the personal knowledge of the writer or with reference to particular sources of information." 1659

Shorter Oxford Dictionary

Introduction

The Vietnam War lay squarely across my path to adulthood.

The era of the Vietnam War turned the United States from the smug, self-satisfied, white-dominated society of my youth into the anxious, dissatisfied, diverse society of today. We tried to change Vietnam. Instead, Vietnam changed us.

This is the story of that period of change as I experienced it. My purpose, though, is to tell a broader story to a wider audience; an audience of those interested in why the United States is the way it is and why we fight so bitterly with each other.

In September 1963, I was kicked out of Yale University.

Knowing that I would soon be drafted, I immediately enlisted for three years in the U.S. Army. The United States was at peace and had been since the end of the Korean War. Serving in the army did not seem life-threatening.

My entire youth had been spent in a pleasant enough world, full of expanding possibilities for people like me. True, some neurotic, fearful adults worried about nuclear war, but for most white suburban

American kids this was a remote, unlikely horror, like getting juvenile cancer or being run over by a bus.

The Yale I left in September 1963 was similar to the Yale I'd entered in September 1960. Yale undergraduates were almost all white males. There were no women undergraduates. Over half of my class was from private schools.

We prided ourselves, as bright young men always do, on being original, but in appearance we were homogenized. We were buttoned-down of shirt; we wore jackets and ties for any sort of vaguely formal occasion without being told to, and our hair was generally short.

In our thinking, we were also much of a muchness. These thoughts included the assumption that most of us would serve in the U.S. military in some form.

In September 1966, I returned to Yale for my senior year after three years in the U.S. Army as an ordinary soldier. The army I left was fighting hard in Vietnam.

Yalies, it transpired, also wanted to fight someone. They simply weren't sure whether they wanted to fight the American army or Washington, D.C. or a selection of their fellow citizens—or with all of these. By 1968 these tensions—and contradictions—would explode.

I'd come directly from my own year of war in Vietnam. I hadn't spent more than a brief period in the United States since 1963.

The Yale I rejoined had socially changed out of all recognition. Not only was the place seething with unrest, most of my new classmates appeared to be Quaker postulants. Instead of finding myself surrounded with would-be corporate lawyers or their equivalents, I was among Gandhi wannabes.

These wild-haired young men proclaimed a passionate refusal to serve in the U.S. military because of their newfound hatred of war. Or because of a burning moral objection to the particular war that America was involved in. Or because of cowardice.

This newfound pacifism was highly selective. These emotionally agitated youths failed to qualify as true Quakers. They were not only in favor of the United States experiencing a bloody defeat in Vietnam, but they also proclaimed a loud enthusiasm for liberating our black—then called Negro—fellow citizens by whatever means necessary, up to and including generous doses of violence on the home front.

Of course, much of this was just talk. Most of the Yale Class of 1967 predictably became big-shot lawyers or doctors or the professional equivalent. But the social atmosphere at Yale and in the country was permanently transformed. Many Americans dislike or distrust each other today because of events that occurred then, even if they are too young or too ill-informed to make the connection.

What happened?

One easy—and partially true—answer is that the Vietnam War shook American society to its very foundations. However, in 1966 the worst of the Vietnam War still lay ahead. Most soldiers who served in Vietnam that year were volunteers like me, not draftees. Suburban white families had little direct contact with the fighting up to that time.

Other upheavals were already taking place, jolting the public mind out of its cozy rut of the 1950s.

Perhaps the election of John Kennedy and his assassination profoundly changed the United States. After all, he was the first Catholic president and the first young president in most people's lifetimes. All college students knew JFK's inaugural slogan, "Ask not what your country can do for you; ask what you can do for your country."

Yet an infinitely greater president of more inspiring—and self-written—inaugural speeches was assassinated without changing our basic social mores.

Sex is more fundamental than politics. Was it the sexual revolution that turned America upside down? Phillip Larkin wrote:

Sexual intercourse began
In nineteen sixty-three
(which was rather late for me)—
Between the end of the Chatterley *ban*
And the Beatles' first LP.

And what about the Beatles and the revolution in pop music? Music mattered in the 1960s; music was a tribal war cry.

Sorting out the contributions of all these shocks in altering our collective and individual psyches is a task for a Gibbon.

Sometimes, though, observing the particular offers a guide to the general. Charting the course of one life may offer insight into what happened to the country.

Shocking events were the norm in the 1960s. No one was unaffected. I was instantly aware of acute social tensions when I was abruptly decanted from the army back into the civilian world of Yale.

What I found at Yale made me adjust all my thinking and carefully consider my own future. By the end of that final year at Yale, I wanted out of the United States. So I left to live in England, not to return for nearly forty years.

During those years outside the United States, at first I didn't talk or even think often about Vietnam. My English friends found it a distasteful subject. My gentle English wife detests war and finds the topic boring.

Occasionally, the U.S. Department of Defense reminded me of the war in an unusual way. Once every ten years or so, the thoughtful folks at Defense send me an Army Commendation Medal with an enclosed letter, stating they are most sorry that my award of the medal was overlooked somewhere deep in the bowels of the Pentagon. But justice prevailed; here is my medal.

And indeed there is a nice box containing the medal and a little green ribbon to go on any uniform I might wear. In the army, we called the Army Commendation Medal the "green weenie" because of the green ribbon.

I now have three of these handsome medals and live in hope for several more before I die. But the arrival of the medals didn't rekindle any enthusiasm in me for thinking about the war.

When, however, our son became a teenager, he began asking the traditional male questions about war. Unlike my English contemporaries, I could answer his questions from personal experience. I tried to answer them, though, with a certain detachment. We visited Verdun together; I didn't want him to romanticize war.

Without warning late one afternoon, he asked me to help him with a school history project about America and Vietnam. Naturally, this paper was due to be handed in the next day. Working late that night on editing his draft, which was well arranged and complete with disturbing photos, I found it hard to get my emotions and thoughts in order.

So, I read Stanley Karnow's lengthy, thoughtful history of the war. I read novels like Jim Webb's *Fields of Fire*. I returned to Vietnam twice. I turned my own experiences over and over in my mind. I dug out my old photos and letters and poured through them. Then I felt the need to write.

The Vietnam War was not the sole reason that the American world I grew up in vanished. Demographic forces alone meant that the confident white Anglo-Saxon Protestant ascendency my parents' generation took for granted would inevitably give way to something different. The United States has always changed rapidly in ways that startle not only the rest of the world but amaze or dismay its citizens.

But, whatever exact role the Vietnam War played in altering the country, my experiences in the army in Vietnam and immediately afterward at Yale certainly changed me.

Background: Yale—and the United States—in 1960

The United States in 1960 was the global dominant economic and military power. At home, the United States was socially a narrow world shaped by three bland, self-censored television networks whose programming was aptly described as "a vast wasteland" or "chewing gum for the mind."

This pre-digested pap perfectly suited Americans, who watched far more TV than any other nation. In public, Americans followed unwritten but powerful conventions in discussing most subjects. A smothering puritan sensibility, for example, censored the nation's ability to talk out loud about sex. In 1963, Lenny Bruce was arrested for saying "schmuck," which is Yiddish for penis, on stage.

At Yale, students generally followed predictable academic paths that led to a profession, assuming that they didn't plan to join a family business, like politics for George W. Bush, or to live off a family trust fund while pretending to work at what was really their hobby.

Before launching themselves into grown-up life, though, most Yalies expected to perform some sort of military service, as a rite of passage for new graduates.

Many Yale families like mine had living relatives who had served in the two World Wars and long dead ones who had popped up in every American war. My father's family had produced an aide de camp for Stonewall Jackson. We weren't at all interested in the military as a career, but we considered military service as a citizen's obligation of manhood.

Yale undergraduates took it for granted that they would either be drafted or serve in the military in some capacity unless they had a legitimate medical impairment like a missing foot, as opposed to the difficult-to-diagnose knee and back ailments that became so common as the Vietnam War intensified.

Going to medical school first was a particularly good way of spending your time in the military as an officer. Plus, military medicine offered a splendid opportunity to make any early diagnostic or surgical mistakes outside the realm of malpractice suits. Doctoring was also a great way to earn a lavish civilian living after the military. Doctors, not bankers, were at the top of the earnings' pecking order back then.

Getting into a top medical or law school was tough. This made Yalies slog away at mandatory courses in history or English in order to get the B plus/A minus average necessary to get into a top graduate school. (Remember: this was prior to grade inflation.) Whether studying the works of Shakespeare or the Napoleonic wars inspired these earnest young men was irrelevant to their futures.

Getting good grades, however, was totally relevant. Naturally, this did not make these bright young sparks keen to challenge the content of the many mandatory courses or indeed to challenge anything taught at Yale. Or to comment on the fact that much of the teaching was dreadful.

Yalies didn't question their world. They were active politically, of course; Yalies always have been. But generally they practiced politics only within narrow limits.

One opening in this closed political world was on the right, where a radical new kind of so-called conservatism was emerging as a reaction to the prevailing intellectual climate of anti-individual collectivism and in opposition to the interlocking circles of schmoozing, venal politicians, corrupt unions, and corporate oligopolies that dominated the United States.

Mussolini would have found much to admire in the America of the late 1950s and early 1960s.

These fledgling conservatives or libertarians were a small minority, even among Republicans. Yale politics followed national trends. People viewing the wild and wonderful antics of Tea Party Republicans today can't grasp how centrist and corporatist were the Republicans of the past. Richard Nixon, for example, leaned on the steel industry to make the steel bosses capitulate to the steel unions in 1960. Nixon wanted the unions on his side for his presidential run.

Nelson Rockefeller, then governor of New York State, led the liberal or Rockefeller Republicans, who were indistinguishable from most Democrats. Rockefeller, like Mussolini, built massive public works. To finance these, and public housing projects especially, Rockefeller launched the funny-money finance schemes that are so devastating now to public finances. Tax and spend was as Republican as it was Democrat in those days.

In the 1960s, Rockefeller benefitted, though not to the same degree as Jack Kennedy, from the total lack of press scrutiny of politicians' private lives. Like JFK and, for that matter Mussolini, Rockefeller considered women as objects to be used when sexually required.

Rockefeller, unlike JFK, lived long enough for the press to lose its inhibitions. When Rockefeller died of a heart attack in 1979 while having it off with a young female aide, the family's initial attempt at a cover-up quickly collapsed and the truth came pouring out.

Yale Republicans in 1960 were mostly Rockefeller Republicans. Any political ideals that deviated much from an unquestioning belief in some sort of Washington-run, highly taxed, corporatist economy were broadly ridiculed.

Please don't call this collectivist faith "socialism." Being a true socialist requires thought, mental energy, and historical and philosophical underpinnings. No, this was a minor, quasi-religious faith, one that all decent, upperclass white people were supposed to accept as a given—just as Christians are supposed to believe in the Holy Trinity and the afterlife, without asking too many awkward questions.

In the United States, this widely held religious faith was known for some peculiar reason as "liberalism." (American liberalism overlaps with "progressivism," the term preferred these days by many "liberals," just to further confuse the public).

Yale Democrats differed little from Yale Republicans. The most promising future politicians in my class were Democrats. The most talented of these would-be politicos was Joe Lieberman, who went on to be the long-term U.S. Senator from Connecticut.

I remember Lieberman well. Young Lieberman was a mid-sized blond kid with curly hair. He was a warm, charming, immensely hard-working guy of no apparent ideology who would chat with anyone. I liked and respected Lieberman as did everyone else. His inert, droning, present-day TV personality never fails to surprise and disappoint me.

In 1963, Lieberman was a clever, funny person who probably knew more people in our class than anyone else. One of life's natural, small "c" conservatives, the son of retail store owners, I would have assumed that Lieberman was a Republican had he not been Jewish. With rare exceptions, Jewish Yalies defaulted to Democrat. This was mandatory for them, like circumcision.

John Kerry, another future senator, was not in my class, but we overlapped. In those days, Kerry looked like a tall, doleful cocker spaniel. Kerry was pompous, aloof, and lacked the slightest sparkle. His future success in squiring and marrying exceedingly rich women is another mystery to me.

If Kerry had any political beliefs then apart from those of any conventional New England prep school goody-goody, he didn't reveal them. As a public speaker, Kerry spoke in a deep, ponderous way and in the broadest of platitudes.

<hr />

In sum, the Yalies of 1963 were boring. As were their parents.

It amuses me to read about how wonderful the "Greatest Generation" was. Whatever the heroism my parents' generation had demonstrated during World War II, the effort had left them empty and full of a desire for a quiet, cud-chewing life. We were a product of the result; a product of the complacent, dullard 1950s that the Greatest Generation created and reveled in.

Why would a young man strive for anything different? Jobs were easy to find. Houses and cars and gasoline were cheap. Early marriage was the norm. Working-class men married soon after high school. Educated men married the girl of their dreams shortly after college graduation or, at the latest, after graduate school. What was there to agitate about?

Yes, we were aware that blacks—or Negroes—had always had a rotten deal in the United States.

President Kennedy talked quite a bit about this, but legally not much new had been done for Negroes before Kennedy's demise in November 1963; the Civil Rights Act barring segregation wasn't passed until the following year.

In any case, it isn't clear how keen Kennedy was in actually doing anything about civil rights, as opposed to simply talking about them. In 1957, like many Democrat senators, Kennedy had voted to pigeonhole Eisenhower's Civil Rights Act by sending it into committee limbo. Fortunately, this move failed.

Kennedy was a wonderful talker. A famous *New York Times* journalist said that, "Kennedy talked like Churchill but acted like Chamberlain."

The real struggle for black equality was going on in the south. We were aware of it in a general sort of way. Eisenhower had sent the army to Little Rock in 1957 to enforce school integration, so the struggle wasn't new to us. I had seen segregated drinking fountains on a school trip to Mount Vernon in the sixth grade. These appalled everyone in my class, including me.

Yalies took it for granted that Negroes deserved equal rights, but I don't remember talking to anyone who proposed to do anything dramatic about this, such as going on a freedom ride or dating black girls.

Though there were blacks in my class at Yale, their number was insignificant. Plus, blacks at Yale usually turned out to be from the tiny, post-Civil War black middleclass or the sons of African diplomats.

America still belonged to the white male, at least in theory. White females had the vote all right, but they were little more represented in the professions than they were at Yale. The concept of equal pay for equal work hadn't spread far outside the world of small circulation political magazines.

Most middle- and upperclass WASP women stayed at home, busy with tennis, golf, and the Junior League. (In those days middleclass meant "of the professional classes or educated" and not "of current or former median income" as it does now. For "middleclass" then, think of lawyers or doctors.)

Actually, male diffidence and male fear of female sexuality, coupled with the American tradition of "momism," made women powerful on the domestic front. The United States of the 1960s was matriarchal in practice. Yalies generally did what their mothers told them to do.

In most of the country, the United States belonged especially to white Anglo-Saxon Protestants. Being born an upper- or even middleclass WASP guaranteed a boy a good start in life. Of course, this obvious truth was seldom publically expressed in such crass terms.

There was lots of talk in WASP homes about "noblesse oblige" and endless speeches at commencements about leadership and responsibility towards the less fortunate. No one questioned who would be doing the "noblessing" or the leading.

In Cleveland when I was growing up, Jews could not join country clubs or the important business clubs downtown. Of course, my parents would explain, Jews had their own clubs that were so much nicer. And some upmarket local Jews were socially accepted, especially doctors and lawyers. My mother only trusted Jewish doctors; my father had a Jewish lawyer.

People from Cincinnati, like my parents, called these acceptable Jews, "German" Jews. In contrast, New York Jews were considered pushy and a pain in the ass, even when they weren't outright Commies or pinkos.

Being a Catholic wasn't so hot, either.

While running for President in 1960, Kennedy had to explain that, if elected, he wouldn't take orders from the Pope. Having an Irish name, though, was OK.

However, being a Catholic with a name ending in a vowel wasn't OK. Having such a name meant that you shouldn't make plans to run a major bank or a large quoted company.

Or hope to be president of a great private university. The pristine WASP president of Yale from 1951 onward was the ineffable and appropriately named A. Whitney Griswold, known to Yale students as Gritney Wiswold. Poor Wiswold was busy dying of cancer so we saw little of him.

How I wish I could claim to have spotted these unattractive features of the United States and taken a heroic moral stand against them.

In truth, I blithely ignored these manifest wrongs since they didn't apply to me. This was also the attitude of my preppy classmates. In our endless debates and bull sessions, I don't remember such unseemly topics ever being mentioned. Yale itself had an unwritten Jewish quota of around ten percent through the 1950s, according to the *Yale Alumni Magazine* of December 1999. No one mentioned this, either.

My ability to take public moral stands was compromised in any case. I was too busy fending off the efforts of Yale to make me into a well-behaved undergraduate. This was a serious struggle that overlapped with my angry, urgent desire to separate myself permanently from my parents and from Cleveland, Ohio—the Mistake on the Lake.

As a school kid, I joked with schoolmates that my biggest worry about a nuclear war was that the Russian missiles would miss Cleveland. I didn't particularly want to be incinerated, but some sacrifices are worth it.

Later, I came to understand how my negative feelings about Cleveland were linked to my negative feelings about my dysfunctional parents. Both had much to answer for.

How to Get
Kicked Out of Yale

Yale and I got off to a bad start.

I had no desire to go to Yale in the first place. My only ambition as a kid was to get out of Cleveland as fast as possible. I had no wish to be a doctor, lawyer, or Indian chief. Organized sports left me cold. Academic work came easily to me, but I saw little point in it.

My joys were endless reading, the company of large dogs, riding my bike, and being outdoors. I was a solitary kid. At my Maine summer camp, aged about eleven, I won a prize for memorizing the names of all the local trees and identifying them by their leaves and bark. Anyone for Asperger's?

Goals in life? What goals? Who needed goals?

If my parents had any suggestions for the future, I ignored them. However, I had the good fortune to have two wonderful grandmothers. One taught me that unselfish love was a possibility, despite the contrary evidence of my parents.

My other grandmother, Nana, was rich and immensely practical. Nana's idea of a perfect Christmas present for a twelve-year-old boy was a set of fine white bath towels. Her three surviving sons, including my father, were wealthy, heavy-drinking duds. This left Nana with plans and ambitions for the next generation. Nana took my future in hand.

At a meeting of a charitable organization, Nana met Frank Boyden, the headmaster of Deerfield Academy in Massachusetts, a famous old prep school. Nana and Frank hit it off at once, possibly because each felt perfectly competent to direct any and all activities of the human race. Or possibly because they were both in their seventies, utterly straightforward, without ulterior motives and totally lacking in any form of doubt or uncertainty.

Once Nana took on board that Frank was running an important New England prep school, she realized this was a good opportunity to remove me from my parental home. She informed Mr. Boyden that I would be attending his school in the fall. The necessary fees and paperwork would follow. Mr. Boyden agreed without further discussion.

Later, reading John McPhee's fascinating book about Frank Boyden, *The Headmaster*, I learned that such an ad hoc admission to Deerfield was typical of Mr. Boyden who ruled Deerfield like his own private empire. Mr. Boyden had been headmaster since 1901.

In due course, Nana informed me that I was going to Deerfield. Since this meant leaving Cleveland and my parents, I was pleased and happily went off alone on the overnight Pullman sleeper train to Springfield, Massachusetts, in September 1957, aged fourteen. Upon arrival the next morning, I treated myself to a movie double-feature in grotty downtown Springfield, then found a cab to share with some other boys going to Deerfield. So this was freedom. I liked it!

Deerfield, though totally controlling, was the perfect school for me. I thrived in its intense, monastic grip. The teachers were excellent. Sports were unending and mandatory, but I found that I liked soccer as much as I had hated American football. I took up skiing, which became a life-long love, second only to my wife and family. And I did well academically.

By my junior year, it was time to apply for early admission to college. I had a vague opinion about where I wanted to go. Never introspective, I still grasped that, though I was independent-minded and academically clever, I was also ridiculously immature.

A small New England liberal arts college would be a happy extension of Deerfield, in my mind anyway. I had a favorite teacher who had gone to Bowdoin, an excellent old college in Maine. Though I'd never even visited Bowdoin, I told the career advisor at Deerfield that I wanted to apply there. The career advisor smiled at me somewhat thinly and suggested having another meeting the following week. Then he called my parents.

In an unusual burst of activity, my mother immediately made one of her few interventions in my academic affairs.

Mother hadn't gone to college and disdained most forms of academic learning. In particular, she had convinced me as a small child that math was a subject that no sensitive, thoughtful person needed to be concerned with. Math was for plumbers and bookkeepers. This attitude did me considerable harm and took years to shake off.

Mother was, however, intensely interested in maintaining her social position. Since by then she was a full-time alcoholic and progressively more agoraphobic, keeping the Thomson's sunny-side up socially wasn't straightforward, even in as unchallenging a social environment as the eastern suburbs of Cleveland. Having a son at Yale would be a major plus.

Accordingly, mother phoned me at Deerfield. This call came so much out of the blue that I assumed someone had died. Mother liked passing on bad news. Otherwise, she seldom phoned.

Mother reminded me that men on my father's side of the family always went to Yale.

"Yale," she claimed, "is in your blood." After all, our family had lived happily in New Haven when my father went back to Yale for his masters' degree after World War II. "How well I remember the elms," mother said. (The elms were long dead of Dutch elm disease, but neither of us knew this. Mother and I hadn't been in New Haven since 1948.)

"Why would you accept something second best?" mother bellowed down the line in her croaky smoker's voice. I tried to be noncommittal, but I didn't have a good counter-argument. And I think mother honestly believed that Yale would be best for me, quite apart from being good for my future CV and for her immediate social needs.

Mother and I knew little about each other. Her great pleasure lay in winding up family members until a blazing row resulted. If they turned on her, well, that was attention, wasn't it? If they turned on each other, well, wasn't that fun to watch? *Long Day's Journey into Night* as played by the Addams family in a new adaptation by Woody Allen. Accordingly, I tried to stay out of her way. Dogs and grandmothers were my sources of emotional consolation.

Deerfield also wanted me to go to Yale. I had the highest score on the verbal SAT in my class, excellent grades, and was active in this club and that society. I would thus be an applicant Deerfield wouldn't have to force on Yale. The career advisor arranged for me to have a pleasant chat with a visiting Yale interviewer. I was given an A rating that guaranteed my subsequent admission. So off to Yale I went.

———◆———

Most people can remember going on a date that went wrong from the first moment. Yale and I shared such an experience.

Deerfield is located in one of the most beautiful and best-preserved eighteenth-century country towns in the United States. It is a national historic landmark. The school is a mix of old and new buildings, but all are built in the appropriate colonial style. The school is surrounded by glorious New England farmland and views of hills. The fall foliage is stunning. Winters are cold and snowy and good for skiing.

In the spring, boys swam and tubed in the Deerfield River, a wide, swift stream that skirts the school. Early on one Sunday morning, I saw my first osprey pull a good-sized trout out of the Deerfield.

Yale is located in New Haven, a decaying industrial dump of a city, graced only by the presence of a great university. Aesthetically, the city of New Haven is a typical American twentieth-century urban wasteland. The Yale campus, though, offers a range of unusual architectural excrescences. This ugly collection of expensive buildings shows the world that Yale has plenty of rich alumni with more money than taste and is also the home of a famous school of architecture.

———◆———

The New Haven my family had inhabited in the late 1940s still had factories and streetcars and elm-lined, leafy streets. World War II had revived the arms industry. Blacks moved to New Haven to take up well-paid factory jobs. The place hummed.

However, even by the late 1940s, it was evident that this weapons-led prosperity was not going to last. The small arms industries of New Haven like Winchester and Remington were the past. The aerospace industries of California were the future. I saw the impact of this on New Haven firsthand, but in an indirect way.

My family employed a black couple, Theodore and Maisie Bones, and their sister-in-law, Mamie. I don't think the Boneses were paid much. Instead they lived for free over the garage behind our old house on West Park Avenue.

Theodore was a lovely man, big and strong and kind. I owe him a lifetime debt of gratitude: Theodore taught me how to read. We would sit on the concrete steps that led down from the kitchen at the back of the house to the driveway. Theodore would produce a Donald Duck comic book and read the captions in the balloons over Donald and Daisy's heads. He sounded out the letters so that I learned to read phonetically.

Maisie was bright and funny and cooked the kind of southern black food my father preferred. She and Mamie liked kids and played games with us.

Theodore was a machinist and worked in an arms factory. But the work dried up. So he decided to move to California and start a new life. I realize now that this was a brave and wise thing to do, but I cried buckets when he and Maisie and Mamie drove off in their old car.

Because of these happy childhood memories, I was not predestined to loathe New Haven or Yale. But I did, instantly.

The unskilled blacks and poor whites that stayed in New Haven, after the ambitious workers like Theodore Bones departed, were left to rot. The city deteriorated fast. Yale did little or nothing about this. Historically, town-gown relations in New Haven stank.

Yale is almost as old as New Haven and infinitely more important in the American scheme of things. Yalies looked down upon the ignorant townies from an early time. Each Yale class used to appoint a class bully. The role of the bully was to lead gangs of Yalies out into the town to beat up the locals. The bully carried a large club of knotty wood that was captured from the townies during one of these raids.

The last class bully was chosen in 1840. He was one Hezekiah Sturges who was recorded as being six-foot-two-inches and weighing two-hundred-and-fifty very muscular pounds. Perhaps Sturges was destined to become a Congregational minister like many Yale students in those days. It is interesting to speculate about the brand of muscular Christianity that Sturges would have administered to his congregation.

It is not clear from the letter I found describing Sturges whether it was he who led the attack on the local spectators which disrupted Yale's commencement day and forced the governor of Connecticut to flee. Inevitably, this sordid scene led to the abolition of the office of class bully. The fighting with the town, however, went on informally. At one stage, the townies allegedly attempted to drag up cannon to shell the Yale campus. The Connecticut militia stopped them.

By the time I reached Yale, much of New Haven was a no-go area for students. There was a strong racial element in this, but the local Italians weren't wild about Yalies, either. They had a saying, "If you can't get a girl, get a Yalie."

Fortunately, there was no reason for a Yalie to go into hostile territory. New Haven only had two or three restaurants, plus a White Castle and several wonderful pizzerias. These were all in relatively safe areas.

The Schubert Theater, where Broadway plays tried out, and the nearby Taft Hotel, where Yale men's dates stayed, were also in a safe area. These rounded out New Haven's limited attractions, unless you counted the train station that could whisk you off to New York City at any time.

Apart from the festering reality of New Haven, Yale itself was not visually pleasing. The university had a gothic makeover in the 1920s and 1930s, paid for by the Standard Oil inheritance of Edward Harkness, whose father was part of the John D. Rockefeller gang.

Most of the colonial brick college buildings of old Yale were torn down and replaced with grey stone mock-gothic extravaganzas like Harkness Tower, which now dominates the campus. Frank Lloyd Wright, when asked where he would like to live, supposedly said, "In Harkness Tower. Then I would never have to look at it."

Students took a somewhat different line on Harkness Tower, singing, to the tune of "O Tannenbaum":

O Harkness Tower, O Harkness Tower,
How we love thy phallic power.
You stand up there so tall and straight,
You make us want to masturbate.
We praise thee now in deed and word,
Too bad you're covered with bird turd.

Yet another of Yale's gothic bell towers is a copy of the most celebrated church tower in Wales.

Architecturally, Yale had the phony feeling of a film set. This put my teeth on edge, despite my fairly limited interest in buildings then or now. Perhaps subconsciously I sensed that Yale, like the United States, wasn't quite what it was supposed to be. Medieval stonemasons didn't create the gargoyles or the fan vaulting. Under the gothic façades were modern steel structures and reinforced concrete.

To complete this Anglo-centric aping of Oxford and Cambridge, a system of residential colleges was instituted at Yale between the wars. These Yale colleges consist of dorms around small quads, libraries, and cafeterias, plus excellent quarters for the master of each college.

Unlike Oxford and Cambridge, the system of one-on-one tutorials in your college was not introduced at Yale. The Yale professoriate has only a loose connection with any particular college. Students treat the colleges as dorms.

In short, the college life I experienced later at Keble College, Oxford, never took root at Yale. Like the mock-gothic architecture, the Yale colleges were essentially pointless, lifeless copies of fine originals.

As freshmen, we were required to live on the Old Campus, the original area occupied by Yale, where a few brick colonial buildings survived. As sophomores, we were randomly assigned to a college, thus ensuring that, again unlike Oxford or Cambridge, no Yale college had any particular social character.

By 1960, Vanderbilt Hall on the Old Campus, my first dorm, was crowded. Using double bunks, four of us were crowded into what had been a small set of rooms for two. This was good preparation, though, for moving into a college as a sophomore, since the colleges were also crowded.

As incoming freshmen, we were sent on our first day to the Payne Whitney Gymnasium to be processed in as Yalies.

With nine squat, massive stories, the Payne Whitney Gym is a truly enormous folly, possibly the largest mock-gothic building in the world. There is space for a running track on its roof. Even if you accept that the United States needs a gothic National Cathedral in Washington like those built half a millennium before in medieval Europe, the rationale for building a monstrous, multi-story stone gothic mausoleum of a gym in New Haven is beyond comprehension.

In those days, as you entered the gym, you walked past a glass cage containing a stuffed bulldog. This was the original Handsome Dan, the first of many Yale bulldog mascots. Encountering this shabby, glass-eyed, stuffed dog was only the beginning of an odd and unpleasant experience.

First, we were given a four-digit processing number and told to strip bare. Then, we were subjected to a series of anthropomorphic measurements: size of cranium; height; weight—the works. Apparently Yale had been keeping such measurements since the nineteenth century.

Second, photographs were taken of us in the nude. We were positioned against a white background and shot from two angles to show our body type and posture. Similar photos, or so we were told, were taken at the other Ivy League universities and at Vassar and the other Seven Sisters.

These photos were theoretically to be used for the study of body types but originally may have been intended to be used for some sort of racial eugenics campaign, according to an article in the *The New York Times Magazine* of January 15, 1995.

Whatever the reason for the photos, not one of us objected. This was surprising, because my new classmates included relatives of Holocaust survivors. You might have thought that these boys would be hyper-sensitive to the implications of being given a number, told to strip bare, then photographed (to see who was circumcised?) and sent on for a physical. Next stop the "shower room"?

The celebrated feminist writer Naomi Wolf, who went to Yale right after Yale turned co-ed, threw one of her famous literary hissy fits about these photos. However, Naomi was not objecting to the photo project, only to a TV comic's joke. The comic said that all the Vassar female photos were stolen to be sold as pornography but then found no buyers.

At Yale, the photo project ended in 1968. For me, the photos were just part of joining a cold, impersonal institution. I saw no hint of a neo-Nazi plot. Certainly, looking around at the average physique of the Yale freshmen I was processed with, it required quite a leap to believe in any *Herrenvolk* superiority of Yalies.

After the physical—"Cough. Bend forward."—we were given a swimming test. Pleasingly, while I was waiting to swim, I watched a number of large, muscular guys who could not swim the length of the large pool and had to be helped out. These, I was told, were football ringers. We were also told that no one could graduate until he swam the length of the pool. This seemed an excellent policy. I wonder if it is still in force.

During processing, no one spoke to us, apart from issuing commands. The whole day was good preparation for the army. Being processed also turned out to be the essence of the Yale educational method.

Classes began. There were many required freshman courses, regardless of your ultimate major. Almost all of these required courses took the form of lectures in large, old-fashioned lecture halls with steep, tiered seating. Attendance was mandatory. You were checked off as you entered.

Senior professors gave the lectures. Without exception, they were god-awful speakers. Most read aloud, head down, from lengthy, much thumbed notes. Some mumbled. Some rambled. The atmosphere was leaden. Questions were rarely asked by any of the hundred or more of us hunched in the hard wooden seats. The man next to you could have been Isaac Newton or the janitor; it made no difference.

Early one snowy morning, I remember trudging up the hill to the old science building for a riveting biology lecture on the "effect of colloid osmotic pressure on water retention in the kidney tubule."

The lecture started promptly at eight. A hundred young men gazed bleary-eyed at a wall of blackboards covered with chalk squiggles. In front of the boards and behind a podium, an over-age star of the biology faculty began holding forth in a nasal monotone.

This learned dude was supposed to be riotously funny, but the only humor I remember from him took the form of scornful, misogynistic comments about the human female.

Luckily, these dismal old professors tended to regurgitate material from textbooks they had written and which we had to buy. I cut as many of these lectures as I dared and passed my freshman courses by memorizing stuff from the textbooks and borrowing class notes if required. (The stuff about colloid osmotic pressure turned up on the biology final so it was fortunate I'd attended that lecture.)

That I had a near pathological hatred of boredom was one of my first intellectual discoveries at university; I was bored beyond belief within days of arriving at Yale. So I went to every movie in town. I read a lot on my own. I walked aimlessly. Finally, I bought a bicycle and did a lot of riding day and night. Riding up to the top of East Rock to see the sunrise or sunset was fun.

Regardless of where I went, there were no girls to meet. Like males from the dawn of time, I thought that a lack of sex was my real problem.

Actually, my real problem was me. I was too immature to fit into the big wide world. And much too shy to have done anything with a girl even if one had fallen naked into my lap. As much as I wanted sex, even more I wanted a mate; a real woman to live with. I felt incomplete.

My three roommates were an ill-assorted lot. We did not play well together.

Phinney Works, who took the upper bunk in our tiny bedroom, was a childhood friend of mine, but we hadn't been close for some time. I was amazed and flattered when he asked me in a letter to room with him.

Works and I had a number of shared bonds. We had spent all our childhood summers in Freedom, New Hampshire, a tiny little town of less than five hundred people. Works's family had originated in

Freedom before moving to Cincinnati. My Cincinnati-born mother had been going to Freedom since her childhood because her mother, my beloved Gigi, was a pal of Works's grandmother.

As children, for a while Works and I were as thick as thieves as our parents no doubt intended. But our worldview was never in sync.

One year, aged about fourteen, Works and I were playing tennis as partners in the Freedom men's doubles final. Without warning, in the middle of the first set, one of the two middle-aged businessmen we were playing against grabbed his chest, slumped face forward on to the court, and was dead before the town doctor could arrive.

I put my wool sweater under the dying man's head. This was not a pleasant thing to do: underneath the red clay dust from the court, his face was chalk white, his lips were blue-gray, and he was barely breathing. Works, who came from a thrifty family, was surprised that I didn't want the sweater back later. He suggested simply having it dry-cleaned to get rid of the red dust, but I ignored this suggestion.

Works and I experimented with alcohol together at the same age. I filched a bottle of scotch from my father's booze cabinet. That evening Works slept over at our house. We managed to gag down most of the bottle—neat—by midnight. Soon after that, such bad things happened to both of us that we had to go out into the backyard rather urgently.

Though we managed the next morning to convince my parents that all the barf in the backyard was due to the dog having eaten something dead, the after-effects of the booze were so dramatic that neither of us drank much again before we went to Yale. This lapse we soon corrected.

Our two other roommates, Ben White and Al Guppy, were from the same Massachusetts prep school but otherwise had little in common. White was a rah-rah fellow of forced cheerfulness and manly enthusiasms who took so well to being regimented by Yale that he could have been a plebe at West Point. Guppy, in contrast, specialized in being morose for no obvious reason. Al was as shapeless as a beanbag and had a shuffling way of walking. Being around Guppy was a downer.

White was the only one of us to graduate after four consecutive years. I took four years, plus a three-year army interlude, but did eventually graduate. Works dropped out during sophomore year, joined the army and was killed in Vietnam as an Army Special Forces officer.

Works used his time at Yale to become physically fit by using the gothic horror of a gym. He went to a special afternoon fitness class that was basically for the swim team but open to anyone.

Works got me to go with him a few times. The famous Yale swim coach Bob Kipputh led the exercise class by shouting which exercise to perform. Kipputh then rapped out the tempo for each repetition of the exercise on the gym floor with a wooden staff. Kipputh would start rapping slowly but soon hit a blistering pace.

I was not sufficiently motivated to stick with this grinding regime, which certainly worked for Works, who went from being a weedy kid to being a muscleman in less than two years. His goal was not to get fit for the army but to lure a girl—any girl—into his bed. Perhaps if Works had succeeded in this ambition, he would not have dropped out of Yale.

In love, as in thriving at Yale, the only success among us was Ben White, who became engaged to Works's bright and lovable younger sister Emily, a lifelong friend of mine. (Emily fortunately had the good sense to drop White and marry a rich Swiss. Alas, Emily died young.)

Guppy's permanent departure from Yale was imaginative.

At Yale, freshmen were encouraged by entrepreneurial older students to buy large white china beer mugs with the freshman's nickname and class year on it in blue letters, along with the Yale crest and motto—*Lux et Veritas*.

One afternoon, Guppy summoned all of us into our small communal room. Without any prelude, he struck a pose in front of the fireplace. He took his beer mug off the mantelpiece and threw it into the fireplace with such force that it broke into dozens of pieces. Then, without a word, he shuffled slowly out of the room. We expected Guppy to return later in the day, but he never resurfaced.

We never heard from Guppy again.

Ben White glued Guppy's beer mug back together, a project that took White weeks. I think his idea was that fixing the mug would somehow also fix Guppy and to induce him to return.

Instead, I wound up with the mug, which I heaved across my college's faux-medieval courtyard and through an open window during sophomore year. This seemed a good move at the time and required a strong, accurate heave to go cleanly through the narrow opening of the mock-gothic leaded window. I was delighted with my throw when the mug disintegrated noisily and this time for good inside the room.

Heaving beer mugs and getting in trouble came effortlessly and naturally to me, unlike attending the mandatory sessions in the French language lab, which I skipped. Fortunately, since Yale taught French as a dead language, featuring such entertaining greats as Corneille and Racine and plenty of written work, these lab sessions didn't count for much grade-wise, but I had to spend part of the summer between my freshman and sophomore years at Harvard, making up the language lab work.

I was glad later when I traveled in France on business for the Morgan Bank that I had done as little as possible in the language labs. I instantly discovered that most of the spoken French taught at Yale and Harvard was perfectly, totally useless. In a typically perverse French way, no Frenchman under eighty spoke French the way it was taught in those learned American institutions.

I can't remember now which of my many escapades led to my being caught and which I got away with. I remember some trouble and a fine after I chopped through a door with a fire axe. But I ran all over the campus naked and drunk on many occasions without consequences. Streaking was a fad at the time.

I did just enough work during my freshman year to avoid being kicked out for academic reasons.

The required academic work was dreary. Having to write twee little essays for English courses about John Donne's imagery made me want to smash things. Or to puke. Raising the level of the world's drivel barometer is demoralizing. Ruining a youthful love of poetry is worse. "Who breaks a butterfly upon a wheel?"

Like my classmates, I wrote essays by the yard. Writing about great villains in novels or who won the Franco-Prussian War was less of a trial than writing about poetry. Also, learning to produce reams of more or less coherent written material about something totally boring and meaningless is good training for would-be lawyers or indeed for anyone who is lucky enough to land a writing job that bills by the column inch.

A few teachers inspired me. Like many ex-prep school students, I had been spoiled at Deerfield by excellent teaching and attentive teachers. At Yale, I quickly recognized that teaching undergraduates wasn't the point of the institution and that my resentful attitude in the face of great learning and scholarship was childish. Still, I couldn't help warming to the few professors who tried, however vaguely, to match undergraduate names to faces.

I adored Professor Gordon Haight who taught the Victorian English novel and was the world's greatest expert on George Elliot. Professor Haight had been one of my father's teachers, and I had known him as a small child. Academically, Professor Haight was a holdover from Yale's former tradition of a broad historical approach to the study of literature. This appealed to me. I could never see the point of separating the life and times of John Milton from the poetry of John Milton. At least Milton's life and times were interesting.

One escape hatch from the required courses in the embalmed world of English literature was accidentally discovering *V.* by Thomas Pynchon. I added Pynchon to the short list of fiction writers like Evelyn Waugh and P.G. Wodehouse whose style and attitude speak loudly to me. I must have read *V.* five times during my first two years at Yale.

Obviously, there were courses that didn't involve writing reams of drivel or sitting through interminable lectures. Being formally introduced to economics and philosophy was stimulating, regardless of the teaching. And the younger professors didn't all use the droning, dismal lecture-hall approach. Some showed actual flashes of interest in teaching undergraduates.

I was fortunate to be taught introductory economics by Jan Tumlir, a Czech refugee from Communism. Doing hard labor in the Czech uranium mines after the postwar Communist takeover had wrecked the professor's health. Without making any specific comments about his experience of Communism, he was a living argument against the collectivist policies believed in, or at least advocated, by so many of the Yale professoriate.

Instead, Professor Tumlir cherished nineteenth-century economic liberalism and ideals like free trade and free markets. He taught us about Ricardo, the great English economist who first stated the law of comparative advantage. Professor Tumlir later became head of economics at GATT, the General Agreement on Tariffs and Trade and predecessor to the current World Trade Organization, but died far too young.

Overall, though, Yale in the early 1960s offered the worst teaching I've ever experienced. The benighted, God-stuffed, over-long rambling sermons in the First Church of Deerfield were delivered better and with more conviction. Semi-literate army sergeants proved to be far better teachers, as did even the idlest Oxford dons. And Stanford Business School didn't give tenure to anyone who received consistently poor student evaluations for teaching.

———◆———

My Yale mischief career peaked as a sophomore with the great water bomb campaign.

Some pals and I discovered that, by using long pieces of highly elastic surgical rubber tubing stolen from a lab and tied to the two handles of a small plastic bucket, we could create a slingshot so powerful that, from the middle of our college's quad, we could fire frozen condoms full of water across Elm Street into other colleges with sufficient force to make a clean hole through a glass window. (Excellent rubber in condoms in those days.)

Two of us held the ends of the extended tubing. Another pulled back the bucket. A spotter yelled back the coordinates of the target and kept watch. We fired a dozen or so condoms, and then ran.

Unfortunately, we soon discovered that Yale used a system of student spies or narks to report on such reprehensible activity. One such nark in our college blew the cover on two of us.

Since the other guy, my frequent boozing pal Bob DeLonza, had a scholarship to lose, we felt that the nark's behavior was despicable. Running a network of student spies for the purpose of stamping out trivial mischief still seems bizarre and unreasonable behavior by an elite educational institution.

We quickly found out who the nark was. DeLonza and I went to the nark's room with a lighted cherry bomb—a powerful illegal firework—inside a feather pillow. We called out the nark's name as we opened his door and threw in the smoking pillow.

Boom! Feathers everywhere. And one terrified nark. But sadly his terror was short-lived.

The nark reported me for this further outrage. Somehow, the nark failed to connect DeLonza, now one of the country's most distinguished research physicians, with this new offense. DeLonza then luckily dropped off the dean's disciplinary radar screen. This left me as a solo act to make the acquaintance of Dean Sam Chauncey, chief campus law enforcer.

Sam Chauncey was only seven or eight years older than I was, but from the first instant of our first meeting it was clear that we were not going to be soulmates. Chauncey was a direct descendent of one of Yale's earliest graduates, thus making him predestined to be a tight-assed puritan. Chauncey's father was the long-term aide of the president of Harvard and the founder of the Educational Testing Service, which administers the SATs.

Though Chauncey was undoubtedly publically committed to the most refined and pure "liberal" sentiments, down deep he was an instinctive conservative autocrat who simply worshipped powerful educational institutions like Yale.

———◆———

Pause here for a necessary definitional clarification.

"Liberal" is a word that appears and reappears in this book. Since the word is used to describe a woolly, quasi-religious but common American frame of mind, I plead guilty to using it in an ill-defined, catch-all way. And, of course, "liberal" as used by John Stuart Mill had a wholly different political meaning in nineteenth-century England. This meaning is still used in Continental Europe, as in the pejorative term "neo-liberal."

Originally, a liberal political outlook meant a belief in the individual freedoms derived from natural law, which were the birthright of every man. (Mill was way ahead of his time and believed that women, too, had such rights.)

In the United States "liberal" has degraded into meaning a belief in welfarism, collectivism, and egalitarianism and hence an enthusiasm for the high taxes and big government that these fetishes require. Therefore, for "liberal," non-Americans should read "traditional, collectivist, European-style social democrat or democratic socialist." American "liberals" are not direct philosophic descendants of John Stuart Mill or William Gladstone and owe more intellectually to Rousseau, Eduard Bernstein, and Continental European political thinkers.

American liberals resent being linked in any way to the word "socialist," of course. And not one in ten thousand has heard of Eduard Bernstein. But note their actions and their political goals and judge them accordingly. Remember, too, that for the most hard-core American liberals, socialism is the love that dare not speak its name.

Chauncey was balding, with slicked back hair, and self-satisfied. I remember him as plump but, checking his photos on Google, Chauncey was not chubby by present-day standards. Just self-satisfied.

In turn, I plainly represented something unpleasant, perhaps even disgusting, to him.

By sophomore year, my grades were not that bad. What I had done was trivial. But I represented a living, breathing assault on his most cherished values. It was clear to Chauncey that I disliked Yale. Worse, I didn't act like someone who felt privileged to be a Yale inmate, despite being informed repeatedly that I was following in the noble, worthy steps of heroic Yalies like Dink Stover, Dean Acheson, R. Ledbetter Cumquat Jr., and Foster Marbles Gumbody.

Though I wasn't on any sort of scholarship, Chauncey reminded me that I was benefitting from the great wealth bequeathed to Yale. This I readily acknowledged. Inconveniently, though, this wealth had been bequeathed to Yale by people who were like my own grasping, brutal, mercenary ancestors. Those grim-faced Ohio capitalists would have despised Sam Chauncey on sight. But we didn't go into that.

It is a shame that I had this run-in with Chauncey prior to learning about *anomie* and *alienation*. I picked up these elegant concepts shortly afterwards during time spent in Greenwich Village. Chauncey would have appreciated something with more of a European sociological flavor as a reason for my lack of enthusiasm for Mother Yale.

Instead, my suggesting that "New Haven is a sewer and Yale bores the piss out of me" was an act of *lese majeste* from Chauncey's perspective. I didn't know that Chauncey was already working on various projects that would use Yale as a tool for noble-minded social engineering.

For Chauncey, dealing with my mischief was like finding and dealing with a blood-engorged tick on a beloved dog. My attitude stank. I was unrepentant. I didn't come from a broken or poverty-stricken home or belong to an oppressed minority. I drank a lot because I enjoyed it. I displayed contempt for the Yale authorities. Worse, I didn't have a scholarship to lose so there was no easy tool for controlling me.

Chauncey sent me to live off campus for some weeks to think about my sins. The dreaded "rustication" was my punishment. He mentioned expulsion but dropped the topic when I was silent and just looked back at him blank-faced. Chauncey had a repellant personality. It was pleasing to look blank-faced at him.

I took this rustication as a good time to learn about New York City. I dossed down with cronies in the Village and went to off-Broadway plays. I drank a lot. I dearly wish that I could say that I smoked grass and inhaled deeply, but none was offered to me. Sadly, I didn't even really know about the stuff or where to buy it.

————◆————

Yes, my behavior was truly contemptible and beyond childish. I knew it even then.

Psychologically, I was waiting for something to happen, which is always the most tremendous mistake. I still don't understand why I never considered transferring to another university or, better, to a small college. But I didn't. I wanted some sort of dramatic event to occur, but I had no idea, not even the slightest notion, of what sort of event would do the job.

I was not alone in this feeling. Once in a while some hitherto passive member of the studentry showed a little spark of life and gave me hope. The son of the most famous member of the English faculty once told me that the English syllabus was boring. I hope that Sandy Mack remembered this when he went into teaching English at a university just like his dad.

Yale, like the country, was profoundly constipated. Events were about to administer a massive laxative to both.

Probably I should have just waited for the laxative to work as did the rest of American society. I could not explain why I was so disaffected. I had no cause to fight for, other than a belief in unlimited personal freedom for everyone. (At that time I was so inexperienced that I actually believed all humans wanted to be free.)

Even for childish me, there were redeeming features about Yale in the early 1960s. Playing college soccer was fun. There were endless societies to join. Every kind of movie from every era and country was shown for free by various film clubs. I sometimes went to three or four movies in a week.

Though I was not alone in my muzzy, inchoate feelings about a need for change, most Yalies thought that this change could be defined and implemented while we sailed merrily along. Maybe all that was needed was a little tap on the rudder? Well, maybe a sharp tap?

Yale was experiencing the dawn of libertarian politics. All my instincts told me to oppose authority so I hung around the fringes of small libertarian political groups. These little groups often used the word "conservative" in their manifestos in deference to the outpourings of William F. Buckley, Jr. but religion didn't feature in their philosophies; they were agnostic.

The artery-clogging, evangelical Christian stuff mandatory for conservatives today had not surfaced. The conservatives, inspired by Bill Buckley and his crew, participated in loose coalitions with religion-loathing libertarians like me. Accordingly, a few of the most active libertarian participants were Jewish.

The libertarians demanded freedom from government economic intervention in our lives, not a reaffirmation of liberty-destroying, religion-based social rules. What people did in their bedrooms was their business. (If sheep or goats were involved, a courteous man spoke to the farmer first.)

Abortion never came up in this all-male setting, but I am certain we would have agreed it was a matter for each woman to decide.

As unworldly Yale students, we sought truth in theories. Our endless arguments and discussions were driven by reading—or skimming—writers like Friedrich von Hayek and Milton Friedman. We found Buckley's obsession with God and traditional religion mystifying and smacking of his love for the Catholic Church and therefore for the likes of Torquemada or Metternich.

We thought that if people were free economically, other freedoms would spontaneously follow. Freeing the markets would set us free. We wanted to smash collectivist, governmental control of the American economy, paid for by ridiculously high rates of tax on the industrious.

Much of this libertarian activity was bumptious and ill-focused; born of resentment toward the smug liberal establishment that we were immersed in. By any measure, libertarian politics were a minority activity. With President Kennedy and Vice-President Lyndon Johnson and the Democrat-controlled Congress striving with some success to turn the United States into a European-style welfare state, resistance often seemed futile, but it was something a free man had to do.

Though among young libertarians there was much talk of opposition to Communism, in truth everyone significant in American politics in the early 1960s was anti-Communist. The Hungarian Revolution in 1956 had inspired us to think that Communism could be toppled. Castro had reinforced our awareness of the danger of Communism spreading close to home.

Being anti-Communist crossed the political spectrum. Bobby Kennedy, for example, made Senator Joe McCarthy the godfather of one of his many offspring and tried to become the legal counsel for McCarthy's committee.

However, it was emotionally and politically necessary for all on the political right to paint the Democrats as soft on Communism. Wasn't Marxist-Leninism simply the ultimate intellectual rationale for the collectivism American liberals so loved? Believing in things like union control of business, anti-free market regulations, high taxes, and moralistic posturing—weren't those beliefs what it meant to be a Democrat? And steps on the road to Communist serfdom?

Yes, we were young and saw politics in vivid black and white.

A more realistic charge would have been that many top Democrats, like Adlai Stevenson, were instinctively "wet" types who cherished global appeasement and who had a naïve, child-like belief in supra-national institutions, especially the United Nations.

When Kennedy sent Stevenson to be our man at the United Nations, Stevenson found endless, creative ways to capitulate. His masterpiece was insisting on pulling the covert American air support for the Bay of Pigs invasion because such air support would offend his little playmates at the United Nations.

The dithering, mincing public manner of Stevenson is brilliantly caricatured in Stanley Kubrick's masterpiece, *Doctor Strangelove.* The great mimic, Peter Sellers, transmutes Stevenson into the shiny-bald, effete president of the United States, Merkin Muffley. As the countdown to the nuclear destruction of the world is ticking, President Muffley-Stevenson is reduced to bleating at his quarreling generals and cabinet members, "Gentlemen, you can't fight in here. This is the War Room."

Anyway, the focus of Yale's neophyte libertarians was domestic. We assumed that the mistakes the Democrats were making were national. We wanted the U.S. government off our backs.

No one anticipated the hellish mess that Kennedy was in the process of creating in a small Asian country. Few at Yale had ever heard of Vietnam, let alone visited it.

Not all of the Yale professoriate was socially cold or hopelessly geeky. Professor Charlie Garside, a historian, made a great effort to befriend undergraduates. Cynics claimed this was because Garside was gay. I saw no reason to believe this was his motive, though Garside had a high camp manner. He simply liked getting to know undergraduates and sharing his ideas and his booze with them. Garside was a kind, friendly man.

Garside could be brilliantly funny even when totally smashed, as he frequently was. He would tell exaggerated tales in his camp voice about the sex lives of the prissy old queens who dominated the English department, for example.

Professor Garside held a come-one, come-all evening in his rooms with more or less unlimited booze once or twice each month. You met all kinds of eccentric people at these soirees. Most of them were very drunk. You staggered between piles of books and stacks of unread student essays, scattered freely about Garside's rooms, which were hot and very crowded. People that you didn't know told you secrets in shouted whispers about other people that you had never heard of.

The setting was like Lotte Crump's hotel in Waugh's *Vile Bodies*. I often woke after one of these evenings on a couch in a strange room. I would figure out where I was, say thanks, and rush back to my college to get ready for classes. (One reason I always loved drinking is that I am not prone to hangovers.)

It was a sad day for Yale when Charlie Garside was refused tenure. Many suspected that his being gay and being friends with numerous undergraduates had a lot to do with this decision. Mingling with the studentry was frowned upon by the senior Yale faculty prior to the upheavals of the late 1960s, when talking with the young became the only way for professors to understand why our cities were on fire and our universities in revolt. Walter Cronkite and the national politicians certainly couldn't tell you.

To the Tables Down at Mory's...

Music was my main distraction from the ennui of Yale campus life. Music was also the cause of my Yale downfall. I do not have a good voice, nor can I read music. My chances of getting into the Yale Glee Club, therefore, were poor. However, I love singing and have decent pitch and a good musical memory. Yale in those days had a second, lesser glee club, the Apollo, which acted as a feeder for the Yale Glee Club.

I wrangled my way into becoming one of the managers of the Apollo. This only meant picking up the sheet music after rehearsals and helping organize our occasional local concerts. Spare-time stuff. I could pick up my musical parts by singing in practices next to someone who could sight read.

After a year in the Apollo Glee Club and a voice trial, I was promoted to the Yale Glee Club as a junior manager. This was thanks to Fenno Heath, the long-time conductor of the Yale Glee Club.

Fenno was an inspired choral conductor, composer, and arranger. He had a fluting, peculiar counter-tenor speaking voice and the habit when conducting of throwing his head back like Leopold Stokowski in Walt Disney's *Fantasia*. Like Stokowski, Fenno wore a beautifully tailored set of tails whenever possible. His manicure was always perfect, too.

But short, pert little Fenno was friendly and liked students. Though he held some sort of title in Yale's music department, he seemed to spend most of his time with the glee club.

Yale has a majestic choral music tradition, which goes back to Gustave Stoeckel of Bavaria, Yale's first professor of music and founder of the Yale Glee Club. Like the tradition of droning lectures in large lecture halls from aged professors, Yale's music owes much to Imperial Germany. Yale's alma mater, *Bright College Years*, takes its tune from the greatest German patriotic song, *Die Wacht am Rhein*, though few Yalies acknowledge this.

Cole Porter, Yale Class of 1913, wrote several stirring Yale football fight songs. If you want to delve into such songs of Yale, there is a fine collection of old Yale songs: *The Yale Song Book*.

Charles Ives, America's greatest composer, also went to Yale. Unlike Porter, Ives mostly wrote church music while at Yale, though bizarrely he wrote a presidential campaign song for William McKinley in 1896. Unlike Porter, Ives played on the varsity football team, rather than writing football fight songs. Going on to make a fortune selling insurance, Ives defied the romantic image of the great composer as an otherworldly wimp.

Yale had many different singing groups. A number sang informally at Mory's, an old Yale institution that was basically a student drinking club. On an evening or two each week, groups appeared mid-evening to sing at Mory's, where you could slurp oysters and drink various fizzy, highly alcoholic punches out of big, silver-plated loving cups while seated at communal wooden tables.

A ritual was associated with drinking punch out of these large old cups. The cup held several bottles of cheap wine, topped up with fruit juice, rum, or vodka. Every drop had to be finished by the last person to drink, accompanied by everyone else banging on the table. The cup was up-ended over his face by the last drinker to prove that it was empty. Since the last drinker was inevitably totally wasted, this fellow usually ended up covered with crushed ice and sticky punch.

Sometimes there was spontaneous, drunken singing by Mory's patrons. Add students with dueling scars, uniforms, and songs in German, and you would have thought yourself in the Kaiser's Germany.

Mory's dark, drink-stained wooden tables had the initials of singing group members deeply carved into the tabletops.

I was pleased to find the initials of my tall, dark, handsome, and deranged Uncle Lew, Yale Class of 1940 and a Whiffenpoof, carved into the Whiffenpoofs' table. The Whiffenpoofs were the most famous and most exclusive Yale singing club.

By my time at Yale, poor old Lew had been institutionalized for a lengthy period for what was called a "complex personality disorder." My part of the family thought that this "disorder" was due to nothing more than Lew's spending too much time around his overpowering wife, Aunt Betty. And to his fondness for the gin bottle.

Eventually, Lew was dried out enough to be sprung from Hartford's euphemistically named Institute of Living. After a period of idle but relatively normal life, and the fortuitous death of Aunt Betty, he moved to Mexico and subsequently scandalized the family by marrying his not-so-young and not-so-thin Mexican housekeeper. Alas, this final escapade overtaxed him, and he died soon after the marriage.

Years before, Uncle Lew had lost several fingers on his right hand through a close encounter with a lawn mower. When asked at parties what he did, Lew held up his hand, paused, and said with a sigh, "Before the accident, I used to be a gynecologist," leaving the cause of the accident to the imagination of his listeners.

Lots of unexpected people turned up at Mory's to listen to the singing. Sometimes I chatted with Professor James Tobin, who went on to win the Nobel Prize for Economics. Apart from being dazzlingly brilliant, Tobin was a cheerful, open guy who liked student music and liked to drink.

One evening, while some group sang "Aura Leigh," Professor Tobin explained to me the role of gold in financial markets with such utter clarity that I have speculated reasonably successfully in the stuff over many years. The professor himself disapproved of gold as a non-productive asset, but he also stressed the role of the irrational in financial markets. Fortunately, the irrational and I get along well together.

The original Mory's closed some years ago, a victim of political correctness and laws against underage drinking. Someone told me that Mory's is now reorganized and has reopened in a politically correct co-ed format. I can't imagine why anyone would go there; the food was always awful so the point was the drunken, macho, song-filled atmosphere.

But Yale music remains wonderful to this day. Even in my churlish youth, I recognized that I was privileged indeed to be exposed to it.

Singing with the Yale Glee Club under Fenno was an indisputable privilege.

Spending time with my fellow student songbirds on a regular basis was a different matter, but initially bearable. My problem was that a certain type of earnest kid—complete with crewcut, impeccably straightened, dazzlingly white teeth and a sports coat and tie—was greatly over-represented in the Yale Glee Club.

These fine young men felt a need to demonstrate their loyalty to America not just by their own example, but by making sure that the actions of other students didn't detract from their own role as self-appointed paragons of patriotic virtue. (It is interesting that individuals of this type, though fervent in their vocal patriotism prior to the Vietnam War, always found some way to sit out the whole lengthy conflict.)

As long as we were travelling around the United States, singing for alumni groups or at well-attended public concerts, these guys and I managed to ignore each other.

Two brothers, possibly Mormons because I think they came from out West, were unusually perfect specimens of such fine young men: severely crewcut; humorless and teetotal; given to prayer; with names like Pyle and Ryle Bigfoot. These two and their disciples dominated the club.

Pyle, the taller of the two, was president of the Yale Glee Club, and Ryle, the shorter, had a title like "vice-president in charge of music stands." Pyle had a splendid manly appearance, due to heavy-framed glasses and a prominent jaw. Ryle was shorter and nondescript. Several others closely emulated Pyle and Ryle. Their key disciple, a stocky, blond kid with a severe crewcut, had a name like Duane Simkins II.

Simkins was either from Indianapolis, Indiana, or Columbus, Ohio, or Moline, Illinois. Choose one; anyplace near a lot of corn and hogs will do.

Duane will do for his first name. This guy was definitely corn-fed and an ex-high school sports star. Being Ohio-born and bred, I knew the type. We disliked each other on sight.

Readers may feel that I am being snotty, snobbish, and unfair to these callow but basically decent young men. And, to be fair, they were merely conventional products of their time.

After all, we all watched the same three TV networks that offered the same schmaltzy programming. All the networks were as sterilized as the shrink-wrapped drinking glasses in an American motel. All the networks offered news minus any real information. Think how different our world might be today if Walter Cronkite had provided us with a few choice facts about Jack Kennedy's sex life, his Addison's disease, or his Mafia connections.

We had grown up in the world of *I Love Lucy* and *Leave It to Beaver*, totally submersed in that mindless California-born pop culture, so well captured in *American Graffiti*. Unlike California, smoking grass was more or less unknown among the mostly east coast Yalies, so we missed out on its liberating effects. The originality and the fun remained in California.

I am looking at our glee club group photo; almost all the songsters have fairly short to very short hair and toothy grins. A fair number wear heavy horn-rimmed glasses. And, though you can't spot this in a photo, many were virgins.

Even though we were college students, our experience of the world was pitifully limited in comparison with that of intelligent high school kids today. Yet the Yalies in the photo took pride in being social yokels. Most liked being little clones of their smug parents.

Nonconformists could pay a high price in the American world of the 1950s we grew up in. Loyalty oaths and McCarthyism were real, however rarely they touched WASP families.

McCarthyism was an extreme. In general, American society in the 1950s and early 1960s merely tried to hammer everyone into the same mold through social pressure, or, as I had experienced, by reporting even minor behavioral deviations to the authorities, who were all too willing to receive the reports.

It is droll to contrast the major trouble I got into for silly mischief on the Yale campus in the early 1960s with the legal obstacles college authorities face today in just trying to flag a psychotic potential killer. "Why should he be suspended? Just because he told a shrink that he wanted to kill his roommate? You can't use that against him or put it in his academic file."

So, there are good reasons why many Yalies of the early 1960s were conformists and toadies. But they are inadmissible as excuses all the same. These guys were bright. Yale was never easy to get into, unless you were the son of a president or a star athlete.

Some were very bright. Pyle and Ryle went on to major professional success, for example. The brothers were ignorant about humanity and about the real world, but not stupid.

In every society, there are always pressures to conform socially. It always takes courage to be different or to accept change gracefully. These Yalies, like their country, would have change forced upon them. Their *I Love Lucy* world had to die. These earnest young men were self-limited human beings; inexcusable in intelligent people who have access to books, music, and films.

In spring 1963, we were told that the Glee Club would make a European tour that summer. For a little more than the cost of an air ticket, we would get to sing all over Europe. This was great news. We started rehearsing many different European national anthems.

We had several excellent soloists. One was a large, handsome baritone who was one of Yale's few blacks. Naturally, though a middle-class guy from a big northern city, this man was assigned to sing a Negro spiritual in the style of Paul Robeson. I can't remember any of the other soloists except for my young pal David Redman, who had the most beautiful tenor voice and an angelic face to go with it.

Redman's true personality was anything but angelic, which was why I enjoyed his company so much. Redman was fiercely intelligent, witty, and sardonic. I think he was the only child of rich, older parents. He also played the piano well; Redman had wonderful musical taste.

All of us begged, borrowed, or stole a tailcoat and a couple of formal white shirts. Add a passport, a toothbrush, and a change of underwear, and we were equipped to fly off to Europe in the summer of 1963.

Musically, the trip was a hit from the start. Fenno was an excellent organizer, and Yale had superb musical contacts all over Europe. We sang in places like the *Musikverein* in Vienna to large, enthusiastic audiences.

Socially, things went wrong from the beginning, but in ways that initially didn't involve me.

Among the general run of Yale undergraduates in those days, quite a few had traveled abroad. Since over half had gone to private schools, foreign travel was no big deal for their families financially. The dollar was rock hard, and Europe was a cheap place to go for Americans. My own family had traveled widely in Europe several times. I had subsequently gone all over Greece and the United Kingdom on my own.

However, it soon transpired that few of my fellow Yale songbirds had ever been outside the United States.

Instead of being filled with pleasure at this mind-opening opportunity to experience something new, lots of the glee clubbers were completely thrown from day one. There were instant complaints about strange food and real or imaginary stomach problems. Some were homesick. We were in the world of "If It's Tuesday, It Must Be Belgium."

In reaction to feeling out of their element, some became gauche and loud. Others were silent but inwardly anxious and resentful.

To their credit, Pyle and Ryle didn't turn into ugly Americans, but Duane Simkins and his followers did. I remember some of their loud comments: "Why are Europeans so funny looking? Why is their television crap? Why are Italians cowards?" Questions like these flew around out of Fenno's earshot but were shared with the local public in train stations and on street corners.

Simkins discovered that in Europe drink was not only cheap but served to anyone who could get his head above the bar. Others made the same discovery. These guys had never had anything stronger than a watery American beer. Now they could buy small bottles of eighty-proof schnapps and nip on them surreptitiously in trains and buses. Then these guys became really obnoxious.

Our first serious problem occurred in former Yugoslavia. We were riding in a bus along the *autoput*, a raised two-lane highway built for the convenience of the *Wehrmacht* during World War II. Simkins and some others were in the back of the bus, drinking.

Someone shouted that we would soon arrive at a pit stop so get the booze bottles out of sight. Without a thought, someone else instantly jettisoned a wine bottle out of a bus window. The bottle made solid contact with the helmetless head of a Yugoslav riding on a moped alongside the bus.

This poor guy swerved off the road, down the embankment, and out of sight. Someone shrieked, "Forget it! These people have heads of stone." Everyone in back laughed. The bus driver sped up.

The two trench-coated Yugoslav secret policemen waiting for us at our stop did not take such a humorous view of what had happened. We were all detained for some time. Calls were made to the U.S. Embassy. Fenno paced up and down.

Someone promptly informed on the person who had thrown the bottle. The informer may have been our bus driver, but my guess is that it was a gutless glee club member. Once identified, the bottle thrower was taken away and only returned to us—drained of color and very shaken—when it was clear that the moped rider was not seriously hurt.

After this, David Redman and I, along with a few others, withdrew from the main group socially. We turned up for the concerts and went to bed in the youth hostel or dormitory at night but otherwise kept to ourselves. This was soon noticed and much resented, especially by Simkins's bottle-throwing clique.

The musical events were thrilling. In Austria, we sang at the Abbey of St. Florian where Bruckner had spent his last years, playing the organ in the glorious church for the monks. In Germany, we sang in small wooden halls that had incredible acoustics. All over Europe, we sang in world famous concert halls.

At every concert, Fenno had us sing several of his own quirky pieces. These went down well. Fenno's compositions were musical settings of modern American poems. They were just tuneless enough to seem clever and original, yet not discordant enough to be unpleasant. The words reminded Europeans of things they liked about America. And we sang each country's national anthem loudly and with real enthusiasm at the beginning of every concert.

Then we reached Italy. We were in Turin for a major concert in an old, elegant opera house. We rehearsed in the afternoon and were told to be back for the concert at seven. To prepare for his solo, Redman wanted real Italian food, not the stuff we were given at our youth hostel.

Redman and I and several others found a splendid fry shop with a black-and-white tiled interior. You went to the counter to ask for a portion of fried fish by weight. Redman also asked for a bottle of Orvieto. And then for another. And then for yet another...

Redman had shown no signs of any interest in serious boozing prior to this. Perhaps he was just sick and tired of doing the same solo, night after night. Perhaps it was the first time he had ever had more than a glass of wine. I think he was only eighteen. I paid no attention to what Redman was doing, assuming he could handle a little wine.

By the time we dragged Redman into the opera house at six-thirty, he was leglessly drunk. Fenno took one disgusted look at Redman and told us to take him to the youth hostel, then to hurry back ourselves for the concert.

Fenno said nothing to me then or later but let it filter out that he blamed me for the incident. For an unknown malicious reason, I had deliberately made the star soloist drunk. This was absurd, but, unwisely, I thought it best to ignore the whole thing.

Subsequently, the atmosphere among the glee clubbers was not pleasant. There was muttering about us "lacking team spirit."

I didn't care because we were coming to the end of the trip. I was going on to meet my English cousin Harry and travel around Franco's Spain, and then fly back to Cleveland. Harry's and my method of travel had been perfected in Greece a couple of years before. We made *Europe on Five Dollars a Day* seem wildly extravagant. We looked at places we visited from the bottom up—the bottom of a wine bottle.

The singing trip was to end in Paris, where we stayed in an austere Catholic youth hostel. Fenno warned us not to smoke or drink in the youth hostel, which was spartanly bare inside and smelled of disinfectant. Redman and I and one other fellow were put in a large room by ourselves. Plenty of large crucifixes were scattered around the youth hostel to keep an eye on us.

Our other roommate was Charles Bobb, a worse influence on the club than I could ever be—notably due to his fantastic enthusiasm for alcohol and his shrewd, snide comments. On the trip, Bobb wore his hair long, lank, and dirty like a British academic. His father was a senior corporate executive who showered money on his son. Bobb, in turn, took having money and drinking as givens; perhaps he, too, was an only child.

———◆———

I knew Bobb outside the glee club because we had both been tapped to join the same underground secret society.

Fraternities were far less important at Yale than secret societies. To confuse matters, there were aboveground secret societies, like the infamous Skull and Bones, and underground secret societies. The aboveground secret societies met in peculiar, windowless stone buildings, called tombs, and were hardly "secret" in that everyone knew who was in Skull and Bones.

Skull and Bones features in many a film and novel as the evil source of plutocratic conspiracies against the American people. In these fictions, older Bonesmen take the new initiates under their wing and launch them after graduation as apprentice members of secret Wall Street and Washington cabals of manipulative right-wing billionaires. This is, of course, the purest nonsense, but it makes for a good tale.

Yalies had a good idea of what the Bonesmen did inside their tomb, which, apart from some ritual mummery, was to get drunk enough to tell each other their unvarnished life histories and hopes and fears for the future. All in all, something like a group masturbating session at a summer camp for boys. Or at a Cub Scout sleepover.

The underground secret societies were really secret in that no one knew who was a member or where they met but, unlike being in the infamous old Skull and Bones, being in an underground secret society was completely pointless; membership offered no social cachet and would not get you a job on Wall Street. I couldn't imagine that we had anything interesting to tell each other, either, but you live in hope.

I had mixed feelings about the whole secret society thing; I am not a joiner of clubs. But the guys who tapped me seemed amusing. We had planned one organizational meeting outside New Haven just before the end of my junior year, but the meeting aborted as we were driving out to our secret meeting place.

On the outskirts of New Haven, a drunk in a Ford crashed head-on into the large Mercedes driven by one of the guys who had tapped me. This Mercedes turned out to belong to the stepfather of the Yalie driver who was instantly plunged into gloom, since, in a quest for total secrecy, he had taken this fine car without his stepfather's permission.

After surveying the wreckage, the guy ran around begging us to tell no one, but clearly he was going to need to tell someone with a tow truck. Sirens indicated that the police were on its way. The rest of us, especially Charles Bobb, thought this attempt to keep the crash a secret pathetic: no one was hurt; it was clearly the drunk's fault, and who were we going to tell?

Anyway, I was glad to share a room with Bobb; we laughed at the same things.

The three of us went out for a steak frites in a bistro and got lightly sozzled on red plonk. Bearing in mind that we had a concert the next day, the last day of the trip, I suggested that we turn in early. Bobb and Redman said that they had never been in Paris before. An early night was a ridiculous idea.

So I went to sleep in our barracks of a room *tout seul*.

Around midnight, Bobb and Redman arrived back in our room. But not alone. They had persuaded a none-too-young *poule* to join them for some traditional Parisian nighttime fun. Naturally, Bobb and Redman wanted me to join in. By then, Bobb and Redman were more than slightly drunk. They had to be to want to do anything sexual with this ghastly woman.

I could see that this was not going to end well, so I got up and went off to sleep in an empty bed in another room.

"Merde! Salauds! Cons!"

I woke to hear ugly screaming in French. Female screaming. Some insanely angry woman was screaming. There were no women in a male youth hostel, were there? I looked at my watch. It was after two a.m. Then, I remembered...

I was the first on the scene. Wearing only their underpants, Bobb and Redman were trying to pay off their prostitute with a twenty-dollar American Express traveler's check. She was protesting that she didn't take traveler's checks at any hour of the night or day and that anyway the agreed price for several hours of fun was fifty dollars in cash. The prostitute seemed to have all the force of logic and natural justice on her side.

When I pointed this out to Bobb and Redman, they told me to please just deal with her. Neither Bobb nor Redman spoke one word of French, and they had no cash. This was going to be a challenge for my rotten, academic French. I was trying to calm the woman sufficiently to commence a rational negotiation when Fenno and the rest of the glee club, led by Pyle and Ryle, arrived in their pajamas.

Everyone began shouting. Pyle thrust out his jaw, looking manly and outraged. Fenno looked stunned and close to tears. The whore was pointing her finger at Redman and then at Bobb. Bedlam...

At that point I slipped away and found another empty bed.

***

The atmosphere in the youth hostel cafeteria at breakfast the next morning was downright hostile. Waves of outrage came off the entire Mormon Tabernacle Choir contingent. Which the three of us ignored since by then we always sat in quarantine on our own. Fenno was busy getting ready for his big event and the end of the tour, so he simply stayed away from us and sat with Pyle and Ryle and their clique.

Fenno was an other-worldly character whose only interest was male choral music. I am sure that he hoped the whole incident would just evaporate. And that he would never see the three of us again after the trip ended.

Once again, it leaked out that he held me to blame for this incident, even though he never spoke to me about whatever he thought I was guilty of. Procuring? This was pure Yale—embarrassed, unspoken accusations. Nevertheless, I still liked Fenno; he was simply a classic academic who had little idea of what was going on in the world outside his head.

The big event was of the greatest significance to Fenno but less so for his songsters, despite Fenno's numerous attempts to explain the importance of what he had arranged for us.

We were to sing at Fontainebleau, just outside Paris, for Nadia Boulanger, a legendary figure in French music who had taught musicians like Aaron Copland, one of Fenno's heroes. We did a quick rehearsal of one of Fenno's compositions. If Boulanger liked it, we would sing more of our repertoire.

I felt awful from lack of sleep. Redman and Bobb were completely hungover. The rehearsal didn't go well. Pyle attempted a man-to-man, Vince Lombardi-style pep talk. Everyone ignored him. We sensed that the trip had effectively ended. On the bus out to Fontainebleau no one talked much.

In 1963, Nadia Boulanger was seventy-six. She had worked with many of the greatest musicians of the twentieth century. It was gracious of her and a real compliment to Fenno that she agreed to listen to a bunch of Yalies. But she was very old. A couple of her people ushered us in to a large concert room. Boulanger appeared and was assisted to a chair. Her eyesight was poor so there was much positioning of her chair and moving us about. Fenno wanted Boulanger to see his hands and his profile. We sang a couple of pieces. Then we were ushered out.

By then it was noon. A communal meal had been laid on for us. The meal was good French food but the menu overall was a mistake. There was a bottle of strong red table wine for every four Yalies. And no water and, worse, no Cokes. This was a serious misjudgment. Everyone except Pyle and Ryle and the few hard-core abstainers drank glass after glass of wine until it was gone. Then we asked for more wine. More bottles were cheerfully brought out for the nice young American students. All the bottles were emptied.

We went out to get on the bus. There was pushing and shoving as we got on the bus, which hadn't happened before. The afternoon was warm. People were dozing as the bus pulled off. The first ten or fifteen minutes of the bus ride back into Paris were quiet. I heard muttered talk in the back of the bus. People were moving around in the aisle of the bus behind me. But everything seemed normal...

Until without warning, Duane Simkins grabbed me from behind and tried to throw me onto the floor of the bus. He attempted to pinion me with some sort of wrestling hold. Others cheered him on but only as observers.

I was forced out of my seat and into the aisle and nearly fell forward onto my face. My guess is that Simkins planned to get me on to the floor of the bus to teach me some sort of lesson with a few good swift kicks. Football locker room stuff.

By now my head was clear. I was in a white rage. I was sick of these miserable, self-satisfied bastards. If fighting was required, I was ready.

Grabbing an armrest, I pulled myself back up and got my legs under me. With a body heave, I managed to throw Simkins back into my seat. I braced my legs against the seat in front and pushed Simkins back into the seat hard, giving him a couple of sharp shots in the ribs with my elbow as I did. Simkins said something nasty and tried to get his forearm around my neck.

I twisted away from him to get some space and then planted my right elbow hard and squarely in his face. I hoped I'd broken his nose but only caught his cheekbone. But this was enough to make Simkins lose interest in continuing the match. No one else wanted to take his place when I stood up and suggested it. I pushed Simkins out of the way and sat down again in my original seat, still shaking with anger. Silence reigned.

The next morning, bright and early, Charles Bobb and I managed to rent a car. We weren't twenty-one so Bobb must have forged something to get the car. We said good-bye to Redman and to a couple of pleasant guys who were bemused by what had happened.

Then Bobb and I drove to Madrid over the Pyrenees. Or rather I drove; Bobb drank all the way. There were no French *autoroutes* in those days so the trip took us a day and a night of steady driving; we only stopped for me to eat and for Bobb to restock with booze. I knew the concept of "road beers," but Bobb took this into a different dimension.

In Spain, Bobb and I split. I had a fun trip around Spain with my cousin Harry, using the *Europe on Zero Dollars a Day* approach we had perfected in Greece. Broken-down rural buses, donkey carts, and hitching rides—we tried them all. I didn't think anything more about the Yale Glee Club tour. My glee club days were over.

When I got back to the United States in late August, I found a letter from Dean Sam Chauncey waiting for me in Cleveland. His committee would like me to report to them just after Labor Day in New Haven. There was no mention of a reason for this meeting.

I didn't think the glee club tour would be of much interest to the Yale authorities. I'd done well academically my junior year. I expected a general warning to finish up my senior year without any further trouble. So, I'd just go back a couple of days early.

My father insisted on joining me for this New Haven jaunt. I will never know his reasons for wanting to come with me. We never did anything together. My father was a successful high school English teacher but a most unsuccessful father. His petulant temper tantrums, often fueled by drink, made childhood an ordeal for his three children.

Father was the youngest child of a rich Cincinnati, Ohio, family of five. His father owned one of the country's largest paper companies and had no interest in children; his mother was busy with good works and not maternal in the least. My father, always known in his family as Bilkers, was raised by a small, dedicated black woman who was part of the family, then sent away to school as soon as possible.

I was taken to visit this interesting old lady, Sallie Dowtin, in a home for old black people in Covington, Kentucky, before she died. This was about 1947. Sallie had looked after three generations of my father's family, starting in 1886. She was small, wrinkled, and frail but had a perfect memory for every detail about the family. Dowtin had been born a slave and must have been about ninety. Since I was only four or five when I visited her, I have only vague memories of her, which I deeply regret.

Unfortunately, this outsourced upbringing turned my father into a physical coward and spoiled brat who couldn't tolerate being thwarted in any form. As a small child, Father was often allowed to eat two breakfasts to keep him from having a temper tantrum. Naturally, his weight was always a problem.

Father was the most perfectly selfish person I've ever known well. (I had an aristocratic British boss who was in the same league. If British libel laws change, I look forward to writing about him.)

Any form of travel brought out the worst in Father. Even a short car journey could be a nightmare. The slightest draft on the back of his neck provoked instant shouting and rage. So, in the days before auto air-conditioning, we three children went everywhere with the car windows of the family's massive, lurching Buick station wagon tightly closed, slumped together in the back seat feeling irritable and sweaty and carsick.

Nasty outbursts followed any questioning of Father's dogmatic pronouncements. These could take the form of anything from a lengthy racist tirade about black people's lack of driving skills—one of his life-long obsessions—to a preposterous, sweeping statement about the imminent collapse of U.S. agriculture due to a shortage of earthworms. Any attempt to ask for facts to support these assertions was met with a screaming fit: "I'm a professional teacher; how dare you question me!"

You might wonder if this infantile streak made Father a poor teacher. On the contrary, by every account he was an excellent, even inspired, teacher. (Aren't most male school teachers' inadequates of some sort? It's a job girly men default to.)

Father taught mostly in good private schools and briefly in one of the best public schools in the country. This was the key to his success. He always worked with ambitious kids who wanted to go to university.

Being selfish and self-centered is helpful in teaching a room full of challenging, hormonal teenagers. The teacher can sock it to them at a nice brisk clip and with a total disregard for their fatuous teenage opinions. If they question something politely, the teacher is pleased. If they object, the teacher just lets it slide over him. The teacher has the daily thrill of a captive audience. If someone laughs at the teacher behind his back, Big Teach has the last laugh when he slaps a large red "D" on the pimple-covered young scholar's next essay.

But there was a positive and original aspect to father's teaching methods. He loved helping kids with speech problems such as stuttering. First, he put the kid on stage to act in an old melodrama. Later, when the kid felt more confident, Father put the kid in front of class to recite Victorian poetry. This method worked. One former stammerer, Austin Pendleton, went on to a fine acting career on Broadway and in films.

Father reserved his nastier side for the home front.

At home, Father used hitting during his rages to ensure our full attention. When I grew into a tall, strong sixteen-year-old, I told Father that if he ever hit me again, I would hit him back. Never much of a listener, Father took a drunken swing at me a few nights later. I stepped aside and biffed him firmly in his large gut. He promptly deflated. After that, we avoided personal confrontations.

My mother was less fortunate. I assume that Father married her mainly to have someone to take the place of his black nanny, though Mother was thought quite a local beauty in Cincinnati when young. Mother had beautiful blue eyes and loved to dance.

She had lost her own father as a small child. She came from a family of provincial gentry, fallen on hard times, and in consequence she worshiped money. Though shrewdly intelligent, she was totally uneducated. So, snagging a spoiled, but rich, brat of a husband worked superbly for her for quite a while.

Until it didn't.

Then she found another, more reliable love—alcohol. At about the same time, she started to lose her marbles. Mother had fears—many, many fears. When I was about twelve, I urged her to see a psychiatrist. This was not well received. Mother had a gut-level fear and loathing of shrinks. When I pointed out to her that she was going down a road that her children couldn't follow, she shrugged.

For her children, bringing friends home was risky.

Increasingly agoraphobic over time, mother stayed inside and got her kicks from stirring the family pot. She had an amazing flair for sensing a topic that would upset someone. She could, for example, sniff out a hidden belief in an oddball religion or unilateral nuclear disarmament in someone she just met. Then she would rubbish that belief.

Or it might be a sexual quirk that she would tease out like a witch hunter, and coyly—but loudly—allude to. Her "gaydar," for example, was superb. Faced with some poor, confused guy who had yet to come out, she would ask him sly, pointed questions about his relationship with his mother. Her code for a gay man was to say, "He has a mother." She fantasized about having a gay son to dominate. Think *Psycho*.

When the person under attack was one of our young friends, we rushed in to defend the belief or quirk, as the friend would be too embarrassed to do so. A screaming row was certain to follow, plus the loss of the friend.

Mother's real life work, however, was the care and humoring of Father. Emotionally this was difficult for her children to accept, but we all understood this reality sooner or later.

Years later, my sister wanted the three of us to spring a dramatic, surprise rehab intervention upon mother, no doubt complete with a straitjacket—size: women's extra small—followed by a refreshing course of electroshock treatments.

My brother and I refused to take part, aborting the intervention. This infuriated my sister who began what now looks like a lifetime of non-speakies with my brother. (I was accepted again as a communicant after some fifteen years of silence.)

Losing contact with my sister was sad. I regret this, but I still fail to see the point of such an intervention. Whether free will exists or not, isn't it necessary to pretend that it does? What degree of mental illness is required to absolve us from treating family members as free to mess up their lives in ways of their own choosing?

For me, it would be emotionally straightforward to go to the supermarket and help seize two or three morbidly obese women from the checkout line for immediate bariatric surgery. Such slow-suicides-by-fat might even later thank you for this intervention. But should you do that to your mother, however grossly obese she might be? Would she thank you in any case?

When Mother died from a fall, possibly caused by being knocked down the stairs by Father, we had to put Father in an assisted-living home. On his own, he could no longer perform the simplest personal tasks. In the home, among other oddities, the staff discovered that Father could not button his shirt; Mother had done it for him. Posthumously, I began to feel sympathy for Mother. Perhaps there was more to her than being an emotionally manipulative drunk.

In middle-age, Mother had a large—six foot square—doll's house made. For the rest of her life, she spent a good deal of time and money on decorating and furnishing this doll's house. Father didn't help her with the practical, hands-on side of this project, but he took great interest in helping select the tiny pieces of furniture and in the choice of wallpaper.

In many ways, playing house together was all they ever wanted to do. Having children was a tedious but necessary part of furnishing their real-life house. They relished collecting things they called antiques but that the average person might consider bric-a-brac. They spent hours together in what they considered antique shops but others might call junk shops.

Individually poisonous they might be, but they loved being together.

On that last night of her life, I suspect that Father did more or less accidentally knock Mother down the stairs in one of his rages. He had done a similar thing before. I doubt that he blamed himself for her death; he probably was also drunk at the time. A truly selfish person doesn't second-guess his own behavior. For Father, what happened wasn't murder or even manslaughter, merely something unfortunate that had happened to him.

Mother had a morbid fear of death, so perhaps her painless end—she never regained full consciousness—was a blessing.

They were both in their eighties when Mother died. In his way, Father missed her. It was all so inconvenient for him afterward.

In my more compassionate moments, I imagine them together again, playing house in some great room in an infernal region. It's damnably hot; hot and horridly humid, but folks from Cincinnati thrive in such conditions. My parents don't mind a thing about the place; they have each other, no irritating and distracting children, and an immense doll's house to play with for eternity.

———◆———

Despite our limited relationship, Father was hell-bent to come to New Haven with me to face this nebulous committee. Perhaps Father felt that, as a teacher who had propelled numerous students in the direction of Yale, he would have some leverage with this committee. Perhaps he just felt that as a Yalie himself, we should stick together. I will never know.

By not talking much, we managed not to argue on the drive to New Haven. Father sat in the passenger seat of my small Volvo and didn't complain about the open windows.

I wasn't exactly glad that Father was with me, but I could tolerate his presence. On the way, Father waxed lyrical about his good old days in splendid downtown New Haven. Since Father considered Cleveland, Ohio, the acme of urban life, I'd learned to ignore his comments about the charms of decayed U.S. industrial cities.

The committee met in a small room in an admin building on the Old Campus. I'd been given no idea what to expect or whether there was anything to prepare for. Sam Chauncey wasn't there, but the by-now-familiar Yale kangaroo court format was in place. I took my seat on one side of a rectangular wooden table, facing my three accusers.

Various charges in connection with the glee club tour were read out to me by a middle-aged administrator I'd never seen before. Two other tweedy types sat with him. I assumed they were all deans. The charges were many but ill-defined. It wasn't clear who had leveled the charges; Fenno or Pyle and Ryle or A.N. Other. It wasn't clear which, if any, Yale rules or regulations I had transgressed. This was beyond rule breaking; this was thoughtcrime.

Obviously, someone had written down notes about my supposed behavior during the glee club tour. When you were suspected of being a deviant at Yale in those days, you could expect to be watched. Someone had been deputized to do the watching.

I wasn't allowed to see the notes, but some of the accusations the dean recited were bizarre. They implied that I had the malevolent organizing ability of a young Trotsky. How do you spread sedition on a glee club tour?

I said nothing. None of this mattered, anyway. It was just for the record. A decision had already been made and rubber-stamped. I was to go away and think about life. I could reapply to Yale at an indeterminate future date. Or not. They wished me well and "please close the door behind you." Father and I left.

Back in Cleveland, I knew that I would be drafted soon after I turned twenty-one in October. I went downtown to the army recruiting office and signed up for three years in the army on September 15, 1963. I had a physical, swore an oath, and was on my way to a fulfilling career as a private E-1.

I had no idea what lay ahead, but I wasn't worried. Self-inflicted gloom was never my thing. Cynical but cheerful; that's my shtick. To this day, I wake happy, hungry, and ready to bite the butt off a bear.

I felt liberated; I counted my blessings. I was born with great advantages. I was a strong, healthy young man with much to look forward to. The big, wide world was varied and fascinating. Some people were lovable and fun. There was so much to learn about and experience.

Dud parents were no reason for not enjoying life. Nor was picking the wrong university.

Suffering from an illness or a bad love affair is different. Loneliness is always hard. Depression is a disease; will-power can't tame it. But the day-to-day crap that people hand out so freely is merely stuff to laugh about. The world is mad.

I swore a heart-felt internal oath. I would not let run-of-the-mill humanity make me feel bad enough about anything to be unhappy. I would laugh at them and their ridiculous, posturing antics. After all, we are all just a bunch of clever apes.

Viewed with cool, rational detachment, life is an endless cosmic joke that offers infinite pleasure and instruction. And at life's end, as in a Looney Tunes cartoon, "That's all, folks."

So, let me offer thanks to Yale and to my parents for helping me grasp these life-enriching and evergreen insights; a liberal education comes in strange forms and from unlikely sources.

Feeling calm and resolute, I boarded an overnight bus in Public Square in Cleveland and went off with a group of newly minted soldiers to Fort Leonard Wood, Missouri.

Learning How to Play Soldier

Fort Leonard Wood, Missouri was built to train soldiers for World War II. Located in an area of low hills, muddy creeks, and scrubby hardwood trees, the base had changed little since then. There were a few permanent modern cinder block barracks, but any training done indoors took place in old, wooden two-story buildings that had outlived their useful lives. Wind whistled through gaps in their thin siding. This didn't matter much since mostly we trained outside.

On arrival, the departing ex-trainees we met in the bus depot told us that Fort Leonard Wood was called either the Garden Spot of the Ozarks or Little Korea. We would hate every minute that we were there. But I didn't hate Fort Leonard Wood; it was all new to me.

After our all-night bus ride, we were herded together by Sergeant Duty who told us that he was our drill sergeant and "not to listen to no bullshit from nobody; he would give us the straight word."

Sergeant Duty was tall and skinny and sounded like a southern hillbilly—which he was.

Over the next few days, Sergeant Duty hustled us through having our heads shaved, teeth inspected, bodies checked out and shot full of injections, and issued with uniforms. The uniforms were a mixture of old and new and not all that ill-fitting.

True, our new belt brass buckles were irritatingly covered with hard protective lacquer that needed to be polished off with Brasso, but much effort and a good deal of care was taken in fitting our two pairs of combat boots. Sergeant Duty supervised the boot fitting. He was a veteran infantry sergeant and told us always to look after our feet. He was an expert about feet.

I know exactly what Sergeant Duty looked like because I have a copy of our graduation-from-basic-training book. On the leatherette cover it is dated 28 November 1963, and in it are pictures of the officers, sergeants, and trainees of Company D, 4th Battalion, 3rd Regiment. Platoon Sergeant Arthur Duty is the spitting image of Randy Quaid, the movie actor. Our company commander was First Lieutenant Joseph Hadley who was thin, black, and super fit. Lt. Hadley led us in exercises, but otherwise we had little contact with him.

My fellow trainees were a random cross section of young American males. Some, like me, were volunteers; some were draftees. We were young—I was one of the older guys at almost twenty-one—and few were married. Most were white, but we had a large black contingent. There were only a few Hispanics.

I had looked carefully at the inner-city black guys on the bus coming down from Cleveland. Some were large and muscular. Did I have to fear these black guys?

From the first, I found that I did not. The black guys hung around together. From their standpoint, having been raised in a black ghetto, this was the first time in their lives they were surrounded by whites.

Even these northern blacks had little experience of the white world. They had every reason to be suspicious of whites, even of trainees like themselves. "They didn't want no trouble."

Not all the black guys were from northern cities. Some were from the rural south. One guy, whom I will never forget, was the most remarkable self-taught, intuitive musician. He was just a skinny kid, but when he played the spoons and sang, the result was so wonderful that you wished for Alan Lomax and his tape recorder to appear on the scene. No one else, not even the other southern blacks, knew the songs this man sang. Everyone stopped to listen.

Some trainees, regardless of skin color, were painfully homesick. In the barracks, there was crying at night after lights out. Some trainees were overaged bed-wetters. The army dealt with this by putting two bed-wetters in the same double bunkbed, then rotating who slept in the top bunk. The idea was that the man in the bottom bunk would ensure that the man on top had a late-night pee. This proved an effective cure.

I kept to myself at Fort Leonard Wood. I wasn't sure what I had dropped into.

I quickly learned that few of my fellow trainees had been to college. None was a graduate. Education was a conversational no-go area. Any revelation of a university background was like suddenly proclaiming that you had a communicable disease. The revelation could lead to boring consequences.

Once, all men with one or more years of university were told to fall out. This resulted in my spending a day opening and closing the door of the dental clinic. As the dental medic shouted "next," I quickly opened the screen door and pushed the guy at the head of the waiting line into the dentist's room. A quick dental exam followed. Gross dental problems were common. One guy was told that all his rotten remaining teeth—about six—needed to be pulled. Unfortunately, I was not around to witness this.

When asked by the dentist, a number of the white, peckerwood trainees admitted they had never used a toothbrush. At this admission, the dental medic gave the young hillbilly a prompt demonstration of the operational use of the toothbrush. With the victim leaning back in the dentist's chair, and the dentist standing tactfully back, the medic forced the victim's mouth open and applied the dry brush briskly to the soldier's gums until they bled.

Just shaving the trainees' heads and ordering them to shower once a day greatly improved the appearance of the typical trainee. Many guys arrived with greasy Elvis-style hairdos and pimply faces. Once their heads were shaved and they started washing, their acne cleared up.

We were given blunt instructions about basic hygiene but never had the famous talk about avoiding VD. Our instructions only covered the need to wash regularly or more often than once a week.

One or two guys didn't buy into the concept of showering. At the urging of a sergeant, one such stinker was hauled into the shower by a gang of trainees—not including me—and scrubbed briskly with a stiff-bristled, old-fashioned wooden laundry brush and a bar of old-fashioned yellow laundry soap. I suppose this was educational for the victim but scrubbing someone raw seemed barbaric to me. But it worked; there were no repeat offenders.

To my utter surprise, I found that my WASP background had prepared me well for basic training. I'd already lived in a tent at summer camp with boys I didn't particularly like. I'd gone away to school years before; I didn't miss anyone but our family dog. Army food was better than Yale's and the army in-processing system no more impersonal than Yale's. Most of my fellow trainees were friendly and much more interesting to me than the suburban types at Yale.

At Yale, I was a sub-mediocre athlete. But in the army I was a near star.

Most of my fellow trainees had never played any sport. Sports were mandatory at my school; they weren't in the nation's public schools. Most of these new soldiers had never run anywhere. At my school we ran all the time, just as we now did in basic training.

The result was that I played end and caught passes in football games. Wearing combat boots, I ran the fastest mile in our training company. Going on marches was no problem after hiking in the White Mountains as a ten year old.

Even better, I'd already learned how to shoot a .22 rifle at summer camp. Later, Phinney Works's father, a World War II major in the army, had taught me how to shoot his World War II M-1 rifle, which the army was still using at Fort Leonard Wood in basic training.

Apart from hitting what you aimed at, the main objective in shooting the M-1 was to keep it from slamming you in the face when you did rapid fire. The trick was not to wrap your right thumb over the stock so that your thumb's knuckle joint wasn't subsequently slammed back into your cheek by the recoil.

Sergeant Duty warned us of this feature of the M-1, but few paid attention. He was a font of hard-won military lore, but most trainees lacked the frame of reference needed to absorb his advice. There was no war going on so the advice seemed academic.

Sergeant Duty would march us out to the rifle range, chanting "Jody choruses"—no doubt like his Confederate military ancestors. A Jody chorus is a marching chant like:

I don't know but I've been told,
Eskimo pussy is mighty cold.

Sound off, one, two,
Sound off, three, four,
Sound off, one two, three, four.

The sergeant chants the verse and the men come in on the refrain, with the left foot hitting the ground on "one" and "three."

Jody choruses make a long march pass quickly. Sergeant Duty kept up this chanting by the hour without repeating a verse. I imagined him in 1863 leading a long column of ragged, brave Confederate soldiers along the dusty roads of Pennsylvania toward their doom at Gettysburg. Sergeant Duty even chewed tobacco. He was fair and, in a limited and military way, considerate.

Whether through instruction or through pain, we all soon learned that any interaction between the human thumb and the M-1 was not pleasant. Another important precaution was to hold back the rifle bolt in a certain way so that it didn't smash your thumb when you were disassembling your rifle. There were lots of guys with bruised cheeks and black-and-blue thumbs after our first week on the rifle range.

I was an OK shot and qualified easily but not well enough for the expert qualification. Something about having to wear a steel helmet while firing threw off my aim.

We all lost weight. My waist shrank. I ate Baby Ruth candy bars by the box. Army food was southern and heavy; pancakes and bacon for breakfast; meat, potatoes, and gravy at other meals. We had treats like greens fried in bacon fat. Despite this unhealthy and filling food, we were hungry all the time. We bought so many candy bars that the PX ran out.

The randomness of the draft meant that I shared basic training with a wide cross-section of American men, somewhat tilted toward working-class men. We were nicely assorted as to size, shape, and color. The truly odd and quirky types were mostly found among my fellow volunteers.

The draftees were a bit older than the volunteers and more homogenized physically, with a couple of exceptions. One poor black draftee with thick glasses quickly proved to be nearly blind. He was sent back home to St. Louis where he made a living as a shoeshine boy. I remember him saying, quite resignedly, that "ah tole 'em an' ah tole em, ah doan see so good. But they is tole me that I gotta come with them so as I did."

One quirky volunteer was little Knock who was supposed to be eighteen but who was more like sixteen and slow mentally. Knock was a "low normal"; a classification the army was well supplied with in those days. Functional illiteracy was not uncommon, either. All through my time in training and later in the artillery, I read or filled in documents for men or helped them write letters.

Knock had a large head on a small body and a fixed, unhappy smile. We assumed that his father or guardian had decided that Knock needed military seasoning. Or just wanted to get him off the farm. This experiment was a failure. Knock couldn't follow even the simplest instructions, despite his own valiant efforts and lots of help from others. Sometimes, we saw him weeping tears of frustration as he tried to put his M-1 back together.

Eventually, I assume that the army washed him out. I imagined an army clerk wrapping Knock in brown paper, tying him up with string, and sending him back to Gomersville, Kentucky.

Knock was sweet-natured and just unfortunate.

Others trainees were much less pleasure to be around. Any believer in the natural goodness of mankind had this belief promptly and aggressively challenged in the army. However, even for cynics about human nature like me, one group proved a surprisingly consistent pain in the fundament.

No, not African-Americans. I never had the slightest trouble with a black American in the army from beginning to end.

No, not the truly poor rural whites from Appalachia, either.

I liked the authentic hillbillies like Yates and his droll cousin, Cordell. Both were stick-thin, but strong, and came from somewhere "down in the holler." They were tough but funny men who liked to tease the rest of us. Cordell claimed to have been born with six fingers on his left hand like all men in his family. However, his daddy had cut off the surplus pinkie with a hatchet when Cordell was "round 'bout eight." And indeed there was a scar on the outside of his left hand.

Cordell and Yates told tales of inbreeding that were as complex as the old song, "I'm My Own Grandpa." I think they made these stories up to amuse themselves, knowing that the rest of us believed anything they told us. However, if we had poked fun at them, violence would have followed. They were proud and independent. Their philosophy was: "Our mothers didn't raise no stupid children."

Men like Cordell and Yates made good soldiers. They knew everything about hunting and being outside in bad weather. Walking up and down hills carrying heavy stuff was second nature to them. Shooting someone probably was, too. They never complained about anything.

My problem was with poor white trash from the south. These guys were from the trailer park and tarpaper shack outskirts of large towns and small cities. Many were, as one black guy explained, "poison mean." To this day, hearing a voice like ex-President Bubba Clinton's—that rasping, nasal, Arkansas trailer park accent—puts me on the alert.

These crackers or gomers were always potential trouble. Racial bigotry lurked just beneath their surface, along with an unfocused anger at the world. So did the suspicion that others were making fun of them behind their backs. They brought this chippiness with them from home; they didn't pick it up in the army. In the army, no one bothered them. Men didn't make fun of other men in the army. Too many guns around, plus you had to sleep in an open barracks with all the other soldiers.

One jerk named Dennis Foxwell, a wiry, smart-ass guy of about nineteen from the outskirts of some town in Arkansas or Tennessee, decided I was dissing him. Foxwell had jug ears, a sly smirk, and that strong rasping accent.

I didn't realize I had offended this cretin until one afternoon out on the rifle range. Already autumn, the weather was cool and overcast. The scrubby trees didn't turn color as they do in the north. The leaves just looked browner and browner. And sad.

We were standing in a small group, waiting to shoot. Without prelude, Foxwell said to me in a flat tone and not as a question, "Why you using them big words." I had never spoken to Foxwell, but it seemed that he didn't like overhearing my vocabulary. I ignored him. One of his friends then also threatened me, but shut up when I snatched up my rifle and told him I was going to plant the rifle butt in his face if he opened his mouth again. And I meant it.

A couple of nights later, some of us spent our first free evening drinking watery three point two percent beer—the only kind available—in the PX annex. When I wandered back into the barracks, there was Foxwell, waiting for trouble. He said something ugly and pushed me. That was the signal. I was being tested. Others gathered around.

I tried to punch Foxwell hard in the face with my right fist but missed. I am not a fight starter and definitely not a boxer. Foxwell grabbed my arm and tried to twist it behind my back. I twisted loose from this hold, knocked him off balance with a shove and rammed him across the room into a store closet with my shoulder. We writhed around inside the closet for what seemed like many minutes but took seconds. He tried to knee me in the balls. I twisted away.

At that point I got lucky and managed to smack him hard across the throat with the side of my hand. It was an instinctive blow; I couldn't have repeated it in cold blood. This ended the fight and left Foxwell gagging and gasping on the closet floor, trying to get his breath. The whole thing only lasted perhaps a minute, but I was covered with sweat and shaking. No one said anything. The observers drifted away.

I don't like fighting. I never started a fight. But somehow I finished all of my adult fights. The way to stop a bully once and for all is to make the bully understand that you are not to be hassled; that if he angers you to the point of violence he will pay. Smashing one of these guys hard in the face or in a soft place is what they understand; words are wasted.

Intelligent, confident men don't start meaningless fights. Too risky. In my rage, I would have cheerfully kicked, bitten, or butted Foxwell to win the fight. I was stronger than he was in any case. Probably had better teeth, too, and certainly had bigger feet.

Fighting was just one of those things; fights were common in the army. No one I knew was ever reported for mere fighting. What are soldiers for?

———◆———

In basic training we were cut off from the world. We had no newspapers. We had nothing but transistor radios for news; there were a few black and white TVs in public rooms, but I never watched. So I was fortunate to watch the unfolding of a major historic event, horrible tragedy that it was.

Toward the end of our eight weeks of basic training, we spent a couple of weeks going out in the field every day. After a week, I began to feel lousy. The constant rain didn't help. I began to cough and couldn't shake it off. This worried me. Since I am rarely ill, I am a whiney, pathetic patient. I reported sick one morning. The medic gave me a couple of aspirins.

The next morning I felt worse. This time I saw the training battalion doctor. He decided that I was indeed ill and put me on light duty. This consisted of loading cases of dummy grenades onto a truck in the rain.

After a day of light duty, I was coughing so hard that it bent me double. I went back to the doctor and asked to be sent back out to the field since the light duty was going to finish me off. By then I had a fever so I was sent to the base infirmary and put on penicillin. The date was November 21, 1963.

By the next morning, I was feeling better. The army ward nurse, who was an officer, had us all up bright and early to clean the ward. Then we were told to lie down again.

A black-and-white TV at the end of the ward was tuned to a daytime soap opera, called I think, *The Brighter Day*. None of us was watching it.

Suddenly, the program was interrupted. A male voice said there were reports that the president had been shot, but no further details were available. We looked at each other. No one believed it. We assumed there was a mistake.

Shortly afterward, though, another message said that the president had been assassinated in Dallas. He was dead. Somber music began to play. We were stunned. No one said anything except "Shit!" Shortly afterward, all the medical staff disappeared. We looked after ourselves for the rest of the day.

As patients, we were ignored in the excitement that followed. Lee Harvey Oswald was promptly arrested. Within hours his connection with the Soviet Union was known. Some military genius immediately decided there was a risk of a Russian invasion attempt or coup. At least, that was the version filtered through to us in the base infirmary.

Fort Leonard Wood was put on full combat alert. The combat forces on the base were mobilized, loaded up in their trucks and armored vehicles, and moved out from the base. Of course, no one had the slightest idea where these trigger-happy GIs should go. So they drove around in circles in the rain for a day and a night, occasionally loosing off a few rifle rounds accidentally, terrifying the already jumpy Missouri civilians.

Finally, these tired, soaked young soldiers were allowed to return to base. The mood remained agitated. No one—including me—had the common sense to reflect that, if the Russians came within a hundred miles of Fort Leonard Wood, which is more or less in the middle of our vast country, it was time for surrender, not for mobilization.

———————◆———————

Despite the fact that the Kennedy assassination soon gave rise to the most elaborate conspiracy theories in the history of the world, its immediate impact on the thinking of ordinary soldiers was limited.

Back in training, I didn't see any soldiers in tears or even shaken. Perhaps the significance took a while to sink in? No, my belief is that the media-driven Kennedy legend soon overtook the reality of the brief, so-so Kennedy Presidency.

Right after the assassination, I heard men say in the PX snack bar that they didn't care much about the whole thing: "It don't mean nothing." No one threatened to bash them for saying this, yet threats of bashing after the slightest hint of an insult were common.

Why was this local reaction at Fort Leonard Wood to the Kennedy assassination so at odds with folklore about what the assassination meant? After all, everyone can remember where they were that day. Or can they? Has this become a communal false memory for many Americans?

First, you have to remember that, with twenty-one the voting age, most of the trainees had been too young to vote in the Kennedy/

Nixon election of 1960. At Yale, my own involvement in that election was limited to helping distribute spoof Nixon posters that read: "They Can't Lick Our Dick" with a scowling picture of Nixon above the slogan.

After the close-run election, which Nixon, like Gore, may actually have won, Kennedy didn't do much for the next few years to capture the imagination of the bottom third of society. Navigating the country into—then through—dire foreign policy messes didn't mean a lot to poor people. Remember that polls always show that at any given time quite a few Americans don't even know who is president. Many poor people never vote.

Kennedy's rapid-fire oratory—stirring to those who listened and believed—was wasted on the part of the population who didn't vote and didn't listen to political speeches. His cool image was wasted on the same people; it played much better on Ivy League campuses, in the eastern big cities and in the suburbs.

Most of my new soldier pals—a random, typical cross-section of America—knew little and cared less about national politics. Now, get them on the topic of invaders from outer space and they were away. But politics? These guys never read anything but trashy magazines, which they called "books" as in "Lemme read that book when you done readin'."

My guess is that Kennedy would not have been considered a great president had he lived. Johnson engineered the great legislative changes of the period such as the civil rights laws, while Vietnam was really Kennedy's mess. It is a shame that JFK didn't live long enough to take the fall for Vietnam.

The ultimate, overwhelming *Legend of Blessed Kennedy the Martyr* owes much in my opinion to the horror surrounding the assassination, which grew and grew over time. The publicity flair of Jackie O and the antics of the other Kennedys kept the JFK story alive, as did the persistent fascination of the media and the professoriate with the Kennedys.

The bungled handling of Oswald and the totally incompetent PR of the post-assassination investigations helped fuel the conspiracy theories, which also kept the JFK myth bubbling away.

Soon afterward, three months after the assassination, two fellow soldiers and I went to Dallas on a three-day pass from Fort Sill, Oklahoma.

The Texas Book Depository was wide open the day we were there and we strolled into it. We looked out of the window Oswald shot from. None of us was a star marksman, but we each, like Oswald, had a good military rifle qualification. Our visit preceded the full flowering of the conspiracy theories about Oswald having an accomplice so we didn't have any theory to prove or disprove.

We concluded that it wasn't that difficult to believe that Oswald got off several well-aimed shots in seconds. Shooting down from a high fixed position at a slow-moving target that is moving away from you in a straight line makes for an easy shot.

That evening, the three of us went to see *Dr. Strangelove*, which, with the cold war at its peak, we found much more interesting and thought-provoking.

After basic training, I was sent to Fort Sill, Oklahoma, to learn how to fire a howitzer. Fort Sill is an old Indian fighting post, where Geronimo ended his life as a captive. Fort Sill is as beautiful as Fort

Leonard Wood is grim and depressing. Fort Sill is on the open prairie. There are few trees and only low rolling hills, so you can see for miles in every direction. The post is huge. Out on the range, even the most incompetent trainee gunners can fire in any direction without harm to man or beast.

Even in January, Fort Sill was sunny and warm, providing you could get out of the constant wind. Firing the old guns was pure fun; soldiering at its best.

We loaded the trucks with ammo before the sun was up; drove out to the firing range and huddled together joking and laughing, trying to ignore the steady, bitter cold wind, standing in a sea of grass that stretched to the horizon. Once the sun was up, and the range officer gave us the go ahead, my team aimed and loaded and fired the old gun we were assigned to, racing the clock to be the first gun to fire.

These 105 mm howitzers dated from World War I. We learned the fundamentals of aiming, loading, and firing them. Firing at a moving target from close range was thrilling, even though we missed the target—the carcass of an old tank dragged along in front of us— every time. This led our sergeant to inform us that a real tank would have killed all of us several times over.

I was with a keen group of guys who mostly were either going to Officer Candidate School (OCS) or to train as warrant officer helicopter pilots. My guess is that the army wanted these bright young army enthusiasts to persuade the rest of us to go to OCS with them. They were certainly a fine group of men and a pleasure to be with.

But my cheerful new Polish pals from Chicago—Nowakowski, Nemchowski, Sosnowski, and Barkis—and I thought that we would take our chances as enlisted men.

Later I often wished that I'd become an officer, though as a young artillery support officer or forward observer you had an excellent chance of getting your name on the Vietnam Memorial. Also,

I strongly believe that every educated person should spend some meaningful time as an Indian before assuming the role of a chief.

Knowing these warm, bright Polish guys made my time at Fort Sill a lot of laughs. Once a gomer started to ride a group of us while we were out on the howitzer firing range; the usual "who you think you are?" stuff. Before I had a chance to say anything to this moron, Bill Nowakowski, a muscular, quick-tempered man, promptly told him to fuck off. With the massive Nemchowski looking daggers at him, the jerk scuttled away like a rodent. We roared with laughter.

Nowakowski tried to call me once after we got out of the army, but I was out and the telephone number he left was lost. I have always regretted this. I went through a lot of William Nowakowskis in the Chicago phonebook once, but failed to find him. I have felt empathy for Poles ever since Fort Sill.

Also at Fort Sill, I made the acquaintance of a wonderful black guy, Howard Jackson. Jackson was a cheerful, powerfully built man from the Deep South, married, and a graduate of Grambling, the famous black college.

Jackson had been drafted. He disliked the army but was going to make the most of it. Like me and the Polish guys, Jackson was resisting pressure to go to OCS. The army wanted black officers badly. Jackson just wanted to be back with his young wife. He was a gentle man in every sense. Jackson always had a smile on his face.

Another warm memory from Fort Sill is musical.

We were not supposed to lie on our bunks during the day. Of course, we did. The old wooden World War II barracks were freezing; wind whistled through them. Lying on your bunk got you out of the wind. I had a lower bunk. One afternoon I was lying on it, reading.

One of the pleasures of the army was having much more time to read than I had at Yale. Rushing off to lectures, writing silly, pointless, driveling essays and getting ready for the endless midterm tests and final exams at the end of each semester took lots of time that could have been much better spent in thoughtful reading and in arguing with my peers. In the army, I always carried a paperback book stuffed into one of the many large pockets of my army fatigue uniform.

The guy in the bunk above me was playing loud music on a transistor radio. I remember exactly what was played. First, there was "Dominique," a huge hit from the one-and-only singing nun, Sister Sourire. As far as I know, this ditty is the only mega-hit Belgium ever produced and probably the only major pop hit featuring a Catholic saint:

Though I'm poor, said Dominique, as he spoke unto the Lord,
I will be your humble servant and your love is my reward.

"Dominique" has a catchy tune and was a big improvement over the usual "I love her but she don't love me" stuff from teen-crush greasers like Bobby Darin or Bobby Vinton.

I had quickly learned to ignore background music; it was literally white noise. Black music was infinitely better but controversial with our military white trash and hence only played when a group of blacks surrounded the radio.

Music, I suppose, always features in culture wars. The musically educated middleclass learn about the war between Nietzsche and Wagner over Wagner's anti-Semitism, Brahms versus Bruckner or about the quarrels between Mahler and his Viennese *fin de siècle* critics. But educated people don't realize that the poor have their own music wars.

In my teens, Cleveland had a station, WJMO, which billed itself as "the black spot on your radio dial." WJMO boasted that it never played music by a white. It made one exception. On the day Elvis died, WJMO played nothing but his songs for the next twenty-four hours. Then, the station reverted to its previous policy.

But that afternoon nearly fifty years ago, I was reading on my bunk, more or less tuning out the music from the Singing Nun, until her song finished. Without any warning, the station put on a song that transfixed me. It was electric! What wild sounds!

Oh, please, say to me
You'll let me be your man
And please, say to me

You'll let me hold your hand
Now let me hold your hand
I wanna hold your hand.

No sound like it had existed before the Beatles. I had never heard such chord changes and harmonies between the voices and the instruments. The sheer drive was astounding.

Pop fans of my parent's age had experienced the peaks of the big bands and Frank Sinatra. My age group caught Doris Day and Patti Page as kids and then experienced the miserable slide downward to the musically illiterate greasers of the late 1950s. The words and music of the pop songs of my late teens were repetitive rubbish. Elvis had a good voice, but the music wasn't his, and the lyrics he sang were the same old thing.

This was totally different. It was new! Something had changed! These four guys had created a new musical world. Sure, they owed a huge debt to Chuck Berry and Bo Diddley and other black musicians. But their sound and their lyrics were their own. The Beach Boys, musical contemporaries of the Beatles, were wonderful and pure west coast America, but this music went places the Beach Boys would never reach.

I listened until the song was over, then jumped out of my bunk and asked the guy in the upper bunk what he had been playing. "Dunno," he said. "But it sure is terrific, isn't it?"

Over the next weeks, little groups formed whenever the Beatles were on the radio. Blacks liked the Beatles' music, too. It was transformative; every pop song that pre-dated the Beatles instantly seemed pointless to everyone but our gomers. They played their country and western music day and night as always.

The only point of country and western music was to drive many of us nuts as it was blasted into our heads from the moment we woke at 0530 hours until lights out. Urban white kids complained about it and blacks simply loathed it, but from Fort Leonard Wood to Vietnam there was no getting away from "Send Me the Pillow that You Dream On" or "Twenty-Four Hours from Tulsa" or "I Fall to Pieces."

One thing I have always feared—with the same intensity that I dread large, hairy spiders—is being seasick. First you think you are going to die, then you fear you won't. Therefore, I was horrified to learn that I was being transported from New Jersey to Bremerhaven, Germany, in an old World War II troop ship. As soon as I learned this, I rushed to the PX and bought many bottles of Dramamine. I planned to take them by the handful.

Immediately after boarding the old tub, my worries skyrocketed when a sergeant gave me my duty assignment for the ten-day crossing. After every other meal, I was to man a garbage toilet in the bowels of the ship. When I reported to the mess sergeant, he urged me to wear old fatigues—and to pay the closest attention to the roll of the ship. He did not explain why paying attention to the roll of the ship was so important. I had learned not to ask questions so I didn't ask why.

The only question permitted was: if ordered to jump, you could ask "how high?"

So after meal number two for our large band of brothers, another private and I made our way down to a small room in the bilge. In front of us was a large, round steel bowl with a heavy lid and a long steel lever at its side. The resemblance to a massive toilet bowl was complete.

Soldiers on KP—kitchen police or a low form of dish scraper—began to bring us large garbage cans of food waste. The other guy and I dumped several cans of scraps into the steel bowl. We put the lid down on the bowl. Looking at each other, we waited for a few seconds. I pulled the lever. Just as I did this, the ship rolled. The lid flew up and we were drenched in seawater and garbage.

As in so many things in life, timing is everything in garbage flushing.

We soon got the idea. Flush well before the roll of the ship.

A luke-warm seawater shower after my first garbage duty got most of the yuck off me. And through Dramamine or some other miracle, I never felt seasick during my army pleasure cruise. A miracle indeed, because once seasickness arrives, it stays. Like guilt, it is the gift that goes on giving. A seasick voyage spent working the garbage toilet would have been something truly unforgettable.

In Germany, we boarded a troop train and went on to Munich overnight. The next morning we were put on buses and sent to Augsburg, my assigned post. Driving along the autobahn, I grew amazed by Bavaria's order and prosperity. By 1964, West Germany had shaken off the ruins of World War II and was in the midst of the *Wirtschaftswunder*, or economic miracle.

Neat fields showing the light green shoots of early wheat were followed by the dark green of small pine forests, where every tree was planted in a neat row and all the under branches were trimmed off. On top of every hill, there was a white church with an onion spire. Below the church was a small tidy town of white houses with brown wooden doors and balconies.

In Augsburg, I was sent to Sheridan Kaserne, an old Luftwaffe base. I was assigned to the headquarters company artillery survey section and given a temporary bunk in a large, high-ceilinged room with a parquet floor. The room was warm from a bank of old-fashioned radiators. Large windows offered a fine scenic overview of the motor pool. The Luftwaffe had lived in comfort, compared with the drafty old barracks at Fort Sill.

The survey team was out in the field on an exercise. I would meet the team the next day and move into its room in the barracks.

Meanwhile, some friendly guys took me to the EM or enlisted men's club that evening. The EM club (for ordinary soldiers under the rank of sergeant) was a cavernous shed that must have been used by the Luftwaffe as a hanger or workshop. Inside it was gloomy, hot, and noisy, but I liked the place right away. A large German beer was twenty-five cents. A whole pizza was a dollar. Both were excellent. There was live music. What more could a private E-1 ask for?

German beer was strong. After a number, I walked woozily back to the barracks. Lights out sounded. We were in the dark. I was in a large room in a single bunk, surrounded by many other occupied single bunks. Without talking to anyone, I soon dozed off.

Suddenly, I was jolted wide awake. Two guys had come in, drunk and angry at each other. I heard rustling in the other bunks. Then someone put on a flashlight. There were no curtains, and some light also came in from the floodlights of the motor pool.

The light was enough for me to see a whippet thin black guy suddenly paste a large white guy on the head with what sounded on impact like a tremendous punch. Whoomph!

The white guy shouted, "You dumb cocksucker, Walker!" The white guy was bigger than the black guy and had a hillbilly accent. There was a little scuffling between them. The white guy grabbed something from the floor. Then all hell broke loose.

Clunk!

The white guy hit the black guy on his chest with a short piece of metal pipe called a bunk adapter, which was used to make two single bunks into a double bunk by joining one bunk on top of another.

Clunk!

The black guy was hit hard again across the side of his face and head. Walker reeled. The white guy pulled a window open. He grabbed something that turned out to be Walker's footlocker and threw it out the window.

Smash and crash!

We were on the second floor. The footlocker hit the ground hard and spread its contents everywhere.

No one said anything. I was terrified. I thought that the white guy was going to throw Walker out of the window after heaving out the footlocker. Was this the racial bad stuff I'd heard about but not yet witnessed? Should I try to save the black guy? No way! The enraged white guy might use the pipe on me. Cowardice was mandatory.

The black guy staggered out of the room, bleeding profusely from his head. The white guy lay down on his bunk and passed out, snoring. The rest of us tried to go back to sleep. I thought, "If this is what barracks life is like, I'm doomed! This is something that precedes a lynching."

In the morning, dawn and clarity arrived early. At 0530 hours, the duty sergeant appeared in our room, banging a piece of wood around the inside of a metal wastebasket. He shouted, "Drop your cocks and grab your socks!" This was our wake-up call. We staggered out to roll call, shivering in the Bavarian morning chill, yawning and shaking off our previous night's drinking.

After headcount, the battalion sergeant major led us—to my astonishment—for a slow jog around the Sheridan Kaserne perimeter. Astonishment, because Big John, as everyone called the sergeant major, but only behind his back, was a man of about fifty, a veteran of World War II, dignified, and tall. (Big John continued to lead these early morning runs until the following winter, when he fell onto his large butt on some ice. Big John was unhurt but, without any announcement, the jogging immediately ceased.)

After the run, we lined up outside the mess hall, until the doors opened and we filed in. Breakfast was terrific, though unhealthy by present day standards. Cereal and milk and canned fruit were available, but as we passed along the chow line everyone went for the sausages, bacon, and pancakes that were swimming in bacon fat on the large flat griddles. These greasy yummies were washed down with large mugs of milky coffee.

Sitting at a long mess table, I asked someone what had happened last night. The explanation was, if not exactly reassuring, not at all what I'd feared. Race had nothing to do with the fight.

Walker, the black dude, was a close friend of the white guy, a hillbilly private named Colley Myers, who was our colonel's jeep driver. Walker was the middleweight boxing champion of our division, the proud 24th Infantry Division. He was also the colonel's personal jeep mechanic.

Myers and Walker always drank together. Each had a terrible temper when drunk but were "the nicest guys you could want to find" when sober. Some little disagreement had occurred while they were walking back to the barracks during the night, but it was now cleared up. First Sergeant Waters, who ran the company, knew about the fight and had settled it—permanently. Others had been as alarmed by it as I was.

And so it unfolded. Walker appeared later in the day with stitches in his face and a cast on his hand. He had indeed landed a terrific blow on Myers's head, but Myers's head was harder than Walker's hand. Myers was unmarked, apart from a hangover. Later I found Walker to be sullen and difficult but harmless. Myers, who was bright and funny, became a pal.

For Its Hi-Hi-Hee
in the Field Artillery…

The next day I joined the survey section and moved into their room in the barracks. The surveyors were a decent bunch, led by a slow-talking, slow-thinking white sergeant from Mississippi, Sergeant Miley Hurley. The other surveyors were white draftees, except for me and for Private Frank Sloan, who was a black draftee and also from Mississippi.

I expected Sergeant Hurley and Private Sloane to be at each other's throats. However, they had worked out a system of mutually assured loathing—MAL—that precluded any actual warfare. Neither did more than the minimum required in any military situation; both were bone idle.

The rest of us did the actual surveying. I only had a few days to learn surveying before we loaded up our survey team trucks and drove off in a massive convoy at fifteen miles per hour to Grafenwohr, the greatest of Kaiser Wilhelm's military training areas, the location of the 24th Infantry Division's major winter training exercise. Our brand-new self-propelled 155 mm M109 howitzers went ahead of us by train since their tank tracks did too much damage to German roads and German farms to allow them to move freely around the peaceful countryside.

Traditional surveying is interesting and fun—in decent weather. Using basically the same methods as the Romans, we triangulated from a known point to locate first the guns and then the target they were supposed to hit. Then, after the guns began firing and the shells were landing close to the target, the artillery forward observer could fine tune where the shellfire hit.

To do the triangulation, the survey team used high school trigonometry. We determined the length of the side of a hypothetical triangle with fifty-foot chains attached to red-and-white striped poles, then measured angles at the ends of the side with a Swiss-made theodolite. In doing the measuring of the length of the side, a lot of awkward walking while holding the red-and-white striped poles was necessary. After we had the data, we huddled in the back of the survey truck working out the results with special printed forms and a book of trigonometry tables.

One of our team, Stackhouse, a contractor in civilian life, was a wizard at the trig calculations. Stackhouse was a stubby, red-headed fellow with freckles and a Brooklyn accent. He laughed a lot. The rest of us raced him to complete the trig form but we never won. However, it was important to have several people complete the same form to make sure we all got the same result. Despite this care, our guns several times lobbed a live round into the outskirts of a small German town. Since this had been happening since before 1914, no one seemed too concerned.

While the gun crews prepared the guns for firing, we huddled in holes for hours. We froze while waiting; no fires were allowed, though we sometimes managed to sneakily burn a smoldering heap of damp wood. Someone with calibrated binoculars watched the impact area where we expected the shells to land. The guns might be a mile behind us.

When the guns were finally ready to fire, we waited, listening to the old-fashioned field telephone. At the moment of firing, someone by the guns shouted, "On the way, wait!" down the line. When the shell was due to land, the voice said, "Splash," and we expected to see an explosion on the target—if all went well.

Stackhouse usually manned the binoculars. If I saw his head swivel away from the target area when we heard "Splash," I'd know that we—or the gunnery officer—had messed up again.

Stuff happens.

Grafenwohr was the perfect setting for a grim film about German prisoner of war camps. Most days, mist covered its ninety square miles of hilly pine forests, interlaced with dirt tracks. Part of Grafenwohr was a permanent artillery impact area, not to be blundered into.

We soldiers lived in long, low one-story cement block sheds in a muddy, open area. There were dozens of these sheds—think of *Stalag Luft Seventeen*.

Like the rest of Germany, Grafenwohr is miserably cold and drizzly in late winter. The only heat in the sheds came from one pot-bellied stove right in the middle of the long, open room. This stove normally burned crumbly soft coal so, apart from not warming the place, the stove smoked up the atmosphere inside the sheds. This interior fug went well with the smoky pollution that hung over the camp, mixed with a fine perpetual dust that no amount of rain removed. We could taste the dust.

Stackhouse thought that this perma-dust was due to the soil having been pulverized over decades so completely by shellfire and churning tank tracks that particles were perpetually suspended in the air.

Since we sat in muddy holes most of the day, the dank cold of the shed at night was depressing. There were showers, but so little hot water that only the first two or three guys to arrive back from the field out of the fifty or more sleeping in the shed got a warm shower. Accordingly, most of us only showered once or twice in the month the division spent at Grafenwohr.

Stackhouse decided to make the stove more effective—the chimney was choked with soot. He was a man of the most practical kind of imagination and a deep hater of the army. His first move was to obtain a blank .50 caliber machine gun cartridge.

We made the best fire possible in the stove. We put bunks across the door of the stove and sat on them so that the stove door could not open. Stackhouse climbed up on the low roof of the shed. He had the blank .50 caliber round and his steel helmet. He screamed, "On the way, wait!" and dropped the blank round down the chimney, putting his steel helmet over the opening of the stove pipe.

We waited a few seconds. Then Stackhouse cried, "Splash!" as the blank round exploded. He held the steel helmet down on top of the chimney for an instant, then whipped it off, and pushed himself away from the chimney. A splendid pillar of flame went a dozen feet up into the air as all the soot ignited at once.

We had a clean stove—a really clean stove.

This was only phase one of Stackhouse's plan. Phase two took place that night when Frank Sloan and I stole several burlap bags full of anthracite from the cookhouse. Mixed judiciously with the soft coal to get it lit, the anthracite soon made the iron stove glow red hot. By the time we left, large flakes of iron were peeling off the stove. But we were warm in the shed in the evening, until the stove burned out in the night.

Booze was readily available at Grafenwohr. A large bottle of beer with a flip-top, which we called a "snapper-capper," cost one Deutschemark or one U.S. quarter at the exchange rate then of DM 4 = $1.

If our enlisted men's club ran out of beer, we traded stuff like sleeping bags with the French in exchange for their strong, coarse red wine. The French were still training with us; de Gaulle had yet to pull France out of NATO. When we returned to base after the field exercise we told the quartermaster sergeant that we had lost our sleeping bags and needed replacements.

At Grafenwohr, all ranks drank heavily. After my first field exercise, I always took a canteen full of vodka with me when we went to the field. You could get water at the mess tent, but vodka was hard to find. As a private, out in the field our officers paid no attention to me and the sergeants were often drunk themselves. No one checked on the canteens we carried.

Some drunken officers got all of us in trouble when a German general's dress hat disappeared from the American officers' club. The German general had paid an evening courtesy call on our big shots and found that his valuable hat, adorned with gold braid and so forth, was missing when he got up to leave.

All hell broke out about this. With much publicity, our general ordered a search of all the soldiers' duffle bags and sleeping bags and even of the sergeants' quarters. No German general's hat was found. This was no surprise; everyone knew that one of our junior lieutenants had stolen the hat but that our general couldn't quite bring himself to order a search of the bachelor officer quarters (BOQ) for fear of finding it.

The drunkenness at night in the sheds was often loud and irritating. One guy got into a fight after peeing on a man deeply asleep in his sleeping bag (aka fart sack). The guy doing the pissing claimed he thought he was in the urinal, but the unpleasantly awakened sleeper thought that the pisser was performing a crude joke. An inconclusive, sleep-wrecking scuffle resulted.

In the brief periods when we weren't playing soldier or cleaning our military kit, we were completely free but only to go anywhere we wanted within Grafenwohr. Men wandered from shed to shed, checking on what kind of gambling was going on and on what was being traded. A vigorous commercial undercurrent existed everywhere in the army.

Watching men shooting craps one afternoon, I ran into Specialist Fourth Class Chandos, who worked for our first sergeant. Chandos was a loan shark and was checking on the activities of his clients, most of whom were our senior sergeants. The craps shooters had pulled a blanket taut over a cot and were shooting dice on it.

Though it was strictly forbidden for soldiers to lend money, and especially not to their non-commissioned officers, this was obviously a great business. The sergeants shooting craps were born losers and were soon cleaned out by a street-smart black soldier. Then they needed a further loan to go on shooting.

Chandos himself only played poker and almost always won since he played exclusively with the battalion's most stupid sergeants on payday. Chandos was a short, funny Greek from some northeastern American city. He boasted that his time in the army was going to buy him a Pontiac convertible. I hope Chandos succeeded in this; he was a friendly, amusing man and only charged 50 percent interest per month. In other companies, the rate was 100 percent.

We immediately liked each other. Chandos was finding that his orderly room job got in the way of his loan business, especially when he needed to work on collections. He asked me if I could type.

Could I type? After churning out all those midnight essays at Yale, I could type like gangbusters. He said that he would work on the first sergeant and get me transferred to the orderly room. I thought this was a terrific idea; the other occupants of the orderly room were the captain and the first sergeant. So it was no coincidence that every time I went there, the orderly room was warm as toast, even when we were out in the field and the orderly room was in a tent.

Chandos was as good as his word. Within months, I made my first upward career move in the army, becoming the orderly room flunky.

In the barracks or in the field, decisions were made in the orderly room. In our company, the captain merely signed off on decisions made by the first sergeant. This was not taught at West Point, but our first sergeant was infinitely more experienced than the captain— and infinitely wiser. I did whatever the first sergeant wanted done. Apart from making dozens of pots of coffee day and night, this work varied a lot.

On a Monday morning, for example, I'd be writing letters for our linguistically and vertically challenged Puerto Rican company commander, when the first sergeant, who in practice ran everything, shouted for me to retrieve Blicksen, our toothless cook, from the custody of the MPs.

Blicksen was toothless because he had barfed out and smashed his army-issue false teeth so many times that the army dentist wouldn't give him another set. Blicksen always chose the same cobbled street running downhill off the Maximilianstrasse for barfing out his teeth. He was a man of consistent bad habits, a typical army cook.

When I picked up Blicksen, he was always covered with bruises and cuts from "falling over a foot locker," according to the MPs. He was also always utterly astonished when I asked him why he liked getting crazy drunk and being beaten up by the MPs. It was just something existential for Blicksen. I would sign in the MP's book that I'd received one cook—well battered—and walk him back to our barracks.

On another occasion, Private Frank Sloane strutted into the orderly room. In a loud voice, Sloane informed the first sergeant that he wanted new dog tags. First Sergeant Herbert Waters had been in the army since World War II. He was a raw-boned, ramrod-straight, and honorable west Texan, uneducated but thoughtful, wiry, and tough. I didn't exactly fear him, but I was careful around him. I never spoke to him unless he asked me something.

First Sergeant Waters looked at Frank Sloane, who was not only black but a mess; his uniform was filthy and his boots were muddy. Sloane had made repeated furtive attempts to grow an Afro, only to be sent promptly to the Kaserne barbers to have his head shaved. Today his hair was a fuzzy tangle, about three days of growth away from getting Sloane sent off to have his head shaved again.

I found Frank droll in his sly, honky-baiting way, but he was one of the worst soldiers in the company. His specialty was what the British army call "dumb insolence." In the race-sensitive American army, Sloane's effort was wasted. People like First Sergeant Waters had decided to humor him as long as he did nothing but act insolent. Frank was hoping to be a martyr for the black revolution, but he was in the wrong place.

"Mornin' First Sergeant," said Frank.

"Yes, Private Sloane?" asked Sergeant Waters.

"I want me new dog tags with mah correct name and religion."

"What new name? I don't have orders for you with a new name."

"Mah name is now Sloane-Bey. I have done become a Muslim. When I get out of this army, I will drop that old slave name completely."

First Sergeant Waters said nothing for a second. Then, ignoring Frank, he told me to order Private Sloane-Bey new dog tags. Sergeant Hurley of the survey team came in shortly afterwards to complain that Sloane-Bey had no right to new dog tags. Obviously, Sloane-Bey had told the survey team that he was going to score one on Sergeant Hurley.

The First Sergeant told Hurley that Sloane-Bey could put whatever he wanted on his dog tags as long as his blood type and service number were correct. I could tell from Sergeant Waters's tone that he was going to play this by the book and that Hurley should scoot. Which Hurley did.

Two tasks were routine. One was preparing the paperwork for company court martials. This was only for petty stuff—major offenders were tried by proper military courts. Whatever the offense, though, the outcome was the same. The culprit was found guilty.

At first this bothered me. But I soon realized that the army didn't try people unless the evidence was damning; it took too much time and effort. There were no lawyers booking hours to collect large fees, only junior officers who hated playing the role of lawyer. Plus, the penalties for petty offenses in the barracks were trivial.

The other regular task related to payday. Payday or "when the eagle shits" was a big deal. We were paid in cash each month. In the morning the pay officer collected the payroll. Armed with a pistol and accompanied by a sergeant with a rifle, the officer returned. A long table would be set up. The men lined up by rank, then by alphabet. Master Sergeant Adams went first each month; Private Zilokowsky went last.

A soldier advanced to the table, saluted the pay officer, stated his name, and was handed his cash. He then did a left face, and I would be waiting for him at the end of the table. Many of the men were heavily in debt. A common reason for this was the purchase of an expensive Bible on credit. This leather-bound good book would be a present for the guy's mother, complete with her name on the cover.

Unfortunately, many soldiers couldn't resist the urge to stop paying the mail order Bible company shortly after mom received the Bible. Captain Ramirez then received threating letters from the publisher in Georgia. In disgust, the captain threw the letters at me, and I dealt with them per regulations.

I loved writing to these scumbag companies who charged a dumb private making around $115 a month an astronomic monthly sum plus compound interest for an ordinary Bible with a fancy binding.

I wrote something like this:

Kennesaw Bible and Souvenir Inc.,
Jock Itch, Georgia

Dear Mr. Grabbit,

I received your letter of 20 May 1965 about an alleged debt outstanding of Private Lemuel Glottal. Your letter threatens legal action against Private Glottal.

However, under the Soldiers' and Sailors' Relief Act of 1940, you have no legal basis for such an action against a serving member of the armed forces. In fact, your company has no legal rights whatsoever with regard to this debt. I would advise you a) to consult a lawyer and b) in the future not to solicit business from serving members of the armed forces.

However, I have spoken to Private Glottal about this matter. Though a serving soldier, Private Glottal does not wish to be indebted. In recognition of this, Private Glottal has voluntarily decided to pay $1.73 per month to your company. In ninety-three months this will discharge his debt.

No further communication about this matter is required. Any such will not be acknowledged.

Faithfully yours,
Captain Raoul Ramirez

On payday, I had an addressed envelope ready for Private Glottal. I took the money from him, issued him a money order, and watched him put it in the envelope, which I'd send off to the Bible company.

By the time such unfortunate debtors had bought their "voluntary" U.S. savings bond and handed me their "voluntary" debt payments—many had several to make—their pay would be much reduced—and reduced even further as soon as they stepped away from the pay line because my pal, Specialist Chandos, waited just around the corner for his debt repayment. He seldom had any problem in collecting; the debtors always wanted access to further loans.

———◆———

During my first year in Germany, payday always proceeded like clockwork. Then, the 24th Infantry Division received a computer. Payday was never straightforward again.

The computer arrived in the form of two large trucks and a large generator towed behind one of the trucks. The trucks were on the usual two-and-one-half-ton all-wheel-drive chassis but had boxy enclosed bodies behind the driver's cab. One truck contained the team of key punchers. This was an IBM computer system and ran on a punched card memory so the team fiddled constantly with the cards.

The other truck contained the reason the generator and the services of a senior warrant officer were needed. In the truck were dozens of vacuum tubes—"valves" to the British—stuck in a tall vertical socket board. Each vacuum tube had five pins in its base. Each pin needed to be in firm contact with the innards of the board. If one pin didn't make contact, the damn thing wouldn't work. And the truck was air-conditioned, a small miracle itself in the army of 1965. If the tubes produced too much heat, the computer flipped its wig.

Many of us had heard of the wonders of computing, but none of us had seen a computer. I was thrilled to examine the brute. Before the warrant officer in charge got sick of us, he showed many of us the innards of this huge new toy. He was so proud of it. It was going to produce a perfect, up-to-date payroll for the whole division every month. No more manual bookkeeping and waiting for updates from army headquarters.

And the computer would have produced a flawless payroll, I'm sure, if we had not taken it out on a brief trial maneuver. After all, we were a mobile division, and our payroll should be mobile, too. The computer trucks were certainly up to going anywhere the division went. And it was only a short maneuver.

The problem was those five little pins. As soon as the trucks moved a short distance, however slowly, on their almost rigid military suspensions, tubes wobbled loose and the computer went down. When the diligent, competent warrant officer and his team tried to push the tubes back firmly into place, some pins always broke and became stuck in the socket board. Time for the warrant officer to get out a small pair of needle-nose pliers.

Next payday, practically every soldier's pay was incorrect. And mostly the errors resulted in an underpayment. The computer's warrant officer was frantic. Our own officers were apologetic. But their apologies didn't produce our full pay. There was muttering. Ugly muttering.

There is no trade union in the army. It is not a democracy. But ultimately every soldier is an American citizen with the rights thereof—like the right to write letters to his Congressman. Also, the army wanted all career soldiers to reenlist, early and often.

So Major General Rowny was apoplectic with rage about this blow to his men. And, therefore, his splendid chief of staff was apoplectic with rage. But the division sergeant major, who, like General Rowny and his chief of staff was a high-ranking Mason, was beyond apoplectic. And his rage really mattered. The division sergeant major spoke for all the men.

Senior officers listened carefully to the division sergeant major. He had powerful friends who were also high-ranking Masons—and based at the Pentagon. His friends had been lowly front-line infantry lieutenants when the division sergeant major was a lowly but brave corporal in the darkest days of World War II. Now his officer friends were senior generals.

The division was ordered from on high to work out the problems with the computer while taking the thing out for weeks on our big annual field exercise. Influential local forces made sure this did not happen.

The last time I saw the two computer trucks, they were up on cement blocks, minus their wheels, in front of division headquarters where General Rowny could watch them carefully and detect any attempt to move them. General Rowny did not like electronic technology. The general liked large infantry formations, heavy tanks, and powerful artillery pieces.

Eventually, our missing pay was made up.

While stationary, the computer worked well. This glitch was my introduction to the kind of computer-caused problem that I spent much of my professional life trying to solve.

Technology, however, and the Cold War were not going to leave the 24th Infantry Division alone. Especially not the 7th Field Artillery of the 24th Infantry Division. We were equipped with mighty, new self-propelled 155 mm howitzers. These could fire a six-inch-diameter heavy shell for more than ten miles. On impact, few things survived a hit from one of these shells. We thought that the 155 mm gun was a terrific and versatile weapon; the "queen of the battlefield." But there was yet another use for these fine weapons, it soon transpired.

Despite the efforts of various negotiation-minded figures in the U.S. government and the successful resolution of the Cuban Missile

Crisis in 1962, the Cold War was alive and well. Soldiers in the 24th Infantry Division, for example, were rotated to Berlin periodically to serve as human trip wires.

If the Russki's overran Berlin and killed our boys, the balloon went up. We worried about what followed. Though we were told repeatedly that our equipment and training were superior to those of the Russians, the same had been true of Hitler's forces. Like Hitler, we found the Russian headcount advantage difficult to overcome, even without the fiendish Joe Stalin to push the Russians forward.

Unless, of course, we went nuclear as soon as Berlin was attacked. The problem with using our strategic nuclear forces, though, was that after the inevitable Russian retaliation there might be little left of the United States even if we "won."

Color me Pyrrhic.

Much thinking went on in the Pentagon about this conundrum. And soon an answer to the problem filtered down to the 7th Field Artillery.

First Sergeant Waters told me one morning to find someone in headquarters company who had a top secret security clearance and who was totally dispensable. I screened through our personnel records. There was only one candidate: Private First Class Paul Godleski, a radio signalman.

I wasn't exactly frightened of Sergeant Waters—well, not exactly—but he was not a man who invited comments from below. So I simply handed him Godleski's personnel file. Sergeant Waters took it and went in to talk with Captain Ramirez. Later that day, I was told to arrange Godleski's temporary and secret assignment to a special training unit for a month.

Godleski was then summoned and told to get ready for a move. Godleski expressed neither any surprise nor any objection. He had impulsively joined the army after a brief stint at a Midwestern college. By the end of his first day in the army, he bitterly regretted this decision, but it was too late. Resignation turned him into a passive observer of the military world. He submissively took whatever came his way. Godleski just shook his head and said, "Shit rolls downhill."

The surprise was all mine, though I had no idea what Godleski was lined up for. He was a pal and a prime drinking crony.

Drinking was the reason for my surprise at choosing him for this secret training. Apart from the seriously alcoholic sergeants, like Sergeant Wyatt of the explosive temper, who ran the motor pool with a 12-inch wrench in one large fist and a bottle of Old Everclear behind the dashboard of his truck, Private First Class Paul Godleski was the finest drunkard in the battalion.

His feats were legendary. Godleski did not hold liquor well. Though calm enough when sober or hungover, when he was trashed his friends repeatedly prevented him from threatening to assault German policemen. Fortunately, the policemen didn't understand when Godleski called them "fucking Nazi Lugerheads" and threatened to castrate them with a bayonet.

Godleski vomited everywhere. He fell out of chairs in bars. He walked into trees. He propositioned plump middle-aged German matrons on the streetcar. But he was likeable and an amusing storyteller, so we tried to keep him out of trouble and on the base by drinking with him in the EM club. Paul had his own table in the club most evenings where he held forth on the lunacies of the army.

None of this was exactly relevant. What was relevant was that if I had to pick one soldier out of the fifteen thousand soldiers in the 24th Infantry Division who combined total drunken irresponsibility with an inability to keep any sort of secret, Godleski was my man.

One month later, Godleski returned. He had something choice to tell us. We had to join him in the EM club that evening. He was buying drinks.

After we went off duty in the evening, a group of us wandered down to the EM club. Though I loved the EM club, it was not a place to go on your own. On base we wore fatigue uniform, which included a green baseball hat. Soldiers could tell which unit we were in by looking at the enameled badge on the front of our hats. Each battalion had its own hat badge.

Once, one of our most retarded corporals started a violent fight with guys from another unit. Buddies of our corporal insanely decided to support him. This escalated into a major brawl outside the EM club.

As soon as someone from our unit came out of the main door of the club, his hat badge would be spotted and he would be attacked. Word of the fight spread inside the club so the rest of us exited from the side doors. After that, I always left with other 7th Artillery people by the side doors. Who knew what might be going on in front of the club?

Inside the club there never was any trouble. Bouncers just stood by the walls; no one wanted to be banned from the club. Soldiers were not allowed off the Kaserne on many evenings, and the club was the only fun place on the base. Vast, smoky, and gloomy, it seated five hundred men or more.

The crooked sergeants who ran the club booked great acts like the Kim Sisters, three cute Korean girls who sang great pop, and even once the legendary Roy Orbison. When there wasn't an act, there was oompah-pah live music performed by local Germans. Any conduct short of chair-busting violence or urinating in corners was tolerated in the club. The crooked sergeants were busily skimming the till and getting kickbacks from their German beer suppliers. They didn't want any petty rules to interrupt the spending of their soldier clients.

When I tooled up at Godleski's table that evening, it was spread with pizzas and bottles of cheap German champagne or *Sekt*. Godleski was feeling expansive and already pissed as a newt.

"I'm gonna start World War III," he screamed. "I got the moves!"

By virtue of his top secret clearance, Godleski had been trained to arm tactical nuclear shells for our 155 mm howitzers. This was the Pentagon's answer to the Russians' numerical advantage. These nuclear weapons were limited in range and blast effect to the battlefield. They could be used, it was assumed, without New York City being vaporized.

Godleski explained the plan. Our howitzers would wait until the Russian infantry thoughtfully massed right in front of us. Godleski would go into a special truck to assemble the various components of the nuclear shell, being especially careful with the sensitive fuse that was set to activate the device to explode some feet above the ground.

Then Lt. McConkey, as fire control officer, would get a special message. The nuclear shell would be loaded into good old Marilyn Monroe, aka gun number one. Another special command would arrive. Fire! Then it would be "on the way wait" and "splash" for the Russians. We would watch the mushroom cloud from a safe distance and then advance briskly through acres of freshly roasted Russki's.

Oh, and we would be issued rubber radiation-proof suits to wear over our uniforms. But we were assured that our anti-nerve gas, atropine injector would fire its needle into our thighs as intended, right through the rubber suit.

We believed this without question because one guy had already fired an atropine injector right through his thumb while fiddling with the powerful, spring-loaded injector in the barracks. So we would confidently drive eastward across the German plains, nice and cozy inside the rubber suits, ready to rock and roll on to Moscow.

All in all, it would be quite a day for the 24th Infantry Division. Something to tell our grandchildren about, assuming that they weren't born with two heads or that the Russians didn't fry us in retaliation.

At the time, the tactical nuclear weapons sounded perfectly plausible. I mean, what the hell…the Pentagon must be useful for something?

Godleski was really fired up. After telling us in a shout, shared with every soldier in the club, that everything we were about to hear was top secret, Godleski stood on the table in his combat boots. Kicking pieces of pizza all over the place, he began to mime the assembly of a tactical nuclear warhead.

He put out his right hand and took an imaginary wrench. He adjusted a heavy sub-component. He put the heavy sub-component on top of another piece. It was fiddly; Godleski used both hands to slowly push the pieces together. Then he slid the assembled pieces into the shell casing. He put the shell in a special rack. Very, very carefully he threaded the fuse into the nose of the shell. He adjusted the fuse. Ahhh…

Godleski picked up the imaginary shell. It was heavy and clumsy. He took a small step. His hands slipped! He mimed the shell landing on the ground nose first and then fell off the table in a fit of laughing, smashing his head against a chair. But Godleski came up smiling. We howled with laughter and ordered more of the cheap *Sekt*.

Occasionally, there were entertaining antics in the barracks. Once Horsch, a yokel private with a horrid, vacant face like a bystander at the crucifixion in a medieval Flemish painting, drunkenly jumped or more likely was pushed out of a high dormer window in our ex-Luftwaffe barracks. I didn't feel bad about this. In fact, I felt quite good about it.

In a previous drunken frenzy, Horsch had bitten me deeply in the right bicep as I and others tried to keep him from attacking Lt. McConkey, our best officer.

We had all been given a half day off for a company picnic by Captain Ramirez, our diminutive Puerto Rican company commander. Captain Ramirez had booked a picnic ground and ordered several large kegs of strong local beer. The picnic was an inspiration of the captain's. Had I—or any soldier—been asked, we would have told the captain this was unwise.

The day of the picnic was Bavaria at its best, a perfect warm summer day, blue of sky with lots of fleecy clouds. All of the company—some one hundred and fifty men—were loaded into our large ammo trucks and driven out to the picnic ground.

Once we were all assembled, Captain Ramirez drew up his five feet six inches and gave us a pep talk. He said something like "we were the best company in the division and he wanted to show us his appreciation." Unfortunately, the captain could barely speak English, which was why First Sergeant Waters or I wrote all his letters. So there was no reaction from the men.

The kegs of beer were waiting along with trays of German wurst and pretzels. We attacked the booze as soon as the captain stopped speaking.

I'd been reunited with Howard Jackson, my large black buddy from Fort Sill, who was now the captain's jeep driver. We grabbed a couple of beers and retreated to the sidelines. We knew that we couldn't drink much and just had to watch.

By the end of the afternoon, all the beer was gone. Some of the men had brought bottles of local schnapps to reinforce the effect of the beer. Subsequently, a number had chundered all over the place. Most of the officers had discreetly left the scene. At seventeen hundred hours on the dot, First Sergeant Waters had us fall in for a headcount. All were present, except for Private Horsch. We had trouble finding him because we looked for Horsch at ground level when in fact he was up in a tree.

Using threats of great violence, we persuaded Horsch to come down. He was in an alcoholic fugue of an intensity that only someone with a single-digit IQ and severe mental problems could achieve. We threw him in the back of a truck, jumped in after him, and pinned him down. As soon as the truck started moving, Horsch went berserk. He had the strength of a fear-maddened animal.

Lt. McConkey was in the cab of the truck behind us. The lieutenant saw what was happening. His truck pulled in front of ours and we stopped. Lt. McConkey walked around our truck and climbed in over the tailgate. He was a thoroughly nice man who, like Jesus, checked our feet for trench foot when we were out in the field in the winter.

"Alright men, I'll handle this," said the young lieutenant. "Release him."

We all piled off Horsch. The lieutenant said, "Private Horsch, I order you to stop this nonsense!"

Horsch stood up and did nothing for a second. Then, without a sound, he went back into Texas chainsaw massacre mode and, with his hands like claws, went for Lt. McConkey's face.

Before the officer was hurt much, we pulled Horsch down again. We beat him until he sobbed and stopped his crazy aggression. Alas, in the process I got bitten deeply in the right biceps, right through my fatigue shirt.

So when Horsch jumped or was pushed out of the high window in another drunken fugue, I felt no regrets. In any case, Horsch survived the fall, minus his spleen.

Howard Jackson and I hung around together when we were in the field. Since we looked after Captain Ramirez and put up his large round tent, there was an unspoken agreement that we could sleep in it, too.

The captain was a decent fellow, who was totally befuddled by the awkward turn his military career had taken. When he went on active duty with an army air defense rocket battery in Puerto Rico, right out of San Juan University ROTC, he had not realized that advancement in the army meant a transfer out of Puerto Rico and career time spent "leading men in the field." His rocket battery role made him part of the artillery, ergo he found himself doing two hard years in the field artillery in Germany.

The captain was undoubtedly up to speed on the use of radar and how to shoot down low-flying Russian aircraft. Unfortunately, he lacked other more basic military skills such as map reading. And on the field phone or on the radio the captain sounded like Speedy Gonzalez. No one could understand him. In turn, often the captain didn't understand his instructions from on high. Like where to go.

Jackson helped the captain with map reading. Many times I saw them bent over the hood of the captain's jeep, with a map spread out on it. Jackson pointed at a landmark on the map with a thick brown finger. The little pot-bellied captain held his hat in one hand and used his other pale little hand to scratch his thinning hair.

Late one day, after headquarters company spent hours driving around a Bavarian forest in circles, it was time to pitch camp. The captain went off to be balled out by the colonel for getting lost again. Jackson and I unloaded the captain's large tent. We wanted to get it ready for the captain's return, since the poor fellow would be minus many chunks off his backside. The colonel was an arrogant, shouting West Pointer who towered over our aimiable little captain.

Jackson was powerful so he went under the tent, poked the pole through the hole in the center of the round tent, raised the tent, and held the pole in place while I drove in the tent stakes and tightened up the tent ropes.

Erecting the tent went perfectly.

I then unloaded the captain's Yukon stove. This was a small but dangerous device that burned gasoline in a special little burner inside a rectangular metal box. The fumes were vented through a collapsible series of corrugated metal stove pipes that emerged awkwardly through a hole in the tent roof. Fuel for it came from jerry cans we carried on the captain's jeep.

The whole stove was fraught with potential disaster. Its saving grace was that it could heat a tent in seconds and keep it warm all night. Since the captain got up every few hours to check on the men and the trucks, this was important to him. As a native of the tropics, he suffered agonies in cold, damp Germany.

Of course, Howard and I made sure the stove burned all night. With luck, unless we were on guard duty or the regiment moved out in the middle of the night, we slept all night in warmth.

To set up the Yukon stove, I inserted a long, thin rubber tube into a special fitting for the mouth of the jerry can and screwed the fitting onto the can. I then fed the tube under the side of the tent. Howard attached it to the stove inside.

At this point three simple steps were required to ignite the stove safely.

The first was to check that the valve on the stove inside the tent and the valve on the jerry can fitting were tightly closed. The second was to invert the jerry can and tie it to a post or tree right outside the captain's tent. The third was to tell the person inside the tent that you were going to open the valve on the jerry can. The person inside could then cautiously open the valve on the stove and light the first droplets of gasoline safely as they dribbled out of the burner.

Very simple really.

Jackson and I had done it dozens of times. Except that this time neither of us performed step one. Both valves were open. So, when I inverted the jerry can, instantly a large pool of gasoline formed in the stove and started to vaporize. And when Jackson shouted, "Is it OK to light it?" I shouted back, "Yeah."

There was a second of silence, then a horrible whoosh. Instantly, there were only long charred strips of canvas and ashes where the tent had been. The heavy tent pole toppled over and hit the ground with a dull thunk. In a panic, I shouted for Jackson. He staggered out of the blackened ruins of the tent, more or less unhurt but minus most of his eyebrows and some hair.

We were laughing out of sheer relief when the first sergeant approached. Even that man of iron smiled dourly. Then he told us to "find" the captain another tent. First Sergeant Waters had a saying, "A good soldier never comes up short." This meant to steal whatever object was missing from another unit. This Howard and I did with complete success.

The story cheered up the captain, too, when he returned from his lengthy visit to the colonel with little of his small backside remaining.

Jackson and I were buddies. I took this as a serious compliment. He ate with me in the mess hall when we were back in the Kaserne. This was unusual. Most black soldiers did not voluntarily eat at the same mess table with white soldiers. I didn't blame them and could guess at their reasons.

A histrionic hatred of honkies like that of Frank Sloane-Bey was not the usual reason. More common was the simple desire to eat with people who wouldn't make comments—accidentally or purposefully—that made you uncomfortable. The country was just emerging from segregation. It was difficult for ordinary blacks and whites to find a non-abrasive way of getting along socially outside of work.

Out in the field, everyone ate out of mess kits and everyone ate together standing. Call it "vertical integration."

Diversions like burning down tents were welcome but infrequent.

I loved Germany but had little time to explore it. When we weren't on maneuvers, I obtained free tickets to the Augsburg opera from the USO. There I discovered *Tannhauser* and found opera, which has thrilled me ever since, a perfect way to escape from tiresome things. Opera and Germany would have delighted me as a student. In the artillery, I couldn't immerse myself in them; we spent too much of the year freezing our butts off out in the forests.

I decided to change my job in the army. This proved much easier than I'd expected. I'd noticed that enlisted men lived better the closer they were to division headquarters. So I maneuvered politically to get out of my artillery battalion. Ordinary soldiers who read and wrote and handled numbers reliably were in short supply. I made a pal at division headquarters by helping him sort out some complex admin problems. He was only a private, but he knew how to pull strings.

After a year and a bit in Germany, I was transferred to division headquarters. There I found unlimited paperwork to do and no fights to watch. This wasn't a good move, I soon decided; the bureaucratic work palled quickly. And I no longer got to drive a truck. Once again I was bored, and boredom is agony for me. Plus, this wasn't soldiering at its finest. This wasn't war. And a new war was unfolding.

*"Every man thinks
meanly of himself for not
having been a soldier."*

I n the summer of 1965 I volunteered to go to Vietnam. Anything for a change. Besides, how could any manly young soldier pass up the chance to go to war? I knew as much about Vietnam as the American public did. Which was nothing. We were fighting Communism in a hot tropical place where the French had fought Communism. Hot—that was important.

The French had failed utterly, but heroic failure is a core part of the French military tradition. Failure was not then part of our military tradition. Even Korea was fought to a draw. We were Americans; we would succeed. And Vietnam was sunny and hot, unlike cold wet Deutschland.

Eisenhower had resisted direct American military involvement in Vietnam but, after being elected in 1960, Kennedy sent U.S. military "advisors" to Vietnam to juice up the South Vietnamese army. More advisors were sent each year but there were never enough to inspire the South Vietnamese army to fight.

We were hooked.

Certain historians claim that Kennedy was tiring of Vietnam at the time he was assassinated. Even assuming this debatable supposition is true, it isn't clear that Kennedy could have pulled out from the morass of hubris and folly in which we were already immersed.

After the Bay of Pigs fiasco, his humiliating meeting with Khrushchev and then the Cuban missile crisis, Kennedy dreaded appearing weak. Plus, the Democrats were already tarred, however unfairly, with "losing China." The Cold War was going strong. The Republicans would feast on the Democrats if they "lost" another country to Communism. Abandoning Vietnam wasn't really an option for the Democrats. And "the best and the brightest" in the CIA and the Pentagon were full of confidence that they could defeat any third world enemy.

Now in 1965, President Johnson was asking for Vietnam volunteers from the Regular Army. Regular Army soldiers had "RA" before their service numbers. Draftees had "US" before their service numbers. Draftees weren't yet being sent to Vietnam. Draftees moaned and wrote letters home. Regular Army soldiers had signed up of their own freewill and were ready to fight godless Communism in Vietnam or in any place their country wanted them to fight.

Hot damn! Our President wanted Regular Army volunteers! Regular Army, that was me: RA15700564. Over six feet tall, 175 fairly fit pounds with a regulation shaved head, a lovingly polished brass belt buckle, and regular bowel habits.

Plus, I knew from a worm's eye perspective how the army worked. Whether sitting in a freezing hole as an artillery surveyor, loading trucks, not "coming up short" for the first sergeant, or covering up for some dim officer, I could handle the real nitty-gritty. I submitted my application for reassignment to the Republic of Vietnam to my boss at division headquarters, Master Sergeant Andy Anderson, the first black American I ever worked for.

In a perfectly just world, Sergeant Anderson would have ended his career as chief of human resources at IBM. A thin, calm, handsome man, Sergeant Anderson ran the personnel side of the 24th Infantry Division in his head. In 1965 we had only rudimentary computers but an endless flow of crazy bureaucratic orders from Robert McNamara's Pentagon. Dozens of madly conflicting personnel policies had to be juggled. Sergeant Anderson was lightning fast and super accurate. Error-free paperwork erupted from his desk. He was sharp.

Even Major General Ed Rowny, our admirable division commander, who not only made live appearances all over the division but actually spoke to ordinary soldiers like me, deferred to Sergeant Anderson's knowledge of regulations and took his advice about personnel issues. I had watched this and knew that Sergeant Anderson was up for promotion.

I also knew that the division personnel team got brownie points for every volunteer sent to Vietnam. I was a perfect volunteer because I still had my combat MOS. Your MOS or Military Occupational Specialty—a numerical code—indicated which job you were trained to perform. Soldiers with an artillery MOS like mine were supposed to be assigned to artillery batteries. My noncompliant role as a typewriter operative was a constant source of possible reproach from above.

I was surprised; therefore, that Sergeant Andy sat on my request for transfer for days. Finally, he summoned me to his desk. We worked in what had been a vast Luftwaffe aircraft repair shop. Massive Albert Speer-era reinforced cement beams loomed over us in dank gloom that the dim fluorescent lights barely penetrated.

"Thomson, this is stupid," said the sergeant. "I am going to put your request for transfer in the circular file."

Sergeant Anderson looked at me hard. I now realize that he was a kind man who was thinking that this imbecile white college boy had life's every advantage and was just doing some damn fool showing off. Sergeant Anderson had been in Korea during the Korean War, probably driving a truck or loading ammo as black soldiers did in Korea. War was no adventure for him.

I don't remember my immediate response, but I convinced him that I wanted to go. Finally, he said OK.

Getting there is half the fun...

After submitting my request for transfer, I assumed that orders would smartly follow. A steady flow of eager volunteers were receiving orders. But mine didn't come. No problem. Above all, I didn't want to spend more weeks of cold, ass-freezing mega-boredom at Grafenwohr. My orders were bound to arrive before the whole division's big move to the training area after Christmas.

I paid no attention to the escalating war in Vietnam. Johnson had approved a request for more troops from General Westmorland, head of MACV, the U.S. military advisory group in Vietnam.

In October 1965, the 1st Infantry Division, considered the best in the army and called the Big Red One because of the large red numeral one on the divisional shoulder patch, began to deploy to bases around Saigon. American troop strength rapidly reached 200,000.

By early December I began to get antsy. I was due for discharge from the army in September 1966. Over the grape vine, I heard that soldiers sent to Vietnam who were due for discharge in less than a year would have their tours extended so that they served a full twelve-month tour in the country.

This sounded highly plausible, given what I knew of the army. So, in the way of bureaucracy, I submitted a request to cancel my earlier request for a transfer to Vietnam. Sergeant Anderson had this approved instantly and fired it off to Washington.

Naturally my transfer orders came through the next day. I was reassigned to the Big Red One as an artilleryman, or "cannon cocker," reporting on or about 1 January 1966. This required immediate action on my part.

Before leaving my job at division headquarters, I organized a small change in those orders. Adventure was all well and good, but there was no way I was going back into the artillery as a cannon cocker. Too much sitting in holes. And too much waiting.

I typed up an order that altered my military occupational specialty to what I was doing at division headquarters. Sergeant Anderson was away on Christmas leave, so I just put the order changing my MOS in among a vast pile of orders that an aged warrant officer signed in due course. Then I ran off the new orders, sorted them into dozens of cubby holes and attached a set to my clipboard.

Once you have transfer orders in the army, you enter a delightful limbo called FIGMO or Fuck, I've Got My Orders.

The orders in those days took the form of a thick wad of mimeographed paper. These were put on a clipboard for show and convenience, and the transferee started the process of clearing his old place of assignment. Each stage in clearing required handing over a copy of the orders and receiving a document in exchange. Field kit like your sleeping bag went back to the quartermaster, for example, in exchange for a sign off. Your rifle was checked off as clean and complete by the armorer. And so on.

With the clipboard as a badge of freedom, you could wander around the base or drink all day in the enlisted men's club without any questions asked.

Getting clearance from the medics was slow. Initially, they didn't have all the inoculations required. Eventually, I was shot up with everything from the plague to yellow fever, and this was noted in my medical file. Then it was off to Frankfurt and onto a series of long, slow military flights to Oakland Airport in California where we would be processed for the flight to Vietnam.

I don't remember much about Oakland because more or less upon arriving there I found myself in a long line of soldiers being processed. My medical file was taken from me. I started shuffling down the line of clerical types and medics, dragging my duffle bag.

By the time I reached the end of the line I had been injected again with everything from the plague to yellow fever. I protested but, separated from my medical file, the medics in the line simply gave me all the injections again.

I suppose I was lucky not to have my gums painted with gentian violet like Yossarian in *Catch22*.

The result was instant chills and fever. Many of the other soldiers seemed similarly dazed and feverish as we hauled ourselves onto a World Airlines 707. We were all wearing only a short-sleeved khaki dress shirt with a T-shirt underneath and khaki dress trousers. Everything else was in our duffle bags. We were supposed to land in our new place of business looking smart.

Within a few minutes after takeoff, the plane was freezing. We were damp and shaking with chills. There were no blankets or pretty stewardesses. Still, shivering passed the time and distracted the worried. At least the seats didn't face backward as they did on the military transport that flew us back from Germany to the U.S.

After many hours without food or drink, we were hustled off the plane for a brief refueling stop in Guam. Humid Guam warmed us up, and we were given candy bars and soft drinks. After many more hours in the air, the pilot told us to prepare for landing in Vietnam. Without circling, we descended steeply and landed hard at Tan Son Nhut in the middle of the tropical night.

Tan Son Nhut at that time was the busiest airport in the world. The single runway was brilliantly lit. While landing, we noticed Phantom jets parked just off the main runway in half-round individual blast shelters. (Some of the shelters were still used to house antique Migs in 1993.) We were herded off the plane into a dingy shed lit only by overhead naked fluorescent fittings. (The lights were still there when I went through the same hall in 1993.)

We were shouted at and hustled through the hall. Another plane with its load of cannon fodder arrived right behind us. After the usual inexplicable and interminable army wait in front of the terminal building, we were told to throw our duffle bags into a waiting two-and-one-half-ton truck and sit on top of them. We clambered up and over the high tailgate of the truck and sat or lay on the duffle bags.

So far, apart from the heat and humidity, the place was just like arriving anywhere as a soldier. But, loving the tropics and the night smells, I completely forgot my chills and fever and felt excited. Men were muttering to themselves along the lines of "Shit, we made it. Shit, it's fuckin' hot."

As we pulled out of the airport, the sun came up with a tropical bang.

Lying on the duffle bags in the cargo area of the trucks, we instantly learned what sweating really means. No one told us where we were going. The trucks ground along in low gear on high-crowned, red-dirt roads while the sun beat on us. We crossed and re-crossed muddy rivers on Bailey bridges. We passed many small shacks with lots of near-naked children squatting under banana trees in front of the shacks in that Achilles' tendon stretching position that Asian peasants of all ages can maintain so effortlessly.

The dripping heat smothered us. We had heard stories about tiny, beautiful Vietnamese children helping the Viet Cong by giving American soldiers Cokes full of poison or ground glass. If such a child had appeared, I would have taken a bottle with fulsome thanks.

No one knew anything about Vietnamese geography so there were loud discussions about the distance from Saigon to various bases whose names had appeared in the army newspaper, *Stars and Stripes*. We finally drove through a little town that was just a crossroads with a Buddhist temple and a straggle of small shanties around it.

This crossroads town, I later learned, was Di An, which provided the name of our camp. Many of the shanties had walls and roofs made of American beer cans, flattened and soldered together. (Beer cans were thin steel in those days.)

Some of the shanties had chicken wire enclosures in front. On the dirt floor behind the chicken wire were low plastic chairs and tables. Across the front of these shanties were colorful hand-painted signs, bearing names like Snack Bar Sexy or Number One Barber. The chicken wire was to show possible GI clients that a grenade would not land beside them while they were enjoying a blowjob or a haircut.

Exotic undersized chickens and little yellow dogs with curled-up tails ran around everywhere. Slender, short, dark-eyed men and women wearing conical straw hats looked at us expressionlessly, as did small black pigs who then went back to rooting in the mud.

Why weren't they all wearing black pajamas as we expected? Many women wore bright red tight-waisted shirts that flared over their hips. The red went well with their gold front teeth. But we drove past plenty of water buffalo standing in the paddy fields so, apart from the people, Vietnam looked more or less like the pictures in *Time*—and it didn't look threatening. Not compared with places like East Cleveland or Spanish Harlem or the no-go zones of New Haven.

Once outside the town and its cultivated fields, there were no houses. The new military road ran in a straight line through abandoned rice paddies on both sides. Lush, green straggly plants and bamboo lined the deep ditches on either side of the road.

We only knew that we had arrived somewhere when the trucks lurched through a break in a long ragged line of coiled concertina wire. MPs stood beside the road behind the wire. (Concertina wire is barbed wire in large loose coils with little sharp blades instead of barbs. It is springy so it isn't easy to cut, but it is easy to be cut by it.)

First stop was the 1st Infantry Division replacement depot or "repo depo." This was a typical army tent city. The tents were in neat lines, but the place was a human dump. There we milled around in little groups, frequently drinking warm, highly chlorinated water out of a Lister bag (a large, suspended olive-drab canvas water sack with a tap). Evaporative sweating made the water in the bag merely tepid instead of blood heat.

A large sign with the motto of the 1st Infantry Division greeted us:

No Mission Too Difficult, No Sacrifice Too Great, Duty First.

No one then or later told us anything about the history of the Big Red One. Some years back, Sam Fuller made a so-so action film called the *Big Red One* for those Americans who were interested in the history. These did not include the 3,151 members of the real Big Red One whose personal mission did not involve returning alive from the Vietnam War—more soldiers were killed there than the division had lost in World War II.

In the repo depo, soldiers just said "fuck that shit" when they looked at the sign.

Incomprehensible announcements came over crackly loudspeakers. Helicopters flew low over us on their way to the helipad kicking up clouds of reddish dust. Ugly human smells rolled over us. And wasn't that noise distant artillery fire?

But who cared? My immediate concern was that the quartermaster had run out of lightweight jungle pants and green canvas jungle boots. How could we look like jungle fighters in black leather boots?

The repo depo was no place to make new friends. Why get palsy with a soldier who might be at the Cambodian border by nightfall? And in a body bag the next day? And if you didn't keep shuffling around looking purposeful, you might be nabbed to fill sandbags or heave ammo onto trucks.

I did chat with Specialist Fourth Class Benito "Benny" Reyes who was also going to division headquarters. Reyes was a cheerful, stocky Tex-Mex with a round, smiley face. He came from a big, extended family in Texas and had a girlfriend, Rosa, whom Reyes planned to marry as soon as he exited the army with all the money he saved by not drinking or smoking.

Unfortunately for cheerful Benny and his long-term plans, the army had interesting short-term plans for him.

After a miserable night, I got my assignment. Division headquarters was only a quick stagger away, with me lugging my duffle bag and M-14 rifle, and rivers of sweat running down my chest and back. My newly issued green jungle fatigue jacket was soon covered with whitish salt stains from sweating continuously.

My new boss was Master Sergeant Marcus Aurelius Cato, a slender, tidy guy who, like Sergeant Anderson, was another bright, competent, and likeable black career soldier. Sergeant Cato informed me that he would reach twenty years in this man's army and retire after his tour in Vietnam.

Sergeant Cato had a burning desire to do this in one piece, complete with arms, legs, and dangly bits. He expected my full cooperation in this worthwhile project. Sergeant Cato had a soft southern voice and, though he didn't talk much, when he did he had the eloquence and diction of a gospel preacher. He was also a great reader, a thoughtful man.

I was immediately put in charge of a new redeployment section. "Redeployment" is army-speak for sending soldiers home. I was also the only soldier in the section, though I was promised a sidekick.

Sergeant Cato explained that, since a lot of the division had arrived in October 1965, their one-year tour of duty would be up by year end. I needed to get them new assignments and make travel arrangements to get these men home without any snafus. I had to then notify the men through their units when this was done. This activity would make me highly popular, said Sergeant Cato, but there were a few problems to solve.

Benny Reyes received a different kind of redeployment job. Benny was put in charge of redeploying the dead. Sergeant Cato explained that embarrassing incidents had occurred back in the states. Parents received the wrong dead soldier. Local newspapers had a fit. Congressmen babbled in synthetic fury. The army looked bad. Someone had to make sure that the contents of the body bag and the attached paperwork were in sync. Reyes was that someone.

I didn't think Reyes would enjoy this job, but he seemed unfazed.

I was also put in charge of a tent, which was on the edge of a large tent city. My tent had an wide, expansive view across nearby bunkers, on to the perimeter's concertina wire and over the cleared earth of the minefield, which stretched out to the edge of the scrubby trees and bush that surrounded the camp.

Bunker on the Camp Perimeter at Di An 1966

The minefield included traditional land mines, plus claymore mines that were electrically set off and large barrels full of gasoline set off electrically as well. Or so we were told. I never saw any evidence that anyone was in active control of this minefield.

The tent was on a raised platform made of the perforated, interlocking steel plates used to create instant aircraft landing strips. From the wear and tear on the canvas, the tent appeared to date from the Korean War. There were two rows of metal bunks inside the tent, with mosquito nets over them.

I dumped my stuff on a bunk under a part of the tent that didn't appear to have any holes in the canvas. Some of the bunks had homemade mattresses bought from the Vietnamese. The mattresses were stuffed with dry grass and were full of insects. We had no bedding and slept in T-shirts and jungle pants. Scorpions and large spiders meant it was a good idea to shake out your boots in the morning before putting them on.

I hung my newly issued M-14 from a nail on one of the two tent poles, where it joined several other rifles. The other rifles already had plastic bags over their muzzles in a futile attempt to stop the rifle bores from quickly rusting however often they were oiled. The bags were not a sign of idleness. Under the circumstances, the men did not need to be told to keep their rifles clean and operational.

Fifty feet behind our tent and just before the first roll of concertina wire was a low bunker made of sandbags. The same interlocking steel plates supported the bunker's sandbag roof. These weren't quite adequate to support the bunker roof, which sagged dramatically in the middle from the weight of the roof sandbags plus a tripod-mounted .50 caliber air-cooled Browning machine gun, just like the ones on our 155 mm self-propelled howitzers in Germany.

Di An was almost perfectly flat apart from ridges where there had been walkways between the rice paddies. Across the perimeter wire and the fire-blackened, cleared ground of the minefield, the grey-green low scrubby tree line began a hundred yards away. This seemed a tad close.

At that moment in 1966, if you had told me that forty-one years later I would fork out thousands of dollars for a holiday in Vietnam, I might have laughed—or sobbed.

Rifle Cleaning in Di An 1966

In camps like Di An and out in the bundu, soldiers worked seven days and seven nights a week. I started work the moment I'd dropped my stuff and returned to the admin tent. Consequently, I didn't meet all my new tent mates for several days.

Sergeant Cato had cheerfully alluded to problems with my new job, one of which involved two large boxes. One box contained several IBM machine rosters—those wide, long, accordion-like paper computer printouts. The other box held dozens of loose 3x5-inch cards, each with a couple of lines of typing.

The machine rosters purported to contain up-to-date lists of all the personnel in the division. The cards contained information that should have been posted to the IBM printouts but had not been. The rosters were useless.

Most cards had an entry like this:

Sassafras, Weldon R. RA13456789 Sgt E5 2nd Bat Cav
DOW Ben Hoa 2/19/66

Or

Crummy, Lamar Gene RA34276565 PFC E3 27th Logistical Co
Med Evac Philippines 2/5/66

DOW meant died of wounds. Med Evac meant being helicoptered out first to a field hospital and on to some place like the Philippines.

Each card represented a miserable soldier who had been killed or wounded or had a truck accident or got VD, but who in any case was no longer part of the Big Red One.

Of course, the wounded man might return and then need a reassignment. And there were many cards that lacked essential information such as the service number of the John Smith or Joe Green.

And there were cards with question marks, indicating that someone had been assigned to the lst Infantry Division but had gone AWOL in Sioux City and had not been seen since. Such a soldier was in military limbo. He might be in a stockade or might even have already turned up in Vietnam and been sent to another division. He might be dead. But the bastard was on our records. I had to track him down.

I took a long ruler and started scratching out the names of the unambiguously dead on the personnel rosters. The ambiguously wounded or missing would have to wait. This was going to take a long time to sort out. Over fifteen thousand men were in the division.

Back in the tent that night, the first soldier I met was Specialist Fourth Class Chuck Byrd.

An army-recruiting ad in those days read, "Share great experiences with other great guys." The picture in it showed a crewcut, high school kid still in civilian clothes meeting his new pals who are wearing smart uniforms. Wow. What fun.

Prior to the 1960s, there was a rich vein of American war films in which a group of perfectly ordinary young white men, who initially look and sound like trailer trash, join the army. After brutal training by a veteran sergeant, they are shipped off to war, along with the sergeant. These unpromising young studs, thanks to their great army training and innate American virtues, turn out not only to be heroes but actually Montgomery Cliff, Frank Sinatra, and Van Johnson. Their sergeant is of course John Wayne.

These exemplars never piss inside the tent or puke all over the latrine and never say muthafucka under any circumstances. Down deep, there is something fine and interesting about each man, which is revealed under the stress of combat.

In battle they save each other from fiendish enemies in hand-to-hand combat, except for poor Van Johnson who gets a terrible but oddly bloodless wound in a mentionable place and dies with his girl's picture in his hands.

Films about Vietnam are generally less emphatic in asserting the existence of innate human goodness because they are less positive about America, not because they take a dim view of human nature. An evil war makes fundamentally good Americans evil; such is their message.

Often in these films, decent small town American kids are turned into savage butchers by events outside their control, like hordes of savage Viet Cong trying to kill them in a night attack. Or because of insane orders from their own fanatically ambitious senior officers, who just "have to take that hill, goddamn it."

That most people, even Americans, might be fundamentally amoral like our ape cousins and hence situational in behavior—good one time and bad the next or generally fairly passive in the face of whatever happens—is not postulated in any American war film that I know.

Full Metal Jacket shows a man deranged by bullying during training. *Apocalypse Now* suggests it is U.S. military leadership that is collectively deranged. The individuals in it are caricatures. *Hamburger Hill*, an underrated film, shows that war is a pointless mess in which individual character is overwhelmed by events. "It don't mean nothing" is the only lesson to draw from that stunning film.

Platoon reverts to suggesting that the army is full of remarkable people. In this case, one sergeant is truly remarkably evil while another is a goodness-filled proxy for Christ. How about that?

My experience of three enlightening years in the army demonstrated that most of the many soldiers I met were utterly ordinary, however closely I examined them. And, all too frequently, in the end they proved to be trailer trash. Not exactly bad people but not too good either and certainly not too interesting, unless you find the people you meet in the men's room of a New York thruway rest stop interesting.

In conversations over the years since my army time, I have learned that educated, suburban white Americans can grasp, and often even accept, the proposition that most people are average. Stating this isn't taken as undemocratic or non-PC or clear evidence of fascist tendencies.

The problem arises in discussing what the average American is like. Suburban college grad types do not comprehend just how low the American average is—and that, by using a modicum of statistical inference, plenty of our fellow citizens are below that already low average. Way below average...

Most people just laugh when you point out to them examples of "average" behavior. American liberals, however, become irritated or even angry. Why? Because they dread the "tyranny of the real." The world should not be the way it is; therefore, people can't be what they appear to be. The truth is hidden and complex but clear to liberals.

While we had the draft, the army was real America. The draft took a cross section of ordinary male Americans on a random basis. Even better, we were told that the draft rejected two men for every one it took. Most of those rejected were rejected for their IQ (or the lack thereof).

Thus, the soldiers I met in my two infantry divisions were pure American reality.

As a corollary, there may be someone, somewhere, of normal IQ who managed to remain a classic liberal after doing time as an enlisted man in the army while we still had the draft. I simply haven't met this severely cognitively challenged person yet.

To remain a true American liberal, this high-minded ex-soldier not only had to retain the belief that all men are basically good (or at least readily and rapidly improvable through the generous application of other people's money) but also the belief that our government is capable of effective, consistent, rational action over a lengthy period;

in other words, capable of being as institutionally competent as the Salvation Army or Wal-Mart.

These tender, transcendental beliefs have to be cherished and nurtured in the face of ugly and continuous empirical evidence to the contrary, administered frontally and in your face from dawn till dusk during several years in the army.

Whatever...

———◆———

To be honest, Specialist Fourth Class Chuck Byrd was a partial exception to the "not interesting" rule. For one thing he was fairly fat. In the army's infantry divisions in 1966, to be fat was to be exceptional. I didn't know a single fat soldier in the 24th Infantry Division in Germany. In U.S. society as recently as the 1960s, young healthy men were seldom fat. A little unfit sometimes but not blob-wobbly, supermarket-checkout-line, type 2 diabetes fat.

The army then had ways of dealing with the potentially fat. In the army, ordinary soldiers ran or marched or dug or moved ammo daily. Senior sergeants were occasionally porky, but this was like a long service medal and hence admirable. Fat officers were kicked out.

But Byrd was as blubbery as he was southern. Moreover, Byrd openly displayed a high ambition. Any ambition among ordinary soldiers above and beyond getting married or getting drunk as often as possible was highly unusual. Byrd, though, aspired to reach the goal of many an ambitious rural southerner.

Byrd aspired to be a shithouse lawyer.

Soldiers recognized this as a high calling indeed, right up there with being an Elmer Gantry-style preacher man, whom the shithouse lawyer closely resembles.

A shithouse lawyer is no mere crooked used car salesman or small town con man. Greatness lurks down this country road.

Consider the finest shithouse lawyer that the United States has produced in my lifetime, ex-President Bubba Clinton. A true shithouse lawyer can instantly read the souls of strangers. "Ah feel yer pane." The shithouse lawyer knows every regulation and how to twist it. "It depends on what the meaning of 'is' is."

The shithouse lawyer is beyond mere dishonesty or petty moral constraints. Just ask Monica Lewinsky. "Ah did not have sex with that woman." Or, better, ask Hillary Clinton.

In civilian life, money sticks to the outstretched hands of a real shithouse lawyer. His honeyed words attract it. In the army, a great shithouse lawyer is a hero to his fellow soldiers and a commanding officer's nightmare.

Byrd aspired to all these goals. He worked hard, very hard, in order not to work, and he cheated the army whenever possible. He told us of his triumphs, of the rules he had brilliantly circumnavigated. But nature had short-changed Byrd.

Byrd was as sly as a weasel but not all that bright. Being a Bubba Clinton requires brains. Plus Clinton's charm is ours forever. Byrd's charm quickly wore off.

———————◆———————

In striking contrast, my next new tent mate turned out to be one of the best people I've ever met anywhere. Jerry Kahle was a stocky, Midwestern guy with a large head and a lot of civilian work experience, though we were about the same age.

Kahle, married, had been working in a furniture store when he joined up before they could draft him. His wife was young and innocent, and he missed her horribly. Kahle was calm and rational in all situations. Not educated, nor intellectual, Kahle was thoughtful and questioning. Above all, he was a moral person. And very clean.

Kahle was to basic virtue as Sergeant Anderson was to excellent administration: virtue poured from Kahle. Without saying or doing anything, Kahle was just good in ways people sensed. If there was a hole to dig, Kahle was the first to grab an entrenching tool. Or, if someone had to go on patrol, Kahle volunteered, though he longed to return to his high school sweetheart of a wife. Kahle kept her picture in his wallet, just like the movies.

Kahle and I had nothing, nothing at all, in common, but we were instantly as thick as thieves. We talked late into the night, night after night—because it was too hot and frightening and humid to sleep—about everything: love; sex; our futures; baseball; and how to tune auto engines.

Encountering Kahle and a couple of other rough diamonds in Vietnam made me reexamine the cynical views I'd formed in the army and at Yale about the quality of the human race. Perhaps I'd tilted a bit too far in the conservative direction. People could not be pigeonholed. However unlikely and unusual, natural goodness was possible.

Jerry Kahle working on our Tent

American conservatives generally kick off from a religious perspective. They believe that man, though divinely superior to animals, is nonetheless innately prone to sinfulness. Whether this flaw is called original sin or attributed to an imperfection in our collective character, conservatives believe that some form of religious belief is essential to guide us onto the road of righteousness.

The proposition that some people—and not those born again or touched by angels—just plain ordinary people—might be good without the help of God, gods, or persons unknown is difficult for conservatives to swallow.

The conservative belief is thus the converse of the liberal belief, traceable back to Rousseau, that man is innately good until ruined by greed, capitalism, not enough welfare money, or a lousy second-grade teacher.

However, spending time as an enlisted man surrounded by randomly chosen draftees led me to reject the conservative hypothesis that humans are fundamentally immoral and hence need social controls imposed from above. People exist, admittedly rare, who are virtuous without benefit of clergy, and consistently so; their virtue is not situational: they are good. This is not the result of Head Start, going to a parochial school, or sound toilet training; they are just good. Kahle fell into this category.

Such naturally good people are just common enough to discredit the assumptions of America's religiously contaminated conservatives.

There are just enough good people to keep the amoral majority pointing in more or less the right direction most of the time, without religion or social tyranny. If left to their own devices and under sufficient financial pressure to work, most people will behave acceptably most of the time. Society can thus bumble along fairly peacefully; individuals can be free from all but the broadest social rules.

If, therefore, you believe that achieving and maintaining such human freedom is the ultimate goal of a good society, everyone should be a libertarian. Wisdom lies in recognizing and accepting that free people are unpredictable and amoral. The world is messy.

Freedom may not translate into success or a good life for any particular individual; fate plays a mighty role. Freedom merely offers the possibility of fulfillment for the greatest possible number. Trying to stretch individual freedom to the limit means accepting that the outcome for some may be awkward or uncomfortable. Or tragic.

But what is the alternative? Tax-financed, government-run schemes of social engineering or collective improvement don't work. Think of busing or welfare. The venal, incompetent mess we call government is certain to bungle any effort at shaping people or sorting out the world's messes.

Government is only useful and defensible as a referee to keep the human race from self-destructive, ape-like behavior. Government activity or controls above and beyond this basic referee role mean that individual freedom sooner or later goes out the window, without any corresponding benefit.

Additionally, American government activism has a nasty global side effect. Our compulsion to right the world's wrongs ensures that, along the way to losing our own freedom, we gratuitously kill lots of foreigners in the name of some hopeless cause. Like drug eradication in Columbia or democracy in Afghanistan—or eliminating nonexistent weapons of mass destruction in Iraq.

Even worse, activist American government policies rot our own national character. Identifying a subgroup as members of a desperately worthy but sadly flawed ethnicity is a prime example of such government-caused damage.

When we subsidize or prop up this or that group, we keep members of the group from becoming free by shielding them from having to deal with their own problems.

Such folk—and not only blacks—remain unable to support themselves or to compete in an effective way generation after generation because the rest of us "help" them. They cannot, therefore, become fully human; their misery is meaningless and not tragic. Turning to drug addiction or crime is their bored, vapid but perfectly logical response to personal emptiness, just as an animal in a cage paces compulsively or chews itself raw.

I went into the army a mild, muddled libertarian because I disliked authority. I believed that people should be allowed to get on with their lives, doing more or less whatever they pleased, as long as they weren't harming others.

I came out of the army a rock-hard, utterly convinced libertarian. Letting people be themselves and make their own mistakes is a categorical imperative. I don't despise my fellow humans—well, not all of them—but I had spent minutes and hours, days and nights, months and years observing average humanity up close and watching our government in action.

Neither was inspiring.

The rest of the tent's inmates were more in line with the dreary army norm. Cubello, for example, day-dreamed of being a Mafia "made-man" or wise guy but only had an ignorant and cowardly personality and a Boston gutter-mouth accent with which to further this ambition. I suspect that Cubello never even made it to prison.

Physically, he was a squatty little toad. Day to day, Cubello worried constantly and loudly about food and about being forgotten by his beloved mother.

Soon, Cubello's mom came through. He was the first of us to receive a food package: many cans of Campbell's condensed tomato soup, a tropical treat.

Cubello had all the unpleasant racial prejudices that later made Boston such an unfortunate choice of location for the introduction of school busing. However, he had just enough brains to realize that making loud racist comments while surrounded by hundreds of large, armed, and touchy blacks was not a good career move. Therefore, he focused on other ethnic groups.

Once Cubello made an anti-Semitic comment. There were few Jewish enlisted men and none in our tent. So I felt obliged to point out to Cubello that the Jesus who featured on the gold medallion around his neck was at least technically Jewish and might not like such comments.

Cubello simply refused to believe this: "You're shitting me! Jesus was no fucking Jew." I thought of suggesting to Cubello that he read the New Testament. This was an obvious impossibility as it would have caused some sort of lasting damage to Cubello's lips. So I suggested he go to the chaplain for a spoken explanation.

Cubello took a bunk in a corner of the tent next to Bob Gaylord, a career soldier, former short order cook, and petty thief. Bob found or stole a one-burner kerosene stove and then began to filch food from the mess hall and cook it for us. So we all liked Gaylord despite personal hygiene deficiencies on his part, such as never changing his green army T-shirt.

Army food wasn't bad as long as the army cooks had nothing to do with it. Gaylord mixed jars of stuffed green olives and anchovies—yes, from somewhere he got dozens of those small flat cans of anchovies—with a stolen gallon can of army beef stew and heated it to tepid on his stove. We craved salty food because of our constant sweating. With enough Tabasco, we thought the salty, fishy stew was delicious.

Time magazine claimed on several occasions that GIs in Vietnam had shrimp cocktail, steak, and ice cream on a regular basis. I suppose that you have to expect a certain level of bollocks from a mass audience magazine, as *Time* used to be. *Time* was printed on a useful quality of paper, though. In Vietnam, if you saw a soldier walking in a purposeful manner with a rolled-up copy of *Time*, you knew where he was going.

Time's reporting of Vietnam had a more basic flaw. *Time*'s main local correspondent, Pham Xuan An, had remarkable sources of information. In *The Making of a Quagmire*, David Halberstam described An as the linchpin of his "small but first-rate intelligence network" of journalists. Halberstam thought that An "had the best military contacts in the country."

In claiming this, Halberstam was certainly correct. An was a colonel, and later a general, in the North Vietnamese Army. An sent invaluable reports about American activities to North Vietnam via the Cu Chi tunnels.

A full description of An's role is in *The New Yorker* of May 23, 2005.

Ray Gonzalez was in the tent for a while, but his habit of throwing away his weekly anti-malaria pill caught up with him. We last saw Gonzalez looking deathly pale, sweating, and shaking with fever as he staggered off to the medics. I remember Gonzalez for his cheerfulness and his "audition for *Grease*" hairdo.

As was always the way in the army, other inmates came and went and were forgotten instantly. Generally, there were about a dozen of us. We didn't have time for socializing. War was much with us.

Just before I arrived, the first sergeant had been shot cleanly through the fleshy part of his upper arm by the Lone Sniper. The Lone Sniper with his AK-47 hid in a barely man-sized hole concealed by the brush under the tree line, right at the edge of the minefields. Every once in a while he popped up from the hole, loosed off a round, and dove back under cover within seconds.

The Lone Sniper was a brave man. Fortunately for us, he couldn't aim a rifle. Apart from the first sergeant's arm, which soon healed, the Lone Sniper never hit anything, but the occasional crack of his AK-47 made us all jumpy. Many futile patrols were sent to look for this guy.

A mile or so from Di An, frequent dramatic air strikes by Phantom jets hit a target in the bundu whose identity we never learned. I have a series of pictures of such a strike. The faded color snaps show the black blob shape of a Phantom jet pulling out of a dive, followed by a shot of trees with a small black mushroom cloud emerging above them. These photos confirm that I would never make a good combat photographer.

We never saw B-52s dropping bombs but sometimes felt the impact of the bombs transmitted through the ground. The B-52s were simply too high to see, apart from their vapor trails, though they were bombing not that far away.

Ordinary soldiers never had much idea of what was going on in Vietnam. We assumed the generals in Saigon or the big shots in Washington knew.

We know now from dozens of memoirs that this assumption was totally false.

In truth, we were probably as well informed about the war from reading the *Stars and Stripes* and listening to army radio as almost anyone else, since we weren't subject to the corrosive and ignorant theorizing from left and right that increasingly filled U.S. home-front media. Plus, we talked all the time with our fellow 1st Infantry Division soldiers who were witnesses of everything that was happening in our key area of the country.

"War is God's way of teaching Americans geography."

Ambrose Bierce

I was frustrated by my own total ignorance about the history of Vietnam. The place was bloody and dangerous, and I didn't really know why, apart from the fact that a mortar round could turn me into hamburger any evening.

My only personal experience of Communism up to that point was during my three years at Yale.

Being a knee-jerk leftist was as mandatory in the 1960s for younger, tenure-minded Yale liberal arts faculty members and their grad students as it is today. The Yale PhD students who graded our tests and essays casually told me, and possibly even believed, that Mao was a rural reformer, Castro a heroic agent of anti-colonial e, and the Soviet Union a vital check on the fiendish excesses of capitalism.

However, Vietnam was outside the purview of the grad students I had contact with. At Yale prior to 1963, Vietnam was like the draft—never discussed.

So I wrote to the Yale Co-op where I'd kept my account and asked the bookstore manager to send me everything he had about Vietnam. Soon three books arrived by army mail. One was a tourist guide to South East Asia, written circa 1947—not helpful. Another was a large format, color picture history of South East Asian art—suitable for a coffee table. But the third was a treasure: Bernard Fall's *Street without Joy*. I still have this book. In Vietnam I read and reread it.

Fall, a French journalist and academic, had served in Vietnam as a French soldier and was obsessed with the French War in Indochina. He also wrote *Hell in a Very Small Place*, a tragic and somewhat romanticized history of the fall of Dien Bien Phu in 1954. Fall had unique access to the French army at all levels, had been under fire all over Vietnam, and must have been a man of stunning courage. Fall died stepping on a mine in central Vietnam near Route One, the Rue sans Joie or Street without Joy.

Fall's thesis was simple. Our war in Vietnam could not be "won" in any military sense, however heroic our effort and however abundant our helicopters. This was not because the majority of Vietnamese wanted to live under Communism. They did not.

The reason was obvious. With their sanctuaries in Laos and Cambodia, and potentially in Mao's China, and with a plentiful supply of Chinese and Russian arms, a large, brave, battle-tempered Vietnamese guerrilla army could not be beaten by a conventional army—or not at a price that a democratic society at home was willing to pay.

Ninety thousand French-led troops died finding this out. The Americans would lose tens of thousands, too, since Fall was already sure when writing the book in 1965 that we would use more or less the same dud tactics as the French. However, despite the misery of the war, Fall considered the struggle noble and worth the slight chance that the Viet Cong or Viet Minh would crack first. Fall loved the Vietnamese and thought that they deserved better than Communism.

Damn! That wasn't pleasant to learn.

At more or less the same time, my mother informed me by letter that Phinney Works had been killed south of Saigon down in the Ca Mau Peninsula—and by his own Vietnamese irregulars.

Works, an army first lieutenant, had been leading a small detachment of Vietnamese militia soldiers when something went wrong. Did they shoot him on purpose? No one will ever know. What difference does it make? Such a death is a constant possibility in an ugly little neo-colonial war.

I imagined my mother's bittersweet pleasure in passing on this tidbit. Her peculiar psychological condition made her thrill in being the bearer of bad news to a family member, though she had liked Works.

I wish I could claim that I brooded in a suitably First World War elegiac way about the hopelessness of the war—of all wars—and about Works's death, but I was much too occupied with my own piece of war. Besides, Works had extended his tour in Vietnam because he liked soldiering so much. He didn't plan to end as a name on the Vietnam Memorial, but Works wasn't someone who planned to die in bed, either. At least not alone in bed.

Though the heat and the stifling pre-monsoon, shirt-drenching humidity wore heavily on us, we put massive energy into digging to protect the perimeter of our camp. Thousands of sandbags needed to be filled.

We worked in little teams of soldiers along with small groups of Vietnamese peasant women to fill them. One person to dig; two to hold the mouth of the bag open. Over and over, shovel after shovel of red dirt. The women came under the supervision of a toothless old man who didn't work, wore an Australian bush hat, and was called Papa-san in the Japanese manner.

Papa-san's young, hard-working sidekick was a woman called Dead Bug because of her shiny gold front teeth. Dead Bug worked like someone driven and, at about five-foot two-inches but all heart and muscle, could out-sandbag any soldier. And she didn't drip with sweat the way we did. Dead Bug was popular for her upbeat personality and hard work.

One afternoon in the blazing sun, a snake bit Dead Bug. Everyone instantly panicked. Brave young American soldiers and stoical Vietnamese peasant women created an instant scene of horror and screaming.

We looked everywhere for the snake because we needed to know what anti-venom might be needed. I remember beating the bushes with an entrenching tool and wondering if the snake was a two-step. The little foot-long two-step, a cousin of the Indian krait, earned a reputation that claimed you took two steps before dying if one bit you.

Since Dead Bug's screaming continued interminably, it became clear that the snake, never found, was harmless. Dead Bug was given a warm beer. She stopped screaming and we all went back to filling sandbags.

Our Vietnamese Allies

In April, a depressing rumor started to circulate. Di An would be attacked or mortared to celebrate Ho Chi Minh's birthday. Even though there was total disagreement as to the exact date of Ho Chi Minh's birthday (May 19), we took the rumor seriously. Learning of this, our captain gave us a pep talk and claimed that the Viet Cong couldn't get near Di An.

We took this comment just as we took all of the captain's comments—as useless insane bullshit.

Though I am more than willing to believe there were brave and competent army officers like Works leading their men out in the jungle, the army officers I had contact with in Vietnam generally were what the British call "wankers." (Think of what teenage boys and male monkeys do in their spare time.)

Knowing what I know now, I believe that most of our military and political leadership stank in 1966, right up to Lyndon Johnson and his band of morality-free technocrats, like Robert McNamara.

Before an ex-marine garrotes me, I am also willing to believe that leadership was better in the Marines. Jim Webb's *Fields of Fire* and Karl Marlantes's *Matterhorn* were revelations to me. Marines were all volunteers and were better trained and had better morale than the soldiers in the army. Naturally, the Marines took horrifying casualties demonstrating this.

Especially as the war progressed, I find it difficult to imagine that any army unit performed like the Marines in Webb's and Marlantes's terrific, disturbing books. In my opinion, the massacre by the ill-led soldiers at My Lai was nothing more than a larger version of what had happened many times before on a smaller scale. Mix typical so-so soldiers with typical so-so officers, after the good, veteran sergeants had rotated home, and you had trouble.

In the army I knew, the sergeants made soldiers perform and behave, not the officers.

Once I was told in midafternoon to take a document over to an officer's tent for him to sign. Inside the tent I found the officer lying on his back on his bunk. His eyes were open, but he was totally stoned. On the side wall of the tent was a large red banner with "Fuck Communism" on it in large black letters. I dropped the document on the ground beside the bunk and left.

Army officers usually didn't understand the men and had limited contact with them. Sergeants ran the army.

Our captain, for example, didn't refer in his pep talk to the attack that we all knew had just occurred in Saigon. Ton Son Nhut Airport had the best security in Vietnam, but Viet Cong infiltrators had blown up lots of planes and helicopters and the oil tanks there. We knew this because Armed Forces Radio soon confirmed the instant rumor. And we could see the oily dark smoke by day and the glow by night from the raging airport fires. So we found the Ho Chi Minh birthday attack story quite plausible.

Our tent also had a collective, bowel-loosening fright late one drunken evening. We were sitting around nursing a communal bottle of warm scotch in the dark, trying to get drunk enough to have a chance of restless sleep, when machine gun fire started coming through the tent canvas just below the tent's crossbar.

Zap, zap, zap, zap…

Byrd said, "Damn. Those insects are loud fuckers," before Cubello pointed his flashlight at the holes appearing in the tent canvas.

The next day we learned we had been machine-gunned by an overenthusiastic patrol of our South Korean allies. The Koreans were at a good distance from the camp, but being machine-gunned feels up close and personal even if the fire is a few feet over your head. The fire could come in lower any second.

At the time, it had us all futilely cowering under our bunks or trying to get under the metal floor plates of the tent.

The next day we agreed to dig a trench next to our tent. As far as I know, there were then no slit trenches in Di An and certainly none near our tent. There wasn't much argument for once and we began digging. This went on sporadically for days. We couldn't go down far because we hit water so we built up the sides with sandbags.

Shortly after we finished the trench, a major explosion outside the perimeter interrupted another drunken night discussing the varied attractions of Saigon drinking spots. With the clear thinking drunks are known for, everyone shouted at once: "It's Ho Chi Minh's birthday!"

Outside the tent, men ran around, tripping over tent wires and screaming "incoming!" We grabbed our rifles and steel helmets and dove into our new trench. We were huddled in the bottom of the trench when fat Byrd jumped in with a shout and fired his M-14 in no particular direction the same instant that his feet landed at the bottom. Geronimo! The bullet passed so close to Jerry Kahle's head that Kahle claimed to have heard the angels sing.

Byrd was out of his mind with fear and funk and booze. He was about to fire again at nothing or into someone's head when we knocked the rifle out of his hand. The next day Byrd denied the whole thing. And nothing had happened really; the explosion was never explained.

Byrd also had started a kind of sexual slap and tickle game with a large black guy named Cookie. Neither made any attempt to conceal this activity.

I suppose you would have had to call it sex, but it was hardly gay. It was never clear whether either man was gay or whether this was a matter of mere availability like prison sex. The two quarreled loudly and shoved each other. It was like watching male walruses out on the rocks. My guess is that in his natural environment Byrd would have reverted to bar waitresses, like Bubba Clinton.

One night, outside the tent in the dark, we heard grunting and snorting. Elsewhere, I might have taken this for animals.

In the army, it merely meant that two or more drunken soldiers were fighting. Most often, it was the cooks or the guys from the motor pool. Sometimes we went out to watch the pointless shoving and insults, followed by the wild swinging punches that missed and the grappling that ended quickly in mindless mud wrestling. Those involved were in a terrific rage and badly wanted to hurt each other but never did. This evening, we ignored the sounds.

Suddenly, Byrd and Cookie burst into the tent. They were having a titanic lover's quarrel. They came barreling through in a shuffling, sumo-wrestler grip from one end of the tent to the other, on the way knocking over a bunch of guys trying to play poker on a bunk. Then they disappeared into the night, bellowing curses.

Everyone was tired of Byrd. We ignored the slob when he told loud stories of how he beat the army by not doing his job, his favorite topic. In his defense, I must admit that Byrd's excuses for whatever he failed to do were always creative, like those of Bubba Clinton, and worth keeping in reserve for future personal use.

But even Byrd was forced to do a lot of work around our tent city.

Life in Di An was grubby at best. Keeping the place from degenerating into a disease-ridden swamp required constant work. The high water table that kept us from digging in was also the reason we didn't have traditional military latrines. We peed into large cardboard tubes dug into the ground. Naturally, these were called piss tubes. Originally, artillery ammo came in the tubes.

We crapped into large metal cans made of fifty-gallon oil drums sawed in half with a board resting across the open half can. Once a day we poured diesel oil into the drums and burned the contents, one of the many reasons our camp reeked like a ferret breeders' convention.

Army engineers built our showers from the aluminum fuel drop-tanks off our jets. The drop tanks were up high on a wooden frame with a pull-chain valve and an improvised showerhead. Once in a while the engineers pumped water into the tanks, but the tanks were often empty when we had enough time for a shower.

There was not much opportunity to sit around drinking in a group, though drink was more or less free and gloriously abundant. We had a beer ration and could get three-two percent beer or soft drinks from a tent PX. Or someone would produce hard liquor from some source or other. Booze was shared freely. As was grass, very strong grass, but I stuck to booze. I never saw anyone shooting up or snorting, but any drug you wanted could be bought in Saigon.

Every few days some Vietnamese guys brought a truckload of large blocks of ice for sale. We bought chunks off the back of their tiny, overloaded, homemade three-wheeled truck. We acquired a rectangular beer cooler made of two layers of old beer cans rolled out into sheets and insulated with a middle layer of torn-up newspaper and hunks of cotton waste. It had a lid made of the same material and, though it leaked, actually kept things cold for hours as the ice melted.

We were told not to use the ice for drinks since it came directly from the Saigon River. This may well have been true, but we convinced ourselves that freezing killed germs and used the ice freely. We had no glasses. You put a large chunk of ice in the metal canteen cup that fitted over the bottom of a U.S. Army canteen, filled the cup with Jack Daniels or a suitable equivalent, and soon it was "good-bye war."

A few soldiers were permanently in a drunken fog, quite an accomplishment on three-two percent beer. Drinking a case of beer a day wasn't unknown. Sweating constantly alleviated the need to pee constantly. No one cared how much you drank as long as you could remain upright and perform the bare basics of your job.

A drunken hillbilly sergeant I vaguely knew shot himself in the leg in what the sergeant claimed was a quick draw competition with himself as the sole competitor.

The clumsy Colt .45 Model 1909 automatic pistol he used doesn't lend itself to a quick draw, though it is perfect for blowing a chunk out of your leg. My guess is that was the sergeant's real goal, but that the extent of the wound took him by surprise.

No doubt the sergeant's even bigger surprise came later when the army shipped him from a Philippines hospital right back to Vietnam to serve out his full tour as an infantry private E-1. Self-inflicted injuries resulted in a court martial and what was called "bad time." Bad time didn't count toward your one-year tour of duty.

Every few days I ran into poor Benny Reyes. We didn't talk about what he was doing. Dealing with body bags in the tropics was never going to be fun. Reyes had forsaken his resolution not to drink and looked puffy and sick. Reyes was having a bad war.

My own work in sorting through the cards and updating the rosters chugged cheerfully along. Sergeant Cato had me promoted to Specialist Fifth Class, a lowly form of sergeant, as a reward. Our captain then immediately summoned me to ask if I wanted to go to Officer Candidate School.

I considered it. Shoving shells into a cannon by hand was not fun, but flying around in a Piper Cub as an artillery spotter officer might be. Trudging through the jungle with an infantry company, ready to call in fire, would be less fun—much less fun—but valuable to the war effort. Or something like that.

But three more years in the army? Too much soldiering. I turned down this offer.

And I got plenty of flying around anyway. Tracking down missing men was like low-grade detective work. Doing it over the military phone land-lines was difficult and could take days. You cranked the phone over and over and hoped that someone somewhere would eventually pick up and then know how to connect you.

Simply going to the unit where the missing soldier was supposed to be and asking a few questions was a snip in comparison. Organizing for men to go home was important; senior people wanted to help and no one questioned me for doing this.

To fly anywhere, just after dawn I went to the airstrip, a long runway in the midst of a sea of the deepest mud. In the operations tent, I asked the flight crews where they were going and then hitched a lift on any plane or helicopter going in the right direction. These were army aircraft so I did not have to be on the manifest as on an Air Force plane. The army's warrant officer pilots told me that the U.S. Air Force was full of such chickenshit regulations. Hell, a war was going on; who needed them?

Air Strip at Di An 1966

I vividly remember flying up country to a remote artillery-fire base. The mission was to find out if a corporal really existed. The plane was a Caribou that had a large, fully open cargo opening at the rear from which we watched the small green fields and our camp diminish at a funny angle as the plane climbed sharply.

No seatbelts; we sat clinging to narrow fold-down benches along the sides of the plane. The plane's load master stood casually in the cargo opening during takeoff, holding on to the canvas rigging on the side of the plane.

Once we were reached three thousand feet, Vietnam became cool for a change. What a relief! Noticing the shot-down helicopters and wrecked aircraft on the ground as we flew over them was thought provoking, however.

The fire base was a cluster of tents and trenches on top of a one-acre hillock about twenty minutes by air from Di An. The hillock was stripped of vegetation and surrounded by claymore mines and the usual concertina wire. The guns were the old 105 mm howitzers I'd trained on at Fort Sill, Oklahoma, dug into circular pits surrounded by low sandbag walls. I have one of my usual lousy photos of the scene.

The first sergeant took me to the missing corporal. The army simply had his name and service number all wrong. The corporal seemed like a nice guy, so I asked him where he really wanted to be reassigned. I had discovered that, if I put a certain letter of the alphabet in a specific column on the updated IBM machine rosters I sent to Saigon, it meant that the soldier had re-enlisted and got the soldier his first choice of reassignment post.

Like this corporal, a lot of soldiers wanted to go to Fort Dix, New Jersey, since it was located at a convenient distance for partying in Manhattan. So to Fort Dix they were reassigned. Some authority must later have wondered why there was a gross oversupply of artillerymen at Fort Dix where there was no artillery.

By the time I had sorted out the corporal, the Caribou had gone on its way to another isolated base. I had to spend the night at the fire base. The guns fired sporadic salvos all night. Whoomph! Whoomph! They were probably firing blind at map coordinates; fire in response to an urgent radio request was more intense.

Ignoring the noise, I drank steadily all that night in the NCO mess, a tent filled with a bunch of friendly sergeants who were bored beyond belief. Any visitor was welcome, and the drinks were on the house.

When leaving the next day, I noticed that dozens of the large brass shell casings from the 105mm rounds lined the path down to the airstrip. The casings were hammered the same precise depth into the ground six inches apart. Visually, the effect was startling and might suit George W. Bush's ranch in Texas.

With each solid brass shell casing costing about a hundred dollars, this odd form of military landscaping was not good news for the U.S. taxpayer. The fire base commander probably dreamed up using the shell casings decoratively prior to a flying visit by a Saigon-based general. Boondoggling American civilians and politicians didn't often go to such potential hotspots as an exposed fire base, though bad things could happen even in sunny downtown Saigon.

In contrast, journalists and Bob Hope, the comedian, went everywhere. The difference between Hope and the journalists was that soldiers hugely admired Bob Hope. Men dated events by whether they had happened before or after Bob Hope came to their base.

Bob Hope had lots of pretty girls in his show and made snappy, relevant jokes that the men remembered and would quote. I had arrived in Di An just after one of his shows, so I never caught his act. Hope wasn't young, and where he went wasn't safe. Hope had guts. No wonder Hope had such a great career into extreme old age.

Working through the cards with their record of GI injuries and deaths made me aware of how dangerous army life could be, even without any help from the Viet Cong. In 1966 there were 6053 U.S. deaths in Vietnam, of which 5008 were deaths in action. (Which puts the total of just over 6000 deaths, or six hundred a year spread over a decade, in Iraq and Afghanistan into perspective, doesn't it?)

I don't have a breakdown of how the other 1,045 noncombat deaths in 1966 occurred. Some were due to friendly fire, a feature in all wars that nonetheless never fails to surprise and anger the American civilian public.

My impression is that in any war, friendly-fire deaths are far more common than official records indicate. Some friendly-fire deaths, as in the recent Tillman case in Afghanistan, may have been deliberately misclassified as combat deaths. Other deaths were not necessarily misclassified as a blame-shifting coverup. Most parents would probably rather believe that their son was killed by the enemy than by his own trigger-happy American buddy.

A lot of accidents and fatalities in Vietnam were due to traditional human stupidity. Putting a dim, grass-smoking teenage soldier behind the wheel of a heavy truck led to many accidents. I was in a truck whose driver swerved deliberately to force poor Vietnamese peasants on bicycles into the deep ditch beside the road. A small misjudgment and we would have joined the peasants. This casual cruelty was not unusual. War is hell because war is stupid.

Plus, there were plain-vanilla American idiots with guns everywhere. I met a guy who was coming back from hospital in Japan after being shot through the leg while driving a truck. His dimbo passenger had a so-called grease gun, a .45 caliber submachine gun, loaded, cocked, and on the passenger's lap. The truck hit a pothole; the primitive safety catch on the grease gun—a metal "tooth" that holds the bolt back—slipped loose and whammo!—the driver got a .45 slug right through the leg.

The grease gun, nicknamed due to its resemblance to the auto lubricating tool, probably wasn't current army issue. All sorts of weapons came from out of nowhere, probably left by the French and resold to us by peasants who had kept them under their beds.

I used to borrow a communal grease gun when I went to the open-air restaurant in the town of Di An. I don't know whose grease gun it was but, with the grease gun and a grenade on the table and my back to the man-high cinderblock wall of the restaurant, I could enjoy my water buffalo steak and fries and feel secure. Naturally, this popular eatery was known as the Buffalo Steak Restaurant. The food was excellent, even if the meat was tough as rubber.

Guns were regularly bought and sold. I bought a snub-nose .38 Smith and Wesson revolver after firing it once into the ground to see if it worked. That was the only shot I fired in Vietnam. Who wants to clean a gun unnecessarily?

Just before flying back to the United States, I bought a pristine Chinese-made AK-47—one recently deceased but careful owner—that sort of thing. But I lost my nerve and handed it in because the army claimed we would all be searched and then jailed if we brought back drugs or weapons. No search took place. I've regretted not keeping such a splendid souvenir ever since.

Finally, in May the monsoon arrived. The relief was huge, even though the violent wind knocked down tents. The rain fell with a tropical intensity and in sufficient volume for us to soap up and have a decent shower. At night there was a breeze so that, if we weren't on guard, we could sleep. All the trees and brush turned vivid rich greens.

And, possibly because rain filled his hiding hole, a patrol caught the Lone Sniper. We saw him standing in the back of a deuce and a half with his arms tied behind his back. He was wearing black PJs and a conical straw hat. At last, a properly dressed VC! Aged about twenty, emaciated and short, his dark eyes and bruised face showed no fear or emotion.

The truck soon pulled away. We assumed the Lone Sniper was turned over to the Army of South Vietnam or ARVN and shot within a day or two. Such men were just local farmers; they had no secrets worth prying out by threatening to drop them out of an open helicopter door. I wondered whether the patrol had caught the right man. But the sniping ceased.

Despite the grotty conditions we lived in and the fri̇̀
disturbing things going on around us, I felt vividly alive an̄
curiosity during my time in Vietnam. We had so little free t̄̄ne that
any break was keenly enjoyable.

One day about noon, Sergeant Cato told me that I had an
overnight pass, effective immediately. This was a complete surprise.
Before anyone like the captain changed his mind, I rushed off to
hop a lift in the back of an army truck for the twenty-kilometer ride
into downtown Saigon. The truck dropped me off at an army depot
where I was assigned a locker, changed into my only civilian clothes,
and was handed a reservation for a cheap, but air-conditioned—air-
conditioned!—civilian hotel.

I left the .38 Smith & Wesson revolver I'd brought with me in
the locker at the depot since large signs there threatened instant
arrest, death, or castration if I went into central Saigon armed.
As usual, this proved to be typical army nonsense; I saw pistols
repeatedly in Saigon, stuffed in belts under loose shirts or stuck in
ankle holsters or just pushed into a pocket. Guns were everywhere in
Vietnam.

I hopped into a cyclo, a three-wheeled, rickshaw-style bike with
the passenger seat in front between the wheels. Riding in a cyclo
was like being pushed face-first into the traffic at truck exhaust
level.

By 1966, traffic in Saigon was out of control. The dreamy French
colonial world of not many years before as described by Graham
Green in *The Quiet American* had vanished. Tiny, little old Renault
taxis, horns hooting constantly, squeezed through the dense pack of
bicycles and cyclos and mopeds. Army trucks and large white U.S.
government agency Fords and Chevys simply drove at a constant
speed through this mess. All the other traffic just had to get out of
the American's way.

Saigon Street Traffic 1966

White-uniformed local police, called White Mice, made vague attempts to direct traffic, with their short arms flailing, waving white police billy clubs in white-gloved hands.

My cyclo weaved in and out of the traffic, turned down sideroads, went past a large colonial French building with Bureau de Poste on the front, and finally dropped me down by the river. I gave the tubercular-looking cyclo driver a wad of flimsy, greasy Vietnamese piaster notes, too much to judge from his pleasure, but my body weight was probably twice his.

We were supposed to spend only the American "military payment certificates" we were paid in. I still have one of these little notes. It is for five cents and was almost as useless then as it is today. As soon as we received these payment certificates, we swapped them for greasy wads of local piasters on the black market.

The purpose of the silly certificates was to prevent our spending dollars, which caused inflation in the local economy, since the military payment certificates were only good—in theory—at U.S. establishments like the big PX in Cholon, part of Saigon. And we did use them at the big PX to buy booze to bring back to share in the tent. But this was trivial spending; in fact, inflation was rampant. In one way or other, tens of millions of black dollars leaked sooner or later into Vietnamese hands and bid up the cost of everything locally.

This inflation and related corruption were key reasons why ordinary South Vietnamese people were demoralized by the war and resentful of the American presence.

Sounds like Afghanistan today? Or country X tomorrow?

I wandered up Tu Do Street from the river. Hookers stood in every doorway. Bars, with wire netting over their front to discourage passing grenade throwers on mopeds, were all crowded. I thought about going into a pizzeria, but decided to stick with my original plan to have an elegant French meal. We all talked endlessly about what we would do in Saigon, so I had plenty of ideas about where to go.

I went into the main square, called Lam Son Square now, but it may have had another name then. After wars end, the victors rename things. For example, what was then Tu Do Street, meaning Freedom Street, is now Dong Khoi Street, meaning Unified Uprising Street. No need for freedom in a people's republic.

Freedom for the Vietnamese was still a possibility in 1966.

In the time of Graham Green, Tu Do Street was the Rue Cantinat, since the French ran things and named the streets for French reasons. The Rue Cantinat was a splendid shopping street for French colonial ladies. What life was like for the local Vietnamese, who didn't shop on such streets, can be grasped by watching *Indochine*—a moving film about colonial life under the French.

The old Hotel Continental that features in *The Quiet A ican* is across the square. In 1966, the Continental was an American quarters. No American officers were in sight on the wide veranda around the hotel. Possibly they were all shacked up inside.

My goal was the roof restaurant of the Caravelle Hotel, then owned and operated by Air France. Night was falling. I took the elevator up to the roof. As an enlisted man, I half-expected to be turned away but was promptly and courteously seated by the French-speaking Vietnamese head waiter. Most of the tables scattered around on the tiled roof, which was open to the sky, were already full, so I was in luck.

For dinner I had crayfish from the river, rice, and a salad with an ice-cold bottle of French Rose d'Anjou. They were excellent.

The other diners were all westerners, including a number of young, attractive American women. Some of the men with the women wore bush jackets and Australian jungle fighter hats. Those were war correspondents. The American civilian officials were dressed like IBM salesmen in white button-down, short-sleeved shirts, dark neckties, and well-pressed lightweight trousers.

As the night darkened fast, I worked on a coffee and a cognac. The Caravelle Hotel was the tallest building in Saigon. Looking inland toward the flat, featureless horizon, you could see the brilliant flash, then glowing descent, of illumination rounds or WP fired from American artillery. Once in a while you heard the low crrrump! of a distant howitzer being fired or the zap, zap, zap! of a machine gun. I was probably watching and hearing the night activities of my division.

I enjoyed the spectacle thoroughly. It was like a First World War night scene, viewed at a safe distance. I savored the cognitive dissonance of coming from a place where I spent my hours digging or crouching in holes or burning shit cans to dine on the roof of a luxury hotel. Saigon wasn't all that safe, of course. However, the Caravelle, as a French-owned property, was most unlikely to be attacked. After the French defeat in 1954, French businesses made a separate peace with the Viet Cong.

Local Saigon businesses had no such exemption. A limpet mine, placed on the hull by Viet Cong frogmen shortly before my arrival in Vietnam, sunk the boat where I ate on my second and last overnight pass, the My Canh floating restaurant. Promptly refloated and moored at the bottom of Tu Do Street, this excellent restaurant offered a choice of live fish that you selected from large tanks.

Eating there, you had the constant awareness that the Viet Cong might pay a return visit at any time. This stimulated the appetite. The prompt service and excellent food were adequate reward for the slight danger. On the My Canh, if you wanted a beer, without looking up or turning round, you just shouted "beer!" or *bam mi bam!* and presto—a frosty Biere 33 would appear on your table. (*Bam mi bam* is thirty-three in Vietnamese.)

You might wonder how I paid for these treats. Even as a midranking soldier, I had plenty of money. Our pay was tax-free, and I received extra pay for being in a war zone. I had virtually no expenses as an ordinary soldier, except for stuff like toothpaste or razor blades, which were dirt cheap at the PX in camp.

I saved most of my pay, partially through money deducted to buy U.S. government bonds. Just as in Germany, buying bonds was more or less compulsory. Each army unit was expected to have close to a one hundred percent participation rate in this "patriotic" savings scheme. Your company commander leaned on you to make sure you took part. It wasn't wise not to.

———◆———

Apart from passes to go into Saigon, the other relief from the war was R&R—rest and recreation. Every soldier was entitled to one per combat tour. You were given a list of possible places to go; you chose one and then waited your turn to go.

I chose Bangkok for reasons that now elude me. Had I gone to Hong Kong, I suspect I might have returned to the Far East after Yale. Even the antiseptic Singapore would have fascinated me. I am an enthusiastic fan of Chinese culture and of the Chinese-in-origin cultures of Vietnam and Korea.

Not that I didn't enjoy my four days and three nights in Bangkok. I stayed in a motel not far from the airport. It had a large swimming pool. I spent most of my first day in the pool, chilling out and trying to feel clean again.

Over the following days, I watched Thai boxing in which every match between the tiny lightweights ended in a TKO. I watched cock fighting, which also resulted in a lot of TKOs. I ate and loved Thai food. I went on the canals and bought a lot of Thai silk from Jim Thompson's shop. I avoided other soldiers.

In short, I did all the tourist things. But Bangkok didn't change my life or strike me as a place I wanted to explore in more depth. Perhaps I was too drained by my time in Di An. Plus, I had no desire to explore the seamy side of Bangkok. There was enough that was seamy in Vietnam.

R*E*S*P*E*C*T

One of my personal regrets about Vietnam is that I didn't meet Donald Miller sooner.

One day I was walking past a tent near ours when I heard Vietnamese music blaring from a radio. This was odd. GIs didn't listen to what they called "gook" music.

Popping into the tent, I found Miller, a tall, thin, hyper-cool black guy about my age, who welcomed me to share the music. Miller was also a Specialist Fifth Class and had been in the army for some time. He spoke articulate, non-ghetto English and was from some big northern city. Miller had a pussy tickler, a tuft of unshaven hair, under his lower lip, but was otherwise a conventional-looking soldier.

Miller and I hung around together. I was bored with the people in my tent, apart from Jerry Kahle who sometimes joined Miller and me on our little escapades. Miller smoked powerful weed frequently but wasn't a serious drinker. Like me, he had a job at division headquarters.

Miller's main interest was the Vietnamese. He loved their music, their food, their differentness. Miller even managed to learn to speak conversational Vietnamese. The rest of us only shouted short phrases like "didi mau" and "soc mau" that were supposed to mean respectively "go away" and "I will hit you," but probably made no sense to a Vietnamese. The tone of our voices did the trick.

One Sunday morning, Miller introduced me to the advantage of being a practicing Christian in the army. Eureka! They had to let you take time off for church. We would nod at Sergeant Cato, slip out of the work tent, zip by the chaplain's portable outdoor altar just to make sure that God's military representative was on the job that Sunday and head out.

Usually, we first went by the USO to grab a free hamburger cooked by really gutsy, middle-aged American women volunteers. Working in that USO hamburger joint right in the center of our camp was infinitely more dangerous than working in a Burger King in the Detroit ghetto or even in Newark. The USO is a civilian-run support charity for soldiers—a bit like the Red Cross. I still give to the USO.

Then Miller and I hitched a ride or caught a dilapidated local bus into the little town of Di An. Miller had met an ancient Vietnamese lady who owned one of the few proper houses, next to the Buddhist temple. She had been a local landowner, was now a widow, and what she made of us was anyone's guess. Miller felt we should pay our respects, so we walked by her house, put our hands together, and bowed to her every time we went to Di An.

Children came from every shack and alley to pal around with Miller. I have a blurry photo of him talking with the kids.

By this time the monsoon had turned the town streets into a muddy mess, and the stench was even worse than in our camp. A few small black pigs snuffled around in the mud along with naked human infants and little white ducks. Rats dodged around corners or peeked out at us from under the hooches.

War had overtaken rice farming as the town's main business activity. There were always South Vietnamese military milling around but we ignored them. Probably some of the ARVN soldiers and some of the locals were night-time VC. We ignored this possibility, too. Miller and I took rifles or a couple of pistols just in case, but we didn't expect anything to happen. Bad for business.

After satisfying his social conscience, Miller felt other needs. I followed him down an unlikely-looking, narrow, twisting, garbage-strewn alley to his favorite house; the kind of house that is definitely not a home. Inside this hooch were three or four youngish Vietnamese women.

Di An was Hicksville for sex workers. As soon as a good-looking girl learned passable English, she went off to Saigon on the next bus. The girls who stayed were not beauties, and conversation wasn't their thing. The boss girl sold us beers with a side shot of whiskey, then put on an American hit like the omnipresent "Send Me the Pillow that You Dream On" or "Twenty Four Hours to Tulsa." Miller always complained and asked for Vietnamese music, but that wasn't part of the deal.

We drank for a while. The heat was stifling, despite a couple of old black French-made electric fans. The music droned on. A girl made dancing movements for a minute of two, then plonked herself down again when we paid no attention. After examining the girls, Miller went off into a back room with his choice. I will leave my role in this undignified entertainment undefined.

Back in camp, Miller soon spent most of his free moments in our tent. So Miller was present when our first draftee arrived.

We were sitting around on bunks during a work break from digging, in sweat-stained green T-shirts, jungle pants, and jungle boots, drinking beer and scratching bites and prickly heat, waiting for the afternoon monsoon rain to cool things off.

Round in the Chamber Miller on the Razzle in Di An

At the opening of the tent appeared a small, pale-white private with an out-of-proportion melon head, carrying an M-14 by its sling while using his other hand to drag his duffle bag along the ground. He was wearing a new, much too large uniform and was completely wasted. From the guy's inarticulate comments, this unmilitary object was actually trained to be an infantry rifleman but, to his immense relief, Sergeant Cato had intercepted this private to work with us in admin.

Gaining confidence, this druggy munchkin soon announced in a slurred voice that he was Private Garner, the offspring of a famous old Virginian political family. Looking at my photos, Garner does indeed look like a younger, dwarf version of a certain venerable and beloved ex-senator, who in those days was merely Elizabeth Taylor's fourth or fifth husband.

Private Garner went on to say that he had powerful connections so we should watch our step. Garner also proclaimed that he had a master's degree in chemistry. Like, wow.

Miller studied Garner for a while and said, "What a weirdo," and left. From that moment no one ever called Garner anything but Weirdo.

Weirdo may well have had political connections; he was good at politics. He was brilliant at pleasing Sergeant Cato while at work, then spending all of his time when out of Sergeant Cato's sight stoned into perfect zombiehood. Weirdo had good moves.

Weirdo woke up in the morning stoned, pulled himself together sufficiently to work fitfully on some admin task for an hour or two, then slipped away to the tent to get more stoned. He went on guard stoned. None of us could figure out what Weirdo was using apart from constantly smoking grass. Perhaps he just got more out of pot than most people or had accumulated so much in his system that he floated permanently a foot or two above the ground.

I was soon completely fed up with him. Keeping our tent livable during the monsoon took constant work, such as digging out the slit trench periodically or just sweeping out the mud. And there were sandbags to fill and shit cans to burn. Everyone else worked hard. Weirdo ducked everything. He just floated away if you told him to do anything.

One morning, I left him alone in the tent. Weirdo promised me that he would at last work on cleaning up our area. Hours later, I was in the work tent when Cubello came in off guard duty. I asked him if Weirdo was working. The answer was that Weirdo was passed out on his bunk. Zonked again.

I stormed back to our tent. The heat of the noonday sun was fantastic. Sweat poured down my chest and back. I was in a total rage.

I decided to kick Weirdo two or three times, then throw him into the trench followed by an entrenching tool. There he would dig out the abundant mud that had fallen in. I anticipated the sheer, raw satisfaction of burying the hard toe cap of my size-twelve jungle boot in his backside.

When I arrived back in the tent, I suddenly had a better idea. Why should this idle, privileged little shit duck out on the war?

I yanked Weirdo off his bunk and onto the floor and threw our fire bucket of water over him. When he was fully roused, I quietly and slowly told him I was going to arrange his immediate transfer as a rifleman to the 3rd Company 19th Infantry up on the Cambodian border. We got KIA cards from the 3rd of the 19th on a more or less daily basis as they slugged it out with the North Vietnamese regular army.

This news frightened Weirdo so much that I left him lying gibbering on the muddy perforated metal tent floor.

Alas, back in the work tent Sergeant Cato refused to let me organize the transfer. Weirdo was too hard to replace. So Weirdo remained stoned and useless for the rest of my time in Vietnam. I had been poised and ready to kick him witless, but somehow the moment had passed. After that, I ignored Weirdo.

I imagine that Weirdo is now a successful Washington lobbyist for the drug industry.

Realizing that Sergeant Cato would say nothing about occasional absences, Miller and I stepped up our trips into town.

Miller needed to get out of the camp as often as possible. A white cracker sergeant from Alabama named Morrells started riding Miller in a traditional racist way. Morrells would softly say "boy" as Miller walked past or he abruptly stopped talking when Miller entered a tent. Sly stuff, nothing you could really pin down. Morrells was a sallow, lanky, feral-looking type—complete with bad teeth—and small town, fuck weasel mean.

———————◆———————

As in the United States generally, racial tensions were mounting in the army during the 1960s. Vietnam brought these tensions right out in the open. Pointless, drunken fights were common among army enlisted men, but the racial ones were serious.

Music was a frequent cause of racial tension. Music had even caused a racial murder at an upcountry infantry base. The enlisted men there had a recreation tent with a generator that powered lights and a boogie-box. One evening, after a certain amount of drinking and smoking grass, the black guys wanted to hear Motown instead of the endless country music. The blacks told the whites to get out and let them have their music.

After an argument, the whites left quietly enough, but next they cut out the generator. At the moment the lights went out, someone, presumably white, opened up through the tent flap opening into the dark with a .45 Colt automatic pistol filched from an officer. The white perps then dropped the pistol outside the tent. A black soldier was killed and several others badly wounded.

In a Nelson de Mille novel, a keen-eyed military police investigator would have helicoptered into the camp to solve this dastardly crime. Of course, it was never solved, though there was a confused mention of the killing in the *Stars and Stripes*, I believe. I heard about it from a guy I was redeploying.

This was an extreme example of the corrosive damage done by race hate, but racially triggered fights were common.

Like small skin cuts, little disagreements turned nasty fast in the heat and danger of Vietnam.

———◆———

Miller seemed to handle what Morrells handed out so the rest of us paid little attention. There was no personnel department to complain to anyway. We all had to rub along together somehow.

But everyone has a breaking point. As Olaf sang in the ee cummings antiwar poem, *The Song of Olaf*: "There is some shit I will not eat." One torrid afternoon, Miller found the shit he wouldn't eat.

I was wandering back to our tent, slipping around in the mud while trying to avoid piss tubes and tent ropes. As I approached my tent, I heard screaming from Miller's tent.

And it was Miller screaming, "Morrells, you motherfucker. You dumb motherfucker. You motherfucker."

This went on and on as a mantra.

I went into Miller's tent and shoved past a small group of wide-eyed guys. Miller had Morrells backed up against a tent pole. Miller's left hand was pushing his M14 into Morrells's chest with the muzzle tucked up under Morrell's chin.

Miller had his right thumb hooked over the trigger of the M14. His right fingers were clenched around the stock. Morrells's head was pushed up and back; his eyes were closed. Morrells was standing on tiptoes to relieve the force of the upward thrust of the muzzle into the soft place under his chin.

The M14 doesn't have a hair trigger, but this was certainly a delicate moment for Morrells.

Especially when Miller dropped his variations on a theme of motherfucker and started wailing over and over, "I got a round in the chamber and it's for you, Morrells."

Miller hyperventilated. His eyes rolled, showing a lot of white. Morrells had already pissed himself, and the growing crowd speculated as to how long it would take before he shat himself. The crowd was completely with Miller. No one liked Morrells.

Some thought it would be interesting if Miller's thumb slipped, and he blew the top of Morrells's head off. Hard, though, to make this look like an accident or suicide.

So a larger group advised caution, pointing out that Miller was a good man who liked female company. Miller wouldn't want to spend the next fifteen to twenty years of his life with nothing but ugly male companions, locked up in Fort Huachuca in the Arizona desert, spending endless days in the fierce desert sun making big rocks into small ones. Not just for the pleasure of blowing Morrells away.

After five or ten long minutes, we talked Miller down. Jerry Kahle got the M14 from Miller. Its safety was off. There was a round in the chamber as Miller had said. Morrells just collapsed against the tent pole.

After that, everyone called Miller "Round in the Chamber," which Miller took as a great joke. I am proud that I knew Specialist Fifth Class Donald "Round in the Chamber" Miller.

———◆———

And the war went on around us.

Most men liked being on guard duty at night. You were alone. In war, solitude is a rare pleasure. On guard alone, you could listen to your little Sony radio with an earpiece. This was, of course, *Streng*

Verboten, but the chances of being caught were slight. The officer of the guard would not want to surprise a trigger-happy sentry.

At night, Armed Forces Radio played stuff like dance music from the thirties and old film scores instead of the endless country and western music. I learned all kinds of wonderful songs during those nights. I heard Ella Fitzgerald and Duke Ellington, Tommy Dorsey and early Frank Sinatra.

Illumination rounds lit up the low, cloud-filled sky from time to time. Things appeared freaky and frightening looking out across the minefield to the edge of the boonies, but, if you sat on the sandbag parapet on the top of the bunker, you had the comforting presence of the Browning .50 caliber air-cooled machine gun close to you.

None of us had ever test-fired the mighty Browning .50 or knew how to clear it if it jammed, but we expected great things from this monster in case of need. So we daydreamed our two hours on guard away, were relieved, and slept for two hours. Then we went back on guard for another two hours. Guard duty continued off and on until dawn.

Patrols were less popular. Di An was supposed to be in a pacified area, but no one outside of Saigon or below the rank of captain believed that this meant anything.

One of our day patrols—a day patrol; a heavily armed patrol right out in the noonday sun!—was ambushed out in the scrub brush a few hundred yards from the main gate. This patrol included most of the members of the division's band. (Bandsmen at division level were just combat soldiers with a musical sideline.) The subsequent jokes about "we lost our trumpet but thank God we still have our tuba" didn't conceal a general sense of shock.

Our divisional commander then decreed that every soldier in the Big Red One should go on patrol. I never learned the name of this major general. Unlike the splendid General Rowny, this general did not mingle with his troops. General Rowny went on to receive many honors, became Lieutenant General Rowny, and was the chief U.S. arms negotiator at SALT II. Virtue is sometimes recognized.

The general's ill-considered command was never put fully into effect. In our company, only a subgroup of semi-volunteers went on patrol. Going on night ambush patrol meant you had the next morning off-duty, theoretically to sleep. Instead, Miller and I and others went into town to do naughty things or just to eat and drink at the Buffalo Steak Restaurant.

So we didn't resist our turn to go on patrol.

Did we also feel that we should take our chances like the poor bloody infantry? I think so, but we didn't discuss this.

Ambush patrols always started the same way. About an hour before sunset, six or seven of us gathered in front of the mess tent. No officer ever went on our little patrols so the senior specialist or sergeant present led the patrol. Leading consisted of being sure you knew where the patrol was going and making absolutely certain that someone at battalion headquarters knew this, too.

It wouldn't do to accidentally run into the Koreans out in the dark. We respected the Koreans.

The patrols followed paths that radiated away from the camp, usually along old rice paddy tracks or the banks of drainage ditches. We went a short distance outside the camp, maybe five hundred yards, to a junction of two paths or a landmark, like a patch of mauve lilies in an abandoned rice paddy that we all knew, and then set up an ambush. At least that was the idea.

So…it is late afternoon. We are milling around in front of the mess tent. Miller isn't going, but Jerry Kahle, Finch, Cookie, and several others are. I am loosely in charge.

We use soot from the mess truck exhaust pipe to blacken our faces. We don't wear steel helmets—too clumsy at night. The company armorer has produced some weapons.

I take a 7.62 mm M60 light machine gun and a couple of belts of ammo. I load a little stub of ammo belt—about ten rounds—into the machine gun. Kahle wears several more belts of machine gun ammo around his neck and carries a metal box of machine gun ammo belts. Every fourth round of ammo on the belts is tracer, so we can see what we are hitting at night if we need to use the M60.

The M60 is based on a Czech/German WW II design and hence is highly reliable. The headquarters company machine gun is well maintained, and we all know how to use it. I am confident I can clear a jam if necessary. The main thing is not to get overexcited and fire off all the ammo aimlessly. Kahle will help to load and to feed the ammo belts.

Kahle and I also have a couple of pistols. Byrd takes the M79 grenade launcher, a now obsolete weapon that fires a small grenade from a cartridge as big as the cardboard core of a toilet roll. Cookie has a number of claymore mines and the wires and electrical firing devices for the mines. The other guys have M14s and lots of rifle ammo. Byrd and Cookie seem to be behaving themselves, but I look at them surreptitiously. Please guys, no slap and tickle tonight. Behave.

At least I don't have to worry about Weirdo. By universal agreement, Weirdo and a number of others are exempt from patrol duty. No one wants to be out in the dark with that crazy, druggy little turd. We will take our chances of the general finding out that his orders that every soldier should go on patrol are being willfully disobeyed.

Everyone is handed two or three grenades. These I pay close attention to. I didn't know then that the future U.S. Senator Max Cleland would lose two legs and an arm through dropping a grenade with the pin out (or was it dropped by his buddy?), but grenade accidents had already featured plenty on my cards.

I make sure that each grenade pin is in tightly and that the grenades are attached securely to each guy's webbing.

Then we set out. We move out through a break in the concertina wire on our side of the camp. After we go, the MPs will close the gap again. We lope along since we must be in place before dark. We have a couple of entrenching tools to do rudimentary foxhole digging.

We reach the ambush spot that we had all walked past before—nothing special about it, just a break in the brush where two paths cross. My fervent hope is that no Viet Cong use these paths tonight. No animals, either. Any movement can cause instant First World War. We are not seasoned combat patrol types, to put it mildly. Anyway, there have been plenty of incidents out in the bundu in which the tail end of an experienced infantry patrol shoots up the men at the front. Mistakes happen all the time in war.

We dig in but only to the extent of scraping shallow depressions. It is still agonizingly hot, even though it will be dark in minutes. We set up the claymore mines. I watch this carefully. The claymore mine is a so-called shaped charge, a slightly curved piece of explosive around twelve by six inches that has hundreds of steel bearings imbedded in it. When fired off electrically, the mine will throw a scythe-like, knee-to-waist-high swathe of small steel balls. Nasty.

One side of the claymore mine says "Front" and the opposite "Back" in large black letters. You might consider this self-explanatory, but, during a demonstration in our German training area, a second lieutenant fired a claymore mine into a crowd of infantrymen. Vietnam came early for those guys. So I am cautious about the mine's placing.

By now it is dark. We huddle together in twos. The idea is not to talk but to keep each other awake. Or to take turns sleeping.

At some point around midnight, we all became aware that Byrd and Cookie have resumed slap and tickle. Muttered comments like "I fucking well told you not to talk to him" and "You can't trust nobody" drifted though the clearing.

It is really dark. I don't know what to do. There is no way I am going to crawl over to them. I imagine Byrd and Cookie shouting or even fighting. Then a burst of fire from Viet Cong AK-47's might end the squabble. And all our little lives. Night belongs to the Viet Cong. I am shit scared.

Jerry Kahle ends the noise. I sense Kahle moving next to me on the left side of the M-60, raising himself on his forearms. Kahle whispers loudly. "The instant anything bad happens I am personally going to shoot you two fuckers with the M-60. Got it? Everyone else just keep your heads down."

Since we are all within twelve feet or so of each other this argument is powerful. Silence reigns until daybreak when we pack up and walk back to camp for breakfast.

Time passes quickly when you are having fun.

After obtaining hundreds of reassignments and sending hundreds of grunts back to the United States for discharge from the army, I had the exquisite pleasure of cutting my own orders to go home for discharge. The army did not extend my enlistment; I got out a few days short of three years as a soldier.

I had a couple of days to collect my thoughts and pick up my civilian clothes before returning to New Haven for my senior year at Yale. Yes, Mother Yale had deigned to take me back after some correspondence.

Before I left Di An, I spent a little time with Benny Reyes. By now Reyes was a shaky, trembling wreck and still had a month to go in Vietnam. Dealing with the dead ruined Reyes's life. I have often wondered what happened to this decent, simple man.

*"If I die in a combat zone,
bag me up and ship me home."*
—*Soldier Song*

V
ietnam caused the deaths of tens of thousands of promising young Americans and physically wrecked many more. Other men were psychologically ruined by Vietnam in ways that weren't always as obvious as the damage done to Reyes.

Still others blamed Vietnam or the army for their own self-inflicted ruin.

It was a bit rich, for example, to hear a drunken hillbilly boast, at the beginning of an all-night booze session, that he had been smoking, drinking, snorting, and pill popping since age nine and then, later the same night, listen to him tearfully whining about how the army had made him a drunk.

Another favorite claim was that the war had ruined a hero's marriage. Oddly, though, the individual claiming marital destruction spent every free moment in Vietnam in a brothel. Then, as the ultimate homecoming present, such a swain arrived back in the bed of his beloved in Crotchrot, Georgia, with a strain of Asian VD that sneered at penicillin.

Americans are self-made people.

Many men rode on the back of their time in Vietnam in some way or other for decades after the war. One such is Senator John Kerry. I have no idea whether Kerry was a hero in Vietnam (though he certainly was a hopelessly inadequate presidential candidate with or without Swift boating).

There is, though, something peculiar about Kerry's war record that is not in dispute but never focused on. Kerry only spent four months and twelve days in Vietnam. I sent hundreds of men home from Vietnam. Unless they were seriously wounded or their time was up, the tour of duty was one year in all cases.

In all cases...

Kerry once claimed that he got the right to an early reassignment because he had multiple Purple Hearts. This is possible; there was some rule about this. But Purple Hearts were given generously in Vietnam. Many civilian Americans don't understand that, if a soldier broke his ankle by tripping over a tent rope during a false-alarm mortar attack, said soldier might get a Purple Heart.

And this reassignment rule required many Purple Hearts. Lots of infantry soldiers and sergeants in the First Infantry Division had multiple Purple Hearts but, unless they were medically evacuated, all served one year. I never encountered an exception.

I think Kerry's "go home early" deal happened something like this...

Setting: Vietnam—a straggle of tents on a riverbank. Moored to the muddy riverbank is a row of Swift boats. It is a muggy, steamy night in March 1969.

A grey-haired, distinguished-looking navy captain is sitting in a tent at a small folding table under a flickering single light bulb. The officer is slapping at mosquitoes while attempting to read an official document. From time to time he looks longingly at the duffle bag under his bunk. The duffle bag houses a nearly full fifth of Chivas Regal. Soon he will be able to curl up with his bottle and try to get some fitful sleep. Sweat runs down his face.

Captain J. Elmore Snotbag Jr. is not a happy sailor. His nautical soul yearns for the command of a big, fighting ship out in deep blue, icy cold waters.

Outside the tent flap, a voice says, "Sir, permission to enter?"

The voice is that of Lt-Commander Arne Swenson, the invaluable executive officer of the Swift boat base. Swenson is solid Minnesota Norwegian between the ears and would not bother the captain without a serious reason.

In his efficient way, Swenson immediately alerts the captain to the problem. "Sir, the officers walked out of the mess tent again. They say they can't take it in this heat. It's too much."

Despite his Annapolis discipline, the captain groans. "Is it Kerry again?"

"Yes, sir. It's the speeches. The officers say the war is bad enough, but Kerry's monologues are worse. And there's something else."

So far the captain is merely irritated. Rows in the officer's mess are a fine navy tradition. Captain Snotbag only wished that flogging, another great naval tradition, was still permitted.

"What else, Swenson?" he says.

"Montoya says he wants an immediate transfer, sir. Montoya won't say anything bad about an officer, but he says that Kerry's speeches in the mess give him terrible headaches."

Damn! The captain rocks back on his stool and nearly falls onto the muddy floor of his tent. Montoya is technically only the mess boy. In fact, not only is he the only living person who can keep the officers' quarters temperamental generator working, but Montoya is also the captain's secret and only source of the vital

Chivas Regal. The thought of a single night without many calming belts of Chivas Regal is unbearable.

This is indeed serious.

"Your suggestion, Swenson?" asks the captain. The great thing about Swenson is that he never brought a problem without a solution and a solution that is always in perfect accord with the latest Department of the Navy regulations.

But this time Swenson says, "Sir, I'm stumped. Kerry gives these speeches that cause instant migraine. They make my teeth hurt."

Swenson pulls a face and continues, "Unfortunately, sir, there is no regulation against this. Kerry just walks into the mess and starts talking about duty, freedom, and the brotherhood of man—that kind of stuff. Never swears or shouts. But it's loud and it's steady. Once he hits his stride, Kerry just goes on and on even after everyone walks out. Kerry doesn't notice. If you listen, you can hear him now."

For a long moment, both officers listen to a deep, droning oratorical cadence that rises and falls above the noise of the generator. Then Swenson says, "There is one possibility. If Kerry requested an early transfer home, I know a regulation that would permit it."

"Why would even a perfect fool like Kerry do that?" asks the captain. All the keenest young navy officers want to be on a Swift boat.

Swenson takes a long instant to reply. "Kerry often says that American children need someone to look up to now that President Kennedy is dead. The children need a hero."

He continues. "Sir, I think maybe Kerry sees himself as that hero. Kerry wants out of Vietnam but wants something heroic on his record first. It's his Kennedy hangup. Kerry has the same initials as the late president: JFK."

The captain sputters. "Kerry is full of it. But you may be on to something. What would make him let us transfer him?"

"I think he wants a medal, sir."

"A medal? Is that all?"

The captain sighs in immense relief.

"Give the posturing dickhead a medal. Didn't he get a splinter in his ass on the last mission? He can have another Purple Heart as well as a medal. Just get

Kerry to write up his own medal citation, but have that rating of yours check Kerry's spelling and grammar. I'll put the citation in tomorrow with a note to a friend of mine at navy personnel in Saigon. It will go through pronto."

The captain smiles thinly and says, "Dismissed, Swenson."

Swenson snaps off a salute. "Yes, sir! Thank you, sir"

You can't beat that Naval Academy training in a crisis, Swenson muses as he leaves the captain's tent. Inside the tent, the captain cuts the light, stretches out fully clothed on his bunk, and gropes in his duffle bag for the Chivas Regal. His fist closes firmly around the familiar neck of the bottle. The captain swigs a mighty slug of booze. And another. He's earned it.

The next day, John Forbes Kerry writes his own medal citation. The naval rating corrects his appalling grammar and spelling and types it up. Captain Snotbag approves the citation. Kerry applies for a transfer that is also approved immediately.

Soon a be-medalled John Forbes Kerry is on his way back to the U.S. of A, into the welcoming arms of Jane Fonda and on to a splendid political career.

———◆———

Unlike the heroic Kerry, I missed out on Jane Fonda and simply went back to Yale via San Francisco Airport and Cleveland.

Two young 1st Infantry Division infantry sergeants and I were discharged at the same time. In full dress uniform we went into the airport bar.

A scowling bar waitress immediately refused to serve the two sergeants. They had spent a year in combat, but they were only twenty. Despite their medals and Purple Hearts, they were refused a drink. I was over twenty-one, but I could tell that I wasn't welcome, either. "No dogs or soldiers admitted." So I left with them.

Welcome home, soldier.

Yale in 1966:
My Joyous Return

Yale had readmitted me without too much fuss. In Cleveland I picked up my pre-army Yale outfit: a Brooks Brothers tweed jacket; a couple of Shetland sweaters and several pairs of chinos and flew back to New Haven, a little over a week after leaving Vietnam. I now had a single room in Morse College, an Eero Saarinen-designed modern fantasy of a college. I was through with tent mates and male roommates forever.

Morse made a different and crisper sort of visual impact than the traditional mock-Gothic Yale buildings since it had a striking, modernistic exterior of corrugated, textured concrete, already much stained and blackened by New Haven's acid rain.

Inside there was lots more exposed concrete, much lighter without the rain stains. Tall, dark-framed windows ran from ceiling to floor. In fact, there was dark wood everywhere that wasn't glass or concrete.

What there wasn't anywhere was a right angle. For a long lost reason buried deep in the dank, Finnish pine-forest soul of the late architect, Saarinen had declared death to right angles. This created highly peculiar spaces and rooms. The snaking, windowless corridors were right out of a German black-and-white silent horror film of the 1920s.

Morse was truly hideous but I liked it. Anything was better than mock-Gothic. The view of the ghastly, hulking, stone-carving encrusted Payne-Whitney gym from my room's narrow slit window was a daily reminder of this truth.

Odd and disconnected would have described my mood. To go from living in a leaky tent in a place where B-52 bombs shook the earth back to an Ivy League college is a bizarre transition. I was happy and shaky, worried and calm—all at the same time. And relieved. Hugely, massively relieved. To return from a nasty colonial war in one piece—intact!—is a feeling difficult to describe.

Having a single room was a luxury, despite another odd quirk. Saarinen had overlooked the longer-than-standard length of Yale beds. Yalies were tall, and their beds reflected this.

In my room you could open the door to the hallway or the door to my closet, but not both at the same time—the bed was too long. So when I wanted to put stuff in the closet, I had to push the bed up against the room's hallway door. Because of the lack of right angles, the bed didn't fit flush against any wall, either.

After my army experience of soldiers coming and going unexpectedly, I didn't rush to make new pals. There were lots of things I would have liked to talk about, but only with someone like Jerry Kahle who would have understood what I wanted to say.

Since I didn't know what to say to these earnest young guys, at first I didn't mention my time in the army to anyone. No one asked me about where I'd been before anyway. Morse, as a new college, had many transferees from other Yale colleges.

My first full day back at Yale, I went for lunch in the college cafeteria. This was a most interesting meal. The ceiling of the cafeteria reaches to the height of the second floor; the room is well lit, with windows from the floor up to the bare cement ceiling, which is supported by angular concrete trusses.

On my way in, I noticed two students sitting at a table covered with anti-war posters just inside the cafeteria. They were raising money for a cause, presumably with the approval of the Morse College master. I decided to investigate on my way out.

Lunch was an improvement over the Vietnam chow line. There, cooks dolloped c-rations into the open halves of our folding metal messkits as we went along the chow line. Inevitably, the various food items got mixed up together, but with c-rations this made little difference to the taste or consistency.

At the end of the meal, we hung our metal knife, spoon, and fork on the handle of our folding metal mess kit, then, holding the handle, dunked the whole mess-kit into in a fifty-gallon galvanized steel garbage can full of boiling, soapy water, followed by a dunk into another fifty-gallon can of boiling rinse water. Special gasoline heaters immersed in the garbage cans made the water boil.

In Morse College, you just dumped your tray and dishes in a certain spot and left them for the scholarship students who earned their keep by performing the Yale equivalent of KP. The experience of spending time in the army as an Indian rather than as a chief made me notice such details. Before the army, I would have ignored them.

On my way out, I chatted with the two scraggily bearded, painfully sincere students at the fund-raising table. They were raising money to send blood to North Vietnam. Peace was their goal; peace gained by showing the Viet Cong that the American people loved them enough to betray our own soldiers.

I asked them, "How can I be certain that money I give will translate into blood arriving in Hanoi?" I pointed out certain logistical problems, like B-52s dropping bombs on the area.

Consternation followed.

This was a totally unfair question, it seemed. Objections on principle they could respond to but not to "this, this cynicism. Why this shit? Like I mean, man—are you fucking with us? Don't you want to do something, anything to help North Vietnam? Like man, what is wrong with you? Don't you get what your country, this fucking country, is doing over there? Can't you feel it?"

They had no answers about the logistics, but they simply had to do something to help North Vietnam. Deep feeling as opposed to deep thinking was involved. These were neither bad guys, nor unpatriotic in their own way. Just earnest, muddle-headed student lefties. Color them useful idiots.

This experience was an eye-opener. These guys didn't care about achieving results from their emotional gesture. Their objective was primarily to feel good about themselves and secondarily to demonstrate their virtuousness to others of like mind. Results were incidental; their motive was pious, like lighting a candle in church.

I'd love to pretend that I felt horror and indignation about this blood drive, but I'd returned fully aware that such follies were happening. Even in 1966, soldiers knew that our little war was a PR disaster on the home front.

Powerful currents of media-fueled public opinion were running against the war. Kennedy might have been able to sell the war he started to the American public, but Johnson came across as an insensitive and ponderous political hack. Johnson's key role in promoting civil rights and creating an embryonic welfare state had already been forgotten, especially by his former allies on the left.

As a result, the old Democrat coalition was swiftly unraveling, with the liberal wing setting off down a brave new path toward electoral wipeout.

The peculiar cultural cringe of east coast establishment liberals made them especially sensitive to the disapproval of the European *bien pensant;* they couldn't bear waking up in the morning knowing that the French didn't love them.

What their own white countrymen thought of them was only relevant if the countrymen were also liberals and college-educated.

As importantly, the liberals had an ever-expanding and expensive domestic agenda planned for the country. Apart from hoping to give every grandmother in Paducah a set of free false teeth, they were going to free our millions of black slaves for the second time. These schemes would be expensive so the money being spent on the Vietnam War was bitterly resented.

Liberals were totally insensitive to the concerns of the American white working class, many of whom had sons or brothers in the army and old-fashioned ideas about patriotism. And who had, until the 1960s, always voted Democrat. But these "Joe Six-Pack" squares were boring and had a dull, one-dimensional outlook on a morally complex world. The white working class could be ignored; they would appreciate the benefits of the Great Society in due course.

But, over and above conventional politics, the United States seethed with rage. Changes in a nation's psyche are mysterious. What was going on went way beyond simple left versus right political controversy. A violent reaction to the constipated American world of the 1950s was in full bloom.

This aspect of what was happening at first pleased me immensely.

This agitation in the atmosphere affected all the students I met. North Dakota State or Texas A&M might still be oases of academic calm, but Morse College and Yale were bubbling with angry causes. Excellent! Though there were still no girls, I reveled in this temperature rise in the studentry.

And, thank goodness, we didn't all look the same anymore. Though the older generation was obsessed with beards on the male young, beards weren't all that common once you looked around a bit. Wild, manic hair was more the thing.

The visual difference from the pre-war Yale of 1963 was more in the variety of clothing and in the variety of long hair-styles, and in how the beholder was supposed to respond, rather than in the amount of facial hair—especially in the desired response, these guys didn't want to look interchangeable, like infantry soldiers or the Kingston Trio. They wanted to tell you something when you looked at them.

So you had the common "I love the workers" style or the basic Bob Dylan clone—the Pendleton-shirted, anorexic lumberjack look. And, to show identity with the people—but with the Russian people—you had the Fiddler on the Roof or Russian peasant type.

Many students were angry—really, really angry—so you had the never-smiling, stubble-faced, T-shirt, and torn jeans "yes, I sleep in my clothes; fuck you" appearance.

Some kids were sensitive—they felt the cruel pain of life and war so terribly intensely—so they wore tattered Sears work clothes and sported a stick-thin, crazy-eyed, greasy-filthy look that proclaimed: "I have suffered a nervous breakdown over this terrible world; I weep for the little people so much; please share the love."

But the preppy, Shetland sweater and chinos look was still popular; I didn't have to ditch my clothes. And there were uncommon looks like the occasional young Einstein with thick-lensed, round gold-framed glasses and frizzy blond Jewfro, complete with a slide rule in a black leather case hanging from his belt. And, as always, there were a few jocks in Yale letter sweaters with muscular necks and Pepsodent smiles.

What you didn't have, beneath the surface, was much of a change in the social background of the students. A smaller percent came from private schools. There were more Jewish guys from public schools. But, public school or private school, Yale in 1966 was still overwhelmingly a place for white, middleclass, suburban boys.

Compared with the army, blacks were still almost invisible at Yale in 1966, despite the brand-new, fervid, vocal desire of so many at Yale to raise, liberate, or merely improve the lot of black Americans.

That the army was already doing these things for hundreds of thousands of typical young blacks was simply beyond the comprehension of these white suburban Yalies—who didn't know any black Americans.

It would be many years before Yale had a sizable, representative cross-section of intelligent black American students, as opposed to a small, self-segregated cadre of handpicked, cosseted, and atypical blacks.

Whites and blacks also mingled far less at Yale than they had in the army.

But at least they didn't fight with each other.

In contrast with the army, I witnessed no overtly gay behavior back at Yale. Probably I didn't know where to look.

———

Over the next months, my new classmates explained to me repeatedly and earnestly how terrible the Vietnam War was. Their opinions were based upon a close study of the TV evening news programs and *The New York Times,* plus the floating gossip at Yale.

By then, I'd let slip that I'd been in the army in Vietnam. Unfortunately, my fellow students already knew everything about Vietnam so I was wrong-footed in any discussion.

If I observed that the densely populated parts of Vietnam were all under our control and that the fighting mostly involved brief, violent firefights out in the bundu that we always won, I found that my listeners simply tuned out.

If I pointed out that at least a third of the South Vietnamese, especially the million or more refugees from the North, clearly did not want to live under Communism, I was speaking as a tool of the capitalist U.S. government.

My recent military experience was completely irrelevant. Obviously, I'd been brainwashed. More of that damn false consciousness...

Hearing my new classmates discuss what they thought was happening in Vietnam explained some of their intense fear of being drafted. Folk memory is strange. The Vietnam of these guys' imagination was based upon World War II films and the war stories they had heard as children from their Uncle George.

They saw themselves hitting the beach on Iwo Jima and instantly being made into minced veal by gigantic hidden cannons up on Mt. Suribachi.

Others, whose moral agitation matched their physical fears, visualized themselves bayoneting poor, defenseless Asian children, at the command of sadistic, racist American army officers, before being killed themselves by the righteous, avenging soldiers of North Vietnam.

I tried to explain to my new classmates that the chances of an Ivy League draftee ending up in an infantry battalion weren't that high and that, even within an infantry battalion, not every soldier was routinely in a kill or be killed position. Unambiguous moral choices are probably as rare in the army as they are in civilian life.

Of course, being any sort of soldier in Vietnam was dangerous. You could be mortared or blown-up anywhere. I'd watched a Jeep spattered with American blood and riddled with Viet Cong-made bullet holes being towed back into our camp, having been hit just outside the camp.

And you might not be cleanly killed. Being badly wounded or maimed were rational possibilities.

Yet even the more realistic fear of being maimed wasn't what gripped these guys. No, fear of a ghastly death might be their overriding concern, but death wasn't the main reason for their dread of the draft. Few could put into words exactly what turned their bowels into jelly.

Because there was no clear, unmuddled reason. Their terror of being drafted involved a complex emotional goulash of sentimental morality mixed liberally with raw fear. The morality was needed to excuse the fear; healthy, intelligent young men aren't supposed to be cowards.

And life is Color and
Warmth and Light,
And a striving ever more for these;
And he is dead who will not fight;
And who dies fighting has
increase.

Julian Grenfell
Into Battle 1915

Deep down, neither fear nor moral hangups fully explained the attitude of the guys I talked to and argued with for hours late into the night during my final year at Yale.

At the most basic, these guys didn't want to face any real uncertainty or gut-wrenching excitement in their lives. Ever…

Their parents had spent a lot of money on schools, summer camp, teeth-straightening, and dancing lessons. The guys had worked hard at school to get into Yale. Sons and parents were united in wanting a solid, predictable, lifetime return on this big investment.

Despite their new freedom from hair and clothing conventions, down deep most of these students still wanted to be doctors or lawyers or worthies at the Ford Foundation. War could block their path to achieving these ambitions. Dead men don't take the LSAT.

What these guys really wanted was the right, as in the Civil War, to buy their way out of the draft. War could seriously delay them in realizing their ambitions. Which was absolutely intolerable and unacceptable.

Dick Cheney, briefly a Yalie before performing the difficult feat of flunking out, neatly summed up this amoral, practical objection to the draft.

When asked why he kept requesting and getting draft deferments until his liability for the draft had lapsed, this great enthusiast for risking the lives of American soldiers said, "I had other priorities in the sixties than military service."

In our usual rambling student bull sessions, I kept finding that, however hairy they might look, my new fellow students almost all wanted the same sort of conventional professional careers as my ante-bellum classmates.

The world might be in flames. The Beatles had blown up the world of pop music. American leaders were regularly assassinated. Drugs were expanding the consciousness of the cognoscenti. However, the real, underlying goals of these fine young fellows remained so obvious and so predictable. These weren't ignoble goals exactly, just petty in terms of justifying draft-dodging.

To fear that death would stop you from writing the great American novel is one thing.

To fear that death would cost you a splendid career as a top proctologist, and so deny you a well-earned mini-mansion in Greenwich, Connecticut, is tougher to sympathize with.

Of course, the world needs proctologists, just as it needs septic tank cleaners; it simply pays more for proctologists. I, for example, became an investment manager in order to feed my family well.

So I understood why someone would live a boring misery of a life in exchange for big money or for power or possibly even for fast cars, fast women, and ski holidays.

It was actually *wanting* to spend your one and only life doing nothing but dull, boring, risk-free things that baffled me. I couldn't understand why any bright twenty-year-old man would want to be a proctologist or trust lawyer or public sector do-gooder so badly that he would lie to himself about why he dreaded the draft so much.

And these were the same young men who were eager—verbally— to fight for the rights of black people. And to proclaim loudly their sympathy for the working class. However, they were quite content to let Donald Miller and Jerry Kahle and hundreds of thousands of blacks and poor working class whites go off to war—any war—in place of them.

The draft brought the Vietnam War to their full attention. Eliminate the draft and student opposition to the Vietnam War would never have come into full bloom. Where is the student opposition to our little wars of today?

Isn't moralistic posturing fun?

It was hard not to laugh openly at these earnest young cowards and hypocrites. Still, I kept my sneers to myself. You never know when you might need a good Yale-trained proctologist.

———◆———

There was one other recently discharged soldier in another college. He had a WASP-y nickname like Chip or Skip or Bing. I think he may have been in the Special Forces. We met once, but we had nothing to say to each other.

Both of us were soon asked to take part in demonstrations for or against the war. I refused. I don't know what Chip did since I ignored all these fatuous demos.

All of this washed over me. I wanted no part of it. I identified with the poor and simple but morally honest men in the army. I felt utterly detached from the Yale student rent-a-mob.

This antiwar mob of students and faculty was full of sick-making cowards and pig-ignorant about the war. A few of its members even cited Jesus as a justification for their pathetic behavior.

The much smaller pro-war gang was hysterically nationalistic and equally ignorant about the actual war. A few of its members even cited Jesus as a justification for supporting the war.

Some confusion somewhere…

Bright College Years (cont.)

Ileft Yale in 1963 cordially disliking Yale and New Haven. I returned in 1966 with the same feelings but in a diluted form. I wanted my degree pronto, and I wanted out of New Haven as fast as possible. So I worked fairly hard and steadily. I played a little soccer and rowed in the college eight. I longed to find the right woman, but she eluded me.

I drank a lot, but I didn't do drugs. There was no particular reason for my abstinence; drugs were as available at Yale as in the army. There just seemed to be enough in my life to deal with. I felt a lot of ill-defined anxiety. Sometimes I had stomach pains.

Also, with regard to drugs, there was the painful example of Ivan.

In Morse, we lived in single rooms spaced along a corridor. The corridors ran the whole length of a floor; bathrooms were spaced along the corridors and had through doors at each end. Accordingly,

I met everyone in the corridor in various stages of dress and undress. And so I met Ivan.

Ivan was a big, flabby Ukrainian immigrant. He wore thick glasses and had mad spikey hair. His father had been part of the Ukrainian gang who fought for the Nazis, but Ivan said that was only because his father hated Stalin more than he hated Hitler. Ivan had inherited his father's wacky, unstable personality. But he was warm-hearted and very bright.

All of us living along the corridor kept a vague eye on Ivan when he began experimenting with drugs. Every kind of drug. Drugs that even Neil Stein, the son of a pharmacist and a star pre-med student, had never heard of. Stein and his friend, David Melnik, were Ivan's primary carers. They also were my new best pals along the corridor.

After Ivan went to pieces, we never found out what he had taken. His meltdown was so quick and so total. By the time we noticed him in the grip—the firm grip—of some powerful substance, Ivan had gone way beyond answering questions. Stein thought the drug was LSD, contaminated with something else.

The day that Ivan flipped, Stein nabbed me coming back from morning classes, and we went into Ivan's room. Melnik sat in the room's only chair, looking helplessly at Ivan. Ivan remained perched on the edge of his bed, jiggling, shaking, and gibbering apprehensively but more or less coherently about seeing demons and weird, frightening colors and shapes. A bad trip.

We tried to get Ivan to drink water, but he pushed us away. Under the flab, he was fairly strong.

I went out to work in the college library. When I came back to take a turn in watching Ivan, he had descended to hell's lower levels. He was mostly silent, still sitting on the side of his bed, staring at the bare concrete walls. Suddenly, without warning, he screamed in anguish. He thought he was going to be rung out like a sponge so someone could drink his blood and eat him alive. But nothing he said made any real sense. Ivan was in the grip of a terror beyond words.

We talked about taking Ivan to the student medical center. We would have had to tell the medics that he had taken an unknown drug, not that anyone medical would have had the least trouble in figuring this out. We were pretty sure that Yale would expel him for this, which might push Ivan over the edge into total despair; he was the eldest son and the bright hope of his immigrant family. We decided to stay with him until the drug wore off.

That night was terrible. Ivan was determined to get out of the building, preferably via his room's window, and we were on the second floor. He went completely psychotic. We had to more or less sit on him for hours. He became really strong. He wept; he pleaded for us to let him out. He was suicidal and would have run into the path of a bus.

By morning, the worst was over. Ivan was drained, pale, and near physical collapse. We brought him food, and he managed to eat a little. He couldn't say much of anything. Then he slept for hours, with Stein, a very kind guy, watching him the whole time. I want to say that Ivan was subsequently as good as new. But he seemed permanently slightly out of focus.

Having watched Ivan's meltdown, later I always refused to try LSD—or any of the psychotropic drugs that kick off with a couple of hours of barfing. Now as for real hashish—that's another matter…

While I was in the army, the Yale authorities had lost interest in their traditional spying on student mischief. They, like the politicians and the police, had discovered the trendy, evil world of drugs. Naturally, they were miles behind the Yale studentry in this discovery.

One day, shortly after Ivan's misfortune, I was attracted to a commotion on the floor above ours—shouting coming down the stairwell—and went up to see what was going on.

Students were standing around, shouting into the open doorway of the floor's utility room. At the back of the utility room, a young white guy in his twenties sat on a stool with earphones around his neck. Wires from the earphones ran up to a metal electrical box on the wall. The guy wore jeans and a T-shirt and looked like an Italian-American pizza delivery guy.

Students yelled, "What the fuck are you doing?"

The guy didn't answer at first, but I guess he got sick of the yelling so he answered, "I work for the New Haven Police Department."

Then it all poured out. The guy was a police technician, out to bust a Morse College drug ring. A little phone tapping would do the trick, or so the authorities were convinced. I guess they assumed that no student ever went into the mop and bucket room.

We were all furious. There was no Morse College drug ring; the idea was insane. And didn't students have rights? Despite my experiences with Sam Chauncey's student narks and the kangaroo courts, I was surprised by the phone tapping. The raw, snoopy idiocy of the whole thing stank.

So we made a vigorous protest to the master of Morse College. Naturally, we were fobbed off with denials.

Student grievances about stunts like this festered at Yale as they did nationally. I was sorry later not to be around the U.S. college scene when the campuses exploded in 1968. I wouldn't have taken part, but watching the destruction, the fires, and the antics, especially those of the pathetic, groveling student apologists among the administration and the faculty, would have given me orgasmic pleasure.

La Trahison des Clercs

Drugs were now a major worry for the Yale authorities, but far more important issues than drugs obsessed them. Wondrous improvements were planned in the composition of the undergraduate student body. A piece of social engineering to rival the nineteenth-century shift away from educating Puritan clergymen was afoot.

The long-serving president of Yale finally died of cancer while I was in the army. Kingman Brewster Jr., an aristocrat of even more impeccable Mayflower lineage, succeeded him.

Brewster was the same age as my mother but seemed much younger. He had landed at Yale as provost, the senior administrative position of the university, during my first Yale interlude, and then was inaugurated in due course as president, so fulfilling the long laid-down plans of the great and the good for this liberal exemplar. (The great and the good are always in the majority on the self-perpetuating Yale Corporation.)

Unlike his austere and long-in-the-dying predecessor, Brewster was gregarious. He went to all sorts of Yale occasions, formal and informal, always dressed in a splendid academic gown if the event was sufficiently important or in a three-piece London-tailored suit if the occasion was lower key or in a beautifully cut tweed jacket, crested tie, and grey flannels if it was just an undergraduate thing.

Out of curiosity, I chatted at various times with Brewster. I don't remember our topics; probably about the football team or something on that level. (The team's record deteriorated while I was in the army.) He had a patrician manner but was not openly unfriendly or unusually arrogant by the standards of his social background.

Of medium height, King Brewster had a square, reddish face and a good head of greying hair. He wore both a wedding ring and a large signet ring on his left pinky. There was a hearty air of "I know what's good for you" about him and a glow that told the world that King had eaten many fine meals with highly important people. And had drunk many a fine wine.

For such a prototypical liberal establishment figure, though, King Brewster had a most odd background—not in being a Republican; there were lots of Republican liberals in those long lost days.

However, as a Yale undergraduate in 1940, King was the leading student isolationist in the country and a fanatical supporter of Charles Lindbergh. Lindbergh by 1940 had become an ardent fan of Nazi Germany and in consequence a demonic opponent of America doing anything about Hitler. The fatherless Brewster hero-worshipped Lindbergh and lapped up his "America First" philosophy.

Though evidence is questionable that Brewster fully shared Lindbergh's anti-Semitism and Nazi sympathies, King bought the whole isolationist agenda in spades. He founded Yale's own America First Committee after the fall of France in 1940, when Hitler's horrid ambitions were already patently obvious. The Nuremburg Laws against Jews were passed in 1935 and *Krystallnacht* took place in 1938. Thousands of Jews had been driven out of Germany or thrown into concentration camps.

Even after Roosevelt finally backed the British in 1941 with Lend-Lease, and it was clear whose side America would be on, Brewster wrote grudgingly, "I still believe it outrageous to commit this country to the outcome of the war abroad and wish to limit that commitment as much as possible."

Or, in other words, "Carry on, Hitler."

Pearl Harbor ended American isolationism. Brewster, however reluctantly, joined the navy and served as a pilot through the war. After the war, he went to Harvard Law School where he subsequently taught, while showing no interest in any form of scholarship or indeed in reading much of anything.

King seems to have caught the attention of the east coast establishment's talent spotters at this stage. His judgment might be flawed, but his pedigree was impeccable and his political and social opinions sound; he was "one of us." King had a keen sense of which way the wind was blowing even if he didn't have much sense otherwise.

On top of this, King was a prolific, if platitudinous, platform speaker. Here is a typical example from 1965: "Our world and our country as well as all of us individually are in quest of ourselves."

Well, whoopee.

Students always wondered why King Brewster hadn't gone into politics. He looked and sounded born to play the part of a U.S. Senator and later showed that he had access to enough money to carry off the role of U.S. Ambassador to the United Kingdom, a big ticket item. My guess is that he realized there was much more scope for social engineering as the unelected president of Yale than in any electoral role. And no ignorant, lower-class voters to humor.

The United States is an educational meritocracy—of sorts. Getting into Yale, Harvard, or Princeton and managing to graduate with even the most feeble degree is enough to give anyone a good shot at worldly success or at least at living an upper-middleclass life.

Once accepted in one of these places, graduating is more or less guaranteed, barring a major personal meltdown or serious moral turpitude. President Bush the Second, Senator Kerry, and Tony Thomson all proved this axiom by graduating from Yale, despite hiccups like dud grades or being naughty.

There are many routes to graduation. As a family tradition, various Kennedys managed to slip through Harvard with the help of hired nerds who took their exams and ghosted their essays. No doubt similar examples can be found in the other Ivies.

Something like ninety percent of the value of an Ivy League education is gained by being admitted.

If you learn something in one of the Ivies, despite their custom of disdaining undergraduate teaching, it's a bonus. Educated or not, Ivy League graduates rise to the top nationally. This should be no surprise; teaching quality has little or nothing to do with this success.

If you start with the brightest and most ambitious young people in a vast county, they are likely to do well in any case, even if they waste their time doing mindless academic busy work for four years.

Add the social kudos of an Ivy League degree, and an individual, no different in any way from the thousands that the Ivies arbitrarily reject, can soar. If you want to be president, going to Yale or Harvard sharply narrows the odds. So, change the Ivy League admissions criteria and over time you change the country—at least at the margin.

Thus, with great gusto, King Brewster set out to change Yale's admission policies.

My old nemesis, Sam Chauncey, was assigned to determine how to make Yale co-ed. Eventually, Chauncey succeeded after several false starts. Beginning in 1969, Yale's freshman class was co-ed.

Prior to that event, Yale had fiddled with trying to lure Vassar to New Haven as a marriage partner. The notion was that mating with Vassar would make Yale co-ed after a fashion and avoid having too many women physically on the Yale campus. Luckily for Vassar admirers, the Vassar faculty realized that, immediately after consummating the affair, Yale would swallow them as a snake swallows a frog. Vassar vetoed the merger.

Co-education was ultimately such a no-brainer that even the many Neanderthals among the Yale alumni couldn't block it. Yale alumni couldn't avoid having daughters. Telling these bright girls that their presence would pollute Yale caused many a ruckus at upmarket dinner tables around the country.

More controversially, R. Inslee Clark Jr., known as Inky, was assigned by Brewster to make incoming freshman classes much more socially diverse. This proved more far more difficult to achieve than co-education. I never met Inky, though on paper he appears to have exhibited the same priggish worthiness that made Sam Chauncey such a perfect 1960s academic establishment prototype. But things didn't work out as well for Inky.

Inky got off to a hot start in 1965. Apart from admitting more Jews—long overdue—and more boys from public schools, Inky wanted to reduce the number of "legacies" or boys from families that had always sent their sons to Yale. Inky had no plans to reduce the number of legacy jocks and sports ringers; the legacies he planned to eliminate were boys who were more or less qualified for admission but lacked any personal star quality.

Initially, Inky separated these pedestrian legacies into two groups: those boys from good, solid but publically unknown Yale families and those boys, like George W. Bush, who were from families that meant something nationally—the sons of the seriously rich or the famous. Inky apparently decided to favor only the sons of the moneyed or the prominent as legacies.

Thus, some of what Inky wanted to do was simply pragmatic; some was misunderstood.

In particular, the youthful Inky grossly bungled presenting the details of his policy to the great—and well-connected—New England prep schools like Andover that would be most immediately affected by it. Parents chose schools like Andover as conduits to get their sons into places like Yale.

With impressive speed, Inky created outrage and uproar. By 1966, a special alumni committee was formed to investigate Yale's admissions policy. Soon, girls were in but Inky was out. Legacies from traditional Yale families temporarily climbed back up as a percentage of the incoming freshmen.

Inky and Brewster had run smack into a yet to be solved problem that has dogged all the top private universities in the United States and Oxford and Cambridge in the United Kingdom.

In some egalitarian dream world, universities like Yale would function as totally meritocratic leadership academies, drawing on the most diverse pool of talent in the nation and only charging tuition fees to a small number of rich kids who would pay through their nostrils for the privilege of being admitted.

In recognition of this vital public service, grateful American taxpayers would generously support the Ivies while not interfering in their administration. The right of the existing, establishment bodies like the Yale Corporation to manage their institutions would stay firmly in place.

Unfortunately, really existing Yale in the 1960s was financed chiefly by its alumni and by the income from the massive endowment long-dead alumni had donated over centuries. Maintaining this support and encouraging future alumni giving were tediously vital for Yale.

Even more tedious was the fact that the existing alumni moneybags were white and upper-middleclass and unwilling to accept that, barring some miracle, their college-bound offspring were unlikely to get even a once over by Inky and his admissions team.

These tiresome alumni completely lacked the vision to embrace a diverse and totally meritocratic Yale. Instead, they locked up their checkbooks.

So poor Inky was toast.

Facing up to the issue, Brewster schemed to get money from the government to replace alumni funds. He had moderate success in this, but the government funding had strings attached, which predictably have grown more restrictive over time.

The result is that the Yale of today has to be exquisitely sensitive to political concerns in Washington.

At the time this is written, Yale is facing the possible withdrawal of $500 million in annual federal funding due to violations of Title IX of the Higher Education Act. This act specifies blandly that "no one be excluded from participation in, be denied the benefits of, or be subjected to discrimination under any federally supported education program on the basis of sex."

What terrible things has Yale done to merit this investigation?

The full shocking details are not available, but it appears that Yale failed to control its male students sufficiently. Apparently, male students have repeatedly done frat boy things like running around outside the women's' dorms shouting, "No means Yes! Yes means Anal!" This has caused shock, horror, and incipient prolapsed wombs among female Yale students.

Damn! All fans of Yale should thank the Lord God of Hosts that the frat boys didn't deny the Holocaust or—horror upon horror—publically utter the "n" word!

Though the groveling letter, dated April 15, 2011, sent in connection with this grave situation to all Yale alumni by the current Yale president, one Richard C. Levin, is worthy of President Merkin Muffley in *Doctor Strangelove*, the enjoyment given by this letter should not blind us to the fact that Yale has lost much of its former independence through pursuing diversity and a national leadership training role.

Oxford and Cambridge are even more in the pocket of the British government, which is agitating for Oxbridge to take more students from the traditional British working class or lumpen proletariat. Protests by Oxbridge that their admissions staff are searching high and low but can't find enough student proles with such entry-level academic skills as competent reading, writing, and math don't seem to be convincing the British government.

He who pays the piper calls the tune. Prole quotas for Oxbridge are on the way.

———

Over time, though, Yale has indeed become much more diverse. King Brewster and Inky broadly made the social changes in admissions policy they planned stick. Yale is no longer primarily a finishing school for WASPs nor are the other Ivies.

Diversity certainly opens doors. Thus Princeton pre-qualified Michelle Obama to be first lady, rather than some brighter, but less fashionably disadvantaged, girl.

Well…no doubt there are more inspiring examples of the benefits of diversity.

Some method of affirmative action for blacks in Ivy League admissions must be the right thing to do, even if it can't legally be called affirmative action. A Barrack Obama has to be judged by wider criteria than mere grades and College Board scores. To paraphrase Joe Biden, Obama's very own vice president: clean, articulate mulatto liberals don't grow on trees.

And balancing the various non-black minority groups whose progeny would more than qualify for admission even in fair, open competition is also necessary. If the 1950s quotas for Jews were morally wrong, so would have been a one hundred percent Jewish freshman class at Yale.

Today, large numbers of Asians have highly competitive test scores and grades. Few would argue that any one subgroup should be massively overrepresented, even if all their thousands of applicants are well qualified. So someone has to juggle the qualified into an elegantly diversified freshmen class.

Appearances matter; there have to be Indians and Chinese in Yale class photos.

King Brewster felt as strongly about not fighting Communism militarily as he had about not fighting Nazism. By 1966, Brewster was as opposed to the Vietnam War as the most vocal peacenik, so he stopped academic credit being given for the ROTC officer-training program. And he voiced his opposition to the draft frequently. These gestures achieved little, so his own direct contribution to undermining the nation's commitment to its armed forces was modest.

Better—and offering more amusement—than anything antiwar that Brewster did personally was his appointment of William Sloane Coffin Jr. as chaplain of Yale.

Coffin was a passionate WASP do-gooder from an old New York Social Register family. Coffin was quirky in a number of ways, especially in his intense belief in his own highly political brand of intellectual content-free, muscular Christianity. His peculiar career included a stint in the CIA, as well as Yale Divinity School. His list of left wing causes was endless, as was his energy. Apart from being totally manic, he was an athletic and musical guy with a big head, a strong jaw, and large horn-rimmed glasses.

I found him highly approachable but completely goofy in conversation; to me, he was like someone on speed. Religion leaves me cold, so that side of Coffin was wasted on me; I saw only his antics. Like Brewster, Coffin was vain and perfectly devoid of humor or self-deprecation.

Students assumed then that Coffin took himself, and every word that came out of his mouth, as God-inspired. Such a person clearly requires no earthly justification for whatever he does or for the consequences of his actions. Now, I think that Coffin was deeply confused and neurotic, possibly even mentally disturbed, and needed the constant distraction of cause-mongering activities to make his turgid, tangled sex needs bearable.

Yale students respected Coffin as much for his keen interest in young, attractive women as for his civil rights activism. I used to see him from time to time riding around Yale with a long-haired young woman on the back of his expensive motorcycle. It was never the same young woman twice.

Though a demon for personal publicity, Coffin enjoyed the same immunity from press scrutiny of his sex life as did other 1960s big shots like the Kennedys. He also lived high on the hog through his establishment contacts. Monogamy and poverty were never core elements of his religious beliefs.

One year, Coffin wangled an all-expenses paid State Department tour of India. According to his biographer Warren Goldstone in *A*

Holy Impatience, Coffin demonstrated a quite unholy impatience on this trip. During a stop in Teheran, Coffin illustrated his selective approach to the Ten Commandments. Coffin was accompanied by his current wife—he had a number—with whom he was having difficulties:

> While Eva slept, Coffin sneaked off the plane and scrawled a note he gave to a French officer to deliver to Manya Stromberg (by then widowed but still working in the French embassy and well-known to the French community), suggesting a rendezvous in Paris...

The man had style.

Goldstone is a sympathetic biographer of Coffin, almost a hagiographer. So it is with obvious discomfort that Goldstone recounts the saintly, but muscular, Coffin using a karate chop on a later wife during a drunken quarrel:

> He (Coffin) took her to the hospital in the morning. His one judo chop had given her "a huge black eye," she remembered. "My whole face was swollen." He had also given her a hairline skull fracture.

Goldstone also acknowledges the belief of some observers that, like his saintly pal and fellow peacenik, Bishop Paul Moore of New York, Coffin secretly swung both ways sexually. Bishop Moore managed to have nine children and several wives, while accumulating a world-class stash of gay porn and various gay lovers.

Bats right; throws left—with an asterisk against his batting average? The Right Reverend Bishop Moore had the unusual distinction of being posthumously outed by an outraged bisexual daughter. Try and top that!

Coffin was never outed. Goldstone claims that Coffin was merely affectionate towards his male friends. And that his vodka drinking binges were only sporadic and that Coffin could "hold his liquor like few others."

All that should matter, we are told, was Coffin's public, noisy, and florid "spiritual life" and his passionate, wacky support of every cherished left-liberal cause.

Wonderful…

At the time I returned to Yale, Coffin's main prank was promoting draft card burning. This was a symbolic gesture, related to burning the American flag in public or to feminists burning their bras. Draft card burning was hugely irritating to the dimmer sort of traditional American, though it had no effect in getting anyone out of being drafted. The draft card was only a little piece of paper like a Social Security card. The number on it was what mattered.

Publically, Brewster consistently supported Coffin in his many idiocies. Privately, Brewster let other, more petty-minded types in the Yale administration refuse to allow Coffin to turn the university chapel into a sanctuary for draft resisters.

Overall, Coffin represented a now more or less vanished type; a throwback to a Civil War abolitionist who was just made for the crazy, violent 1960s. Like an abolitionist, Coffin carefully avoided John Brown-style violence himself but was always ready to support a would-be John Brown.

Outside matrimony, he was a fervent peacenik and fan of nuclear disarmament and took the attitude that "if a man of peace like me could get my hands on that fucking bomb, I'd ram it down their ugly throats."

Brewster shared Coffin's neo-abolitionist obsession with black civil rights, sometimes called "radical chic." In fact, Brewster is now remembered solely for his remark about the Black Panthers' trial in New Haven.

The Black Panthers were a quasi-national group of self-proclaimed black revolutionaries. Suspecting one of their members of being a FBI informer, the New Haven Panthers had kidnapped, tortured, and murdered this brother.

Inconveniently, several local Panthers were immediately arrested and promptly confessed to the murder. Even more inconveniently, one of the Panthers' national leaders was visiting the local branch when the murder occurred, leading to him being charged as well. This unleashed a storm at Yale.

Since the murder was in reaction to the spying activities of the FBI, Coffin instantly concluded that all the Panthers involved were innocent. Blacks had no rights and hence could do no wrongs. Q.E.D.

Coffin thundered, "All of us have conspired to bring on this tragedy by law enforcement agencies by their illegal acts against the Panthers, and by the rest of us by our immoral silence in front of these acts."

Brewster then chipped in with "I personally want to say that I'm appalled and ashamed that things should have come to such a pass that I am skeptical of the ability of black revolutionaries to achieve a fair trial anywhere in the U.S."

Brewster was correct in thinking that the vast majority of American citizens wanted all the Panthers locked up and the key thrown away. The FBI was reflecting this democratic preference in trying to protect society from violent agitators.

Public opinion, however, was never of the least concern to Brewster who showed at all times a total contempt for working-class white Americans. In this, Brewster was not alone. Upmarket liberals dismissively referred to such whites, often of eastern or southern European origin, as "ethnics" or "hard hats."

Back to the Panthers…

That some of the New Haven Panthers in this case were guilty of killing the informer was never in question. This fact was merely the ultimate inconvenience. Working out a way around it caused all concerned great problems. Luckily, the American legal system didn't fail the nation; the lawyers found a satisfactory fudge.

Whatever the doubts of Brewster, the Panthers got off scot-free or received short sentences in the chaotic trial that followed. You might think that Brewster would at least be tarnished by this affair, but he sailed through it, to be welcomed later by the British as our ambassador to the United Kingdom, despite his inglorious past as a Nazi appeaser.

Henry Kissinger got off a pleasing comment about Brewster after the Panther affair. He mused aloud to the Shah of Iran that Brewster was the one man whose assassination would benefit the whole United States.

You couldn't make it up…

My frustration at watching the antics of King Brewster, Sam Chauncey, Inky Clark, and Bill Coffin, plus their backers in the east coast establishment and its media mouthpieces, was caused as much by what they didn't do as by what they did.

What they wanted to do was clear enough. These self-anointed leaders felt that young WASPs didn't deserve any special role in the future of the country. Therefore, the academic institutions that WASPs had created, like Yale, could simply be reformed to exclude the sons of all but the richest and most prominent WASPs. Such a "pull up the ladder behind us" strategy is often consciously or unconsciously favored by snobbish hierarchies.

What did they hope to achieve? This is less clear; their objectives were muddled, but a pattern emerges when the changes in admissions' policy are linked to the kind of society that 1960s liberals desired.

Their motives were in the truest sense "conservative." They wanted Yale to be more of a leadership training school but a training school for leaders of a massively enlarged nanny state. Demographics meant that this would require a broader social mix of nannies.

The desired result was to produce in volume the same sort of worthy, high-minded people as Brewster and Coffin themselves, but more varied in sex and skin color. These folks would run the United States along the lines that Brewster and Coffin and their clique thought righteous.

And it worked...

In so many ways, President Obama represents a triumph for the policies that Brewster and those like him at the other Ivies put in place in 1960s.

Obama hints in his autobiography that he owes a great deal to affirmative action. But he owes even more to having a personality that fits perfectly into the Brewster plan for pushing limp-wristed, rainbow-hued liberals into "public service." The moment of the nation's "wets" had come; they were called from on high to rule over us. Uriah Heep would get the girl at last.

Many people have commented upon Obama's behavioral resemblance to Jimmy Carter; he is often described as "Carter in Blackface." To further this soft-boiled image, Obama has just compared himself to a "jilted bride'" after one of his many failed negotiations.

Few have commented upon Obama's even closer character resemblance to President Merkin Muffley-Stevenson. Yet all the similarities are there, right down to the connection with Illinois.

That determined, steadfast, thoughtful way of speaking that overlays a basically dithering, indecisive personality and huge ego. That refusal to be stampeded by mere worldly events. That superficial air of rationality that conceals an irrational sense of moral certitude. That desire to excuse the inexcusable. And, above all, that need to appease and to compromise.

Can't you just see Obama in the War Room as the Iranian ICBM is about to reenter the atmosphere above Washington, DC? The generals and admirals are shouting at each other, demanding retaliation or some decisive action but Obama just murmurs, "Gentlemen, please, no fighting in the War Room." Then, he turns back to the teleprompter and continues his uplifting address to the nation until Washington is vaporized.

———◆———

My hope had been that the upheavals of the 1960s would lead to a much looser, freer American society, not to a much bigger, busy-body government. I wanted radical change in places like Yale; a libertarian revolution first in student thinking and ultimately in the way people lived their lives. The goal was the creation of the first human society of radically free individuals.

Such a transformation would have required the admission of a much broader range of personalities to Yale who would push the boundaries of the intellectual world. That was not at all what Brewster and his ilk wanted. Instead, their focus was on admitting students with the same personalities as the would-be proctologists, corporate lawyers, and Ford Foundation executives of yesteryear but wrapped in a different external package.

Admitting lots of right-thinking, do-gooder students—whether black, white, or polka-dot—to be traditionally processed by Yale and the other Ivies was a way of guaranteeing that the *de haut en bas* essence of the method wouldn't change.

Currently, apart from looking everywhere for transgendered Hispanics, Ivy League admissions criteria all stress doing lots of prim, dreary good works in high school and being a high school class valedictorian. "I've greased the wheels on more wheelchairs than you have and I have a higher GPA! I get the microphone at graduation! Suck it up, retards!"

These are not the characteristics of thinking, unconventional individuals or of Albert Einstein. They are the characteristics of Hillary Clinton.

Diversity reinforces adherence to the prevailing liberal ethos in the Ivies. Affirmative action by whatever name means that those admitted partially or largely for reasons of skin color and social background and paying nothing for the privilege—"need blind admission"—have every reason to accept cheerfully whatever is on offer. It's a good career move.

Why would an Obama care about crap teaching or a boring syllabus or want to challenge left-of-center academic orthodoxies? Who refuses a free ice cream cone?

Society fortunately has made more progress toward freedom than the world of academe. Many excellent libertarian freedoms have emerged, even if we are still infantile about drugs. Yet libertarian social progress hasn't altered American society as much as I had hoped.

My wife and I recently had the privilege of attending a touching gay wedding. Our gay friends are not young; I wish them the greatest happiness in whatever way they want to live out the remainder of their lives.

However, I had naively expected that if gays were free to come out, they would not want to live like an updated version of Lucy and Desi—or Ozzie and Harriet. Yet even young gays seem pointed in that direction.

Perhaps a lingering 1960's vision of a Kurt Vonnegut world of rich and varied multiple sexes living in complex new ways still haunts the aging me?

Better, perhaps, just to salute any expansion of human freedom and not dwell too much on *plus ca change…*

———————

When Brewster and Co. pulled the plug on the chances of plain vanilla WASPs to get into Yale, there was some collateral damage to Yale and to society.

If Lamont Cranston III is not going to get into Yale barring a miracle, why should Lamont "Big Bucks" Cranston II, Yale Class of 1970, be expected to go on financing Yale? This is a real problem because the newbie Yalies, while tastefully diverse, so far tend not to be the great earners down the road that the old WASPs were. And possibly not as inclined to donate anyway, though the jury is still out on this.

Do we want the Ivies and Stanford to be financed by the nation? This would put them, however indirectly, under the control of the great minds in the House of Representatives. The dire problems of the once splendid California state universities illustrate what this might mean on a day-to-day basis.

And then there is the military and its relationship with American society.

After Brewster & Co. made the draft unworkable, there was no other, moral reason for WASP sons to feel an obligation to serve in the military, any more than a young man from any other elite social group should feel an obligation. Of course, this ensures that the clever and the privileged miss their best and often only chance to really know ordinary white people, let alone to know ordinary black people.

But who needs to know ordinary people in order to know what to do for them? Or to them? What the masses needed was "public service" and that would be provided by this new, diverse elite.

Serving in the military no longer counts as "public service."

Public service is that service performed by high-minded civilians, mostly based in Washington and paid for by the taxpayer. Such public service, even if useless, short-term, self-serving, or simply used as a passport to a lucrative legal partnership, is superior to anything else a young man or woman might do.

Becoming an academic in a nonscientific field or a charity honcho or an ecological NGO executive is probably just about OK, as long as you contribute generously to Yale alumni fundraisers. Becoming an army general or the CEO of Caterpillar, however, clearly puts someone beyond the pale.

Cutting off the army from the rest of society harms all of us. Ending the draft, a consequence of our Vietnam angst, also ended our tradition of citizen soldiers. Our soldiers are now recruited for money and drawn from unrepresentative small towns, inner cities, immigrants, and minorities. To a lesser degree this is also true of our military officers. Soldiers today are outside the mainstream of society and are in a sense paid mercenaries.

So now we can fight dirty little colonial wars wherever the president sees fit without irritating student protests. Is this healthy for a republic in the long run? What if our centurions get bored with the antics in Washington? Are we priming the nation for a Caesar?

Why write about this long ago stuff now?

Because it still matters; it is still smoking hot. As a society, we no longer trust our government, and that shapes our lives and our collective destiny.

The reason we don't trust our government is because the battles on the home front that started during the Vietnam era are alive and well.

Think: red state versus blue state. Think: budget deadlock. Think: the right to an abortion versus the right to life. Think: food stamps versus welfare cuts.

Think, above all, about the populist pushback against the entire *bien pensant*—our liberal elite and the Washington permanent establishment. Many Americans, including those with no connection to the Tea Party, feel an ill-defined but burning sense of betrayal.

The mistrust of elites that sank American liberalism as the dominant political force was not just due to our loss in Vietnam and the inept failure of "the best and the brightest," but also caused by people and events at places like Yale in the 1960s.

The fatuous leftism of the Brewsters and the Coffins made traditional east coast liberals the butt of endless sarcastic jokes. Nixon didn't create public disgust with peacenik liberalism; he only funneled it. Liberals' own follies convinced the public not to trust them.

The result is that while J.F. Kennedy is still heroically admired, J.F. Kerry is considered a pompous buffoon. If people today vote for such clowns, it is in exchange for IOUs promising entitlements and freebies, no longer out of any belief in the idealistic piffle that comes from their mouths.

Alas, traditional liberalism didn't die from ridicule. It retreated wounded into a corner from whence it bleats its resistance to change. The rest of us can't go forward until this braindead "conservatism" that weirdly operates under the name of "progressivism" finally is taken off its taxpayer-funded life support system. For now, the nation is gridlocked.

Above all, we live today with the turgid, ongoing all-American saga called "diversity." Almost everyone is in favor of this, but there is little agreement about its practical implementation. Could Yale, for example, be meritocratic and "need-blind" in its admissions and still be "diverse?"

Ah…diversity, so many love the sound of the word. Even I sometimes feel fuzzy and warm thinking about it. The feeling is like listening to *Blowing in the Wind* decades ago during an evening spent sharing a Thai stick.

But what does diversity mean?

Diversity isn't about how many Changs or Patels—male or female, gay or straight—get into Yale since diversity trumps meritocracy. There are no op-eds in *The New York Times* about this. Every brilliantly well-qualified Chang or Patel has the same lottery-like chance of getting in as part of the Asian quota. (And it certainly isn't about doing anything for white trailer trash since no one gives two hoots about them.)

As in arguing about the cause of the Civil War, diversity drags in all kinds of issues, but somehow—ultimately—diversity is about blacks; it is about sorting out the old wrongs done to black Americans by giving them new rights. Which often means doing new wrongs to non-blacks. And so it goes…

Widening the pool of potential leaders of society to include people of every conceivable class and background must be ethically correct in some cosmic, ethereal sense.

But is our mindless, emotional pursuit of diversity practical or wise? Certainly the quest produces many comic and perverse effects, like electing an unusually inexperienced, but mellifluous, mulatto liberal as president.

However, apart from providing public amusement, does the pursuit of diversity help us as a nation? Can we measure any practical benefits, as opposed to cherishing a faith-based belief that diversity is always a "good thing"? Are we a more effective nation than we were before we embraced diversity as a goal in itself? Is a society that can't accomplish much of anything a better society than another that can, but appears monotone in group photos?

Why is it that we can't seem to get our act together as a society anymore? Are we too diverse to care about the nation? Or to have common goals above and beyond a desire to watch the Superbowl on a big screen with plenty of beer and a group of pals?

Are we just too ignorant about each other? After all, the United States is more segregated now by geography and by class than it was in the 1970s. There is no institution anymore that mixes us together as a society.

Attending an orderly middleclass public school in a typical American suburb is no substitute for spending nights in barracks with a randomly selected group of your countrymen.

Living in typical middleclass enclaves on either the east or west coast before and after going to Yale guarantees that today's Yale alumni know little or nothing of their struggling countrymen—white or black—in places like Ohio.

Who now leads the United States? Who should we listen to?

Certainly not to our venal, "kick the can down the road" politicians. Poll after poll shows our national politicians as generally despised. Their feeble political efforts speak for themselves.

Do our "Men of God" have something to say? But which men, or women, of God? And which God or gods? We are spoiled for choice.

Should we listen to a radio or TV prophet? Walter Cronkite has no obvious successor; today's mouthpieces all plead tendentiously in favor of one gang or other.

This sort of speculation leads to an indelicate question. Were there, perhaps, advantages for the United States in having the WASPs lead society? For me, the jury is out on this; I grew up with these people and know them all too well.

Clearly, though, society may benefit from having an identifiable group out in front. At the least, it makes sniping from the rear easy. It was useful for society to have nice big targets on the backs of a recognized leadership group. Perhaps WASP leadership made society cohesive in a subtle way.

And, looking at their creations like our great private colleges— even Yale—or our Constitution or our legal system or our individual freedoms, did the WASPs do such a bad job of leadership? Will our new diverse leadership do better? Will they maintain our magnificent institutional inheritance, like a free economy?

It's too late now to ask such questions; our past is another country.

Vietnam, drugs, wild music, and civil rights violence weren't the only radical events going on in 1960s America. I witnessed the beginning of a quiet revolution at Yale, executed without consultation or approval by anyone outside a circle of pious, hypocritical do-gooders. We live with the consequences, for better or for worse, to this day.

Sayonara to Yale
(and America)

A t Yale my second time round, a big bonus from my time in the army was having plenty of money.

A second bonus was that I now knew how to deal quickly with dull but necessary stuff, like writing essays, so that I had plenty of time to enjoy the money. I left the army with thousands of dollars in savings, reflecting payment for all the leave I hadn't taken, the pay I had banked, and the proceeds from all the savings bonds soldiers were coerced into buying. This was a lot of money for a student in 1966 when Yale's basic board and tuition was around $3000 p.a.

I bought a green Volvo, found it underpowered, so had the engine modified and Koni shock absorbers installed. The result, as anyone could have predicted, was a slightly faster Volvo that wouldn't stay in tune and had a teeth-juddering ride. I loved it all the same.

In a perverse way, I missed the physical side of the army and Vietnam, even the asshole-puckering moments. One weekend, I joined my brother to parachute in Orange, Massachusetts. The first jump was such a wonderful thrill that I landed shouting with joy.

However, when I was about to make my second jump, the man who was to jump before me panicked while sitting in the open side-door of the single-engine Cessna.

With the guy's static line hooked up and him in the way of the rest of us, we had to circle the airfield until the whimpering jerk was coaxed into jumping. It was considered too risky to pull him back into the plane from his "legs dangling in space" perch in the doorway.

I found myself longing to kick him out the door in the style of a jumpmaster in the 82nd Airborne because his fear was contagious. By the time he finally let go and went out the door, my own parachute jump was a fearful anti-climax. I didn't go parachuting again.

———◆———

Academically, Yale was more or less acceptable. After the time I'd spent freezing my ass off sitting in frozen holes or filling sandbags under the broiling sun or working in a tent night after dripping, steamy, tropical night, I was more than prepared to sit in a centrally heated dorm room, typing out little essays.

Perhaps the deans had been right to send me away to think about the world. Perhaps I'd grown up. Perhaps Yale had changed. More likely, I'd simply learned to concentrate only on what interested me and to ignore the inevitable Yale academic make work. I dropped my English major and switched to history, so there was no more writing about Wordsworth's cloud imagery to choke my soul.

I studied modern German history with intense curiosity after my army time in Augsburg and Munich. Professor Franklin Baumer's course on intellectual history brilliantly complemented studying German history. Germans spewed out ideas and took ideas seriously; they chewed on them and rolled on them like dogs. Sometimes, Germans started wars because of ideas they kept for home consumption like *Macht* and *Lebensraum*; other times they exported their war-inducing ideas like Fascism and Marxism.

Best was Professor Robin Wincks's course on British history. Professor Wincks was an inspired teacher and easy to approach and talk with. He was one of those people who are endlessly interested in everything, from the most profound social change to the classic detective novel; he sparkled intellectually. We talked about the historical evolution of British society, what I'd observed of my English cousins, and the enduring similarities of all the English-speaking countries, despite our long separation.

It was well into the year before I could face visiting Phinney Works's parents. But it had to be done.

I'd known Skrow—Works spelled backwards—and Glad Works since Phinney and I were kids. Skrow had taught me to shoot his M-1 rifle, which was a big help in basic training. He was a massive, bullying man who had been a major in General Patton's tank army in World War II. He loved war and talking about war. Patton was his hero.

Skrow had a Browning automatic rifle and a captured German Schmeisser machine pistol wrapped up in oily newspaper in the attic of his summer house in New Hampshire, despite automatic weapons being illegal. Skrow was contemptuous of laws and the federal government. He was ready for the uprising.

Glad was a large, intelligent but somehow fluffy woman who was completely under Skrow's thumb. They had five children.

Phinney, my exact contemporary, was their oldest child, but my real friend was his slightly younger sister Emily, a bright, tall, athletic girl who could run, swim, and play tennis as well as most boys. I could talk to Emily. Phinney was too full of the need to live up to his father's absurd, near-fascist views about society. Skrow wanted to shoot everyone who didn't conform to his John Galt take on the world. Phinney tried to copy this attitude, but it didn't suit him.

It was obvious to me that Phinney dropped out of Yale and went into the Special Forces to prove something to his father. Once when we were about twelve, I stood outside an open window in their house and watched Skrow beat Phinney with the flat of his powerful right hand. Skrow then made Phinney stand to attention and say, "Thank you, Daddy."

———◆———

"All unhappy families are different." Are they? I have always thought this a novelistic conceit but Skrow and Glad certainly lived up to it. They were bizarre.

Skrow was a monster. Many years later, when well into his seventies, he launched himself into an impossible love affair with a much younger, manipulative, married woman. After Glad told Skrow that she was leaving him, Skrow blew his brains out with his World War II Colt .45 automatic pistol, the same one he had carried as a tank commander during the Battle of the Bulge.

But for reasons I will never understand, Skrow was always friendly and kind to me. And Glad was motherly. I owed them something, some kind of sympathy or understanding. They were odd and dysfunctional parents, but so were mine; I was used to weird WASPs as parents.

We had exchanged letters after Phinney's death. They had loved Phinney in their fashion and missed him painfully. They thought I was his closest friend, which I may have been when we were fifteen but had ceased to be well before his death.

During the year I spent sharing a small room with him at Yale, I had only the most general impression of what Phinney actually thought about anything. He was bright but indifferent to academic work and didn't share my exasperation with the pointlessness of Yale's teaching.

Phinney was searching for something. Once, lying in the upper bunk as we were trying to sleep, he quietly suggested that, first thing in the morning, we enlist in the Marines together. I grunted a sleepy "no" and he never mentioned it again. He joined the army on his own without telling anyone.

When I looked at him, and he wasn't aware of this, Phinney often sported a pensive half-smile, which revealed a slightly chipped front tooth. The faint smile made him look whimsically happy, but I know that was a false impression. Otherwise, Phinney went to his death a mystery to me. I wonder if anyone ever really knew him. Skrow, another intelligent anti-intellectual, wrote curious and competent poetry. Perhaps Phinney would have in time.

I did not look forward to visiting the Works, but a visit had to be made. I drove to their big house in Greenwich on a fine spring afternoon.

By this time, Skrow was a successful, senior Wall Street banker. The house was a massive brick and stone effort from the 1920s, probably now long pulled down and replaced with two or three McMansions. Then, it stood stiff and proper at the end of a long drive.

I'd feared tears or demonstrative behavior but, apart from an unexpected hug from Glad, nothing seemed changed. Skrow gave me his usual bone-crushing handshake. He was about six foot three and about two hundred and forty pounds of muscular ex-Yale athlete. The weight he'd put on since college made his eyes look small and his face appear piggy above his thick neck. Coupled with his loud voice, sharp comments, and ugly temper, Skrow frightened people and was certainly not someone to offend.

I didn't experience this side of Skrow. I knew the Works as a mom and pop family act who liked most of all to sit down with their children to eat heavy, traditional Midwestern food; they were all for meat and potatoes, the food washed down with plenty of highballs for the adults. This diet's effect on Glad, a tall woman, was to make her bosomy and broad astern.

A photo of Phinney had pride of place in their living room, placed inside a glass-fronted mahogany box hung on the wall. The color photo was of Phinney in his army green dress uniform, looking grim and purposeful. Inside the box, surrounding the photo, were his Special Forces shoulder patch and his medals, along with his two silver first lieutenant's bars. I looked at these in silence.

I knew that Phinney was buried in the old cemetery in Freedom, New Hampshire, down past the fire house beside the mill pond. I used to fish there, though never with Phinney. Mentally, I made a resolve to visit the grave.

We talked about this and that. I was given tea and the chit-chat ebbed. Skrow had no small talk anyway. He began to question me about the war in Vietnam. He even asked me how I was feeling, a most un-Skrow thing to do. Not knowing quite what answer he expected, I said that my stomach sometimes bothered me. Skrow said this was nothing to worry about. He said that I was of good, old American stock and that it would pass, as indeed it did.

Then he got onto his familiar political hobbyhorse but with a fresh crusading zeal: "Communism killed our firstborn. But we will fight the godless bastards until we win, goddamn it."

I chewed on this statement. Skrow wanted some affirmative response, like "Yes, we will kill and disembowel the Commie bastards."

Remember that this was in 1967, before the Tet Offensive smashed our already waning national resolve and still a time when militarily the war was apparently going fairly well.

There was no reason to believe that we couldn't win militarily. America had never lost a war, though Korea was a scoreless tie. In theory, we could do whatever it took to win. After all, the United States then was the most powerful nation in the history of the world and represented something like 50 percent of the global economy.

However, my own opinion was that, whatever happened militarily, the Vietnam War had already been lost—and at home. What I saw daily at Yale convinced me that American society was no longer sufficiently coherent and mentally tough enough to win a nasty colonial war. The sacrifices of our soldiers were meaningless in the face of the mindless flabbiness and the moral cowardice of our liberal elite.

I didn't interpret this failure in terms of an American version of the German *Dolchstoss* or stab in the back at the end of World War I. No, I thought of it in terms of the Chinese proverb that a fish rots from its head or as a bad collective case of the piles.

America had reached the bread and circuses stage as a society.

Not wanting to come right out and say what I thought about our chances in Vietnam, I muttered something about "not being over-impressed by army leadership," then instantly thought, "this is a mistake."

However, Skrow took this calmly and seemed to agree. But then he savagely blamed the Democrats who were running the war: "The army isn't allowed to run at full speed. An engine isn't impressive when it is idling."

"Idling" didn't jibe with what I'd seen in Vietnam. I thought that our military effort in Vietnam was heroic but misconceived and ill-led. Our army lived in camps like Di An, isolated from the Vietnamese. The contacts with civilian Vietnamese I personally remembered were not suitable for polite discussion in suburban Connecticut, let alone likely to sell the Vietnamese on the merits of Jeffersonian democracy or the free market.

Was the big picture any different?

From my worm's eye viewpoint, our tactics stank. In the 1st Infantry Division, we sent tanks down high-crowned narrow roads through the scrub, with a deep ditch on each side of the road, a perfect environment for ambushes.

The plan was to drop infantry from helicopters in advance of the tanks and crush the Viet Cong between the infantry and the tanks. This was called the "hammer and anvil" tactic. Sadly, the tanks were usually knocked out with mines or the infantry were ambushed before they reached the tanks.

Helicopters flew in infantry to seize terrain that meant nothing, except inside the thick skull of a general in Saigon. This was "search and destroy." Holding this hill or that jungle track would prevent the enemy from doing this or that, or so they believed at MACV.

Yet another search and destroy mission would frustrate a fiendish Viet Cong plan by destroying a cache of rice and a few old rifles. And over and over we lobbed artillery shells like confetti into the bush, killing anything that moved, hoping it was the enemy and not our own men.

The results of these tactics soon turned up on my 3x5-inch cards: DOW or KIA.

Though our army and its tactics were basically not suited to fight a guerilla war, might our generals have done better if Lyndon Johnson had let them fight the Viet Cong with everything we had? Could better strategy have offset our questionable tactics?

Maybe, just maybe…

Now that we know how President Johnson meddled, dribbling in troops and turning the bombing of the North on and off for his own tortuous political reasons, perhaps Skrow's military instincts weren't so wrong.

Who knows what we might have achieved by using our maximum force early in the war. Even if we had failed to crack the will of Hanoi quickly, we might have kept American public opinion on the side of our soldiers for longer. And made it less fashionable to be a draft-dodger or a peacenik. Americans like winning.

We know from an interview in 1969 with General Giap, North Vietnam's battlefield commander, that the North had over 500,000 men killed in action between 1964 and 1968. Since the North had a population of around twenty million before the war, even that tough society must have had some limit.

What if we had pulled out all the stops from 1965 onward? Did North Vietnam have a breaking point?

We will never know.

But that afternoon wasn't the time for a strategic analysis of the war. Glad's face showed me that. After a decent interval, I shook hands with Skrow and hugged Glad. She wept as I drove away. I went back to see the Works from time to time, but the visits always ended on the same down note.

They wanted something that I couldn't give them—a reason.

As the year progressed, I was at a loss as to what to do after graduation. I even daydreamed about getting a commission and going back into the army.

Law school? Beyond boring. Business? Interesting, yes, but what business? I was dabbling in the stock market. Was that a business? Watching the gyrations of my stocks, I found that the market was never tedious or predictable. This was certainly not true of my family's paper manufacturing or my father's dreary career as a high school English teacher. But was I ready to make a living in the stock market?

Fortunately, Professor Robin Wincks took the decision out of my hands. We were talking one day in his book-strewn office. Or rather I was listening; Professor Wincks was a fascinating polymath who wore well-cut English suits with striped shirts and bright colored braces—suspenders in America. He looked like an English merchant banker and sounded like a genius.

Out of the blue, he asked me what I was doing after graduation. I was stumped for an answer. I jiggled in my seat and fiddled with my now long hair.

"I don't know," I said.

"Mmm," said Professor Wincks. "What would you like to do?"

"Well, that is the problem," I said.

"When a student doesn't know what to do, the obvious thing is to go on studying," he said.

"Yes," I said, "but what?"

"You have a good basic knowledge of English history and you talk with enthusiasm about your English cousins," said Professor Wincks. "Why don't you read history at Oxford?"

This knocked me back. I instantly loved the idea, but surely it was impossible. Wasn't it?

"How could I pay for it?"

"Use the GI Bill, of course."

With my mouth hanging open, I stared at this brilliant man who proceeded to explain to me the mechanics of the GI Bill. This freebie from the American taxpayer would fund my studies at any legitimate place of education for years. Oxford or the Ace School of Applied Plumbing; it made no difference.

Naturally, no one on the admin side at Yale had mentioned the GI Bill to me. It took the Randolph Townsend Professor of English History to clue me in.

"How would I get into Oxford?" I asked.

"You would need to apply to an Oxford college. I know just the one—Keble. You enjoy rowing. The ideal student for Keble is an oarsman or a theologian. And my friend, Dr. Campbell, is the history tutor there. If you like the idea, I'll write him a letter."

At that, I practically kissed Professor Wincks's hand. He immediately sent a letter off to Professor Campbell. With that and a few forms to fill in, I was admitted as a senior student of Keble College, Oxford, starting in the autumn of 1967. My future looked interesting again.

Because of sharing Ivan's bad LSD trip, I became close to Neil Stein and David Melnik. They were fine men, warm-hearted and funny. Stein was a good-looking, womanizing extrovert with almost jet-black hair that was expensively cut in the style of Cary Grant. He was a dapper dude who liked to be called "Sean" because it sounded Irish and like an actor.

Stein was verbally quick and could chat effortlessly with anyone. He explained that his family were the only Jews in Centralia, Illinois, a nowhere place. Their family policy was to make friends with everyone and to help everyone. Stein was an excellent student who aced all scientific subjects and wanted to be a doctor.

David Melnik was a jolly, slightly chubby guy who loved to eat and to crack jokes about his home town, New Britain, Connecticut. He noted that people in New Britain had an unusual accent that turned New Britain into "Nuh Bri-annnn." He also claimed that the girls in New Britain held all sorts of state and national records for ugliness. So New Britain men were never choosy.

Despite this potential advantage, Melnik was much less successful with girls than Stein but tried hard.

After a drink or two, Melnik burst into wonderful, vulgar songs. To the tune of "Humoresque," Melnik strolled down the streets of New Haven singing:

Was it you that did the pushing,
Put the stains upon the cushion,
Footprints on the dashboard, upside down?

Was it your sly woodpecker,
That got into my daughter Rebecca,
Now I think you better leave this town!

Stein and I replied in song as loud as possible:

Yes, 'twas I that did the pushing,
Put the stains upon the cushion,
Footprints on the dashboard, upside down.
But ever since I had your daughter,
I've had trouble passing water,
So I think we're even all around.

We attracted odd looks, but no one said anything.

Stein and Melnik wanted more than anything to go to the Montreal Expo, the 1967 World Fair that had just opened. I had obtained a summer job with a small newspaper in Cleveland, but I had just enough time to go with them to Expo before I started work.

After the graduation ceremony, which I skipped, we set off in my Volvo. As we drove north along the two-lane, rolling highways of the period, we listened to the radio. The date was June fifth.

Before we left, we had known about the tension in the Middle East. Now the region had exploded into a major war. Israel launched a violent and highly successful pre-emptive attack on Egypt, destroying the Egyptian air force on the ground. Shades of *Blitzkrieg* or Pearl Harbor. Jordan and Syria jumped in and were destroyed in turn.

Stein and Melnik were enthralled. I was pleased, too. In those naïve days, everyone believed in the *Exodus* movie myth about the creation of plucky little Israel, which had taken "a land without a people for a people without land." If only…

Stein and Melnik proclaimed their disappointment that, although Jewish, they would not have the opportunity to fight for Israel. They went on in this vein as the miles passed, and we switched from one silly little radio station to another, trying to learn the latest on the battles.

Since Stein and Melnik had already told me they were going to do whatever it took to avoid the draft, short of maiming themselves, I asked them to describe the circumstances in which they would fight for the United States.

This produced silence, then halting comments. Essentially, barring a replay of World War II with Hitler returning as quarterback, there were no circumstances in which they would voluntarily serve in the American military.

I didn't take this too seriously, since I already knew what they would say. Why would a Jew want to serve in the military of an often anti-Semitic country that so recently had discriminated against Jews in many walks of life? Plus, they both came from Eastern European families that probably had ugly memories of granddad being drafted to serve in the Tsar's army or of being oppressively taxed to pay for the Tsar's army.

Indirectly, Stein and Melnik were making a much more fundamental point; one I didn't grasp fully until much later. Most of our social or ethnic groups could think of their own particular excellent reasons for not wanting to take part in America's wars.

As the United States became increasingly diverse, and the promotion and protection of diversity became a major goal of society, there was no good reason for a member of any social group to feel a call to serve in the army as a matter of general civic duty. The melting pot was over; multiculturalism was the new game. I do my thing; you do your thing.

War is somebody else's thing.

This side effect of diversity wasn't something new. Even in the existential struggle of the Civil War, many wealthy New Yorkers and Democrat "Copperheads" felt that it was perfectly proper to skip the draft and, for three hundred dollars, to buy their way out of serving in the Union Army.

"Please daddy; rent me an Irishman."

The working class draft riots in New York and elsewhere in 1863 weren't because the northern cause was immoral or illegal. Those modern objections to war were absent. The reason for rioting was diversity; many young males lacked enough social identification with their new country to overcome their fears. Call it "a lack of military ardor" among the recent immigrants, if you like euphemisms. Plus anger at the ability of the rich to buy themselves out of the draft.

The South was different. About twenty-five percent of southern white men of military age—all volunteers—were killed in the Civil War. The WASP whites of the mostly rural South could still hear the call of a distant bugle that many in the already diverse, industrial North had ceased to respond to.

In any case, we all thoroughly enjoyed Expo '67. I went back to Cleveland to work on the *Sun-Press* for the summer. Journalism was fun and a nice prelude to the joy I felt when I left Cleveland for good in the fall to go to Oxford.

There were good, rational reasons for opposition to the Vietnam War.

Some thought, like Eisenhower, that fighting land wars in Asia was militarily insane. History is on the side of Ike.

There were emotional reasons for opposition to the war, which didn't involve mere cowardice and draft-dodging.

Some Yalies subject to the draft probably believed all the guff about imperialism and evil and moral imperatives—though bear in mind that these were convenient beliefs to hold at the time—which so many American liberals, and not just King Brewster and Bill Coffin, stuffed into the students' eagerly receptive, pointed little heads.

I simply could not respect the country that let such scum buckets speak for it. Or the sad dolts that responded to them.

Bumper stickers said: "America, love it or leave it." I didn't hate America, but I certainly didn't love it; too many of the American elite filled me with contempt. So I left.

Vietnam Revisited—1993

Deprived of American military support, the Republic of South Vietnam collapsed in 1975. For the rest of the twentieth century, a reunited Vietnam lived under Communism.

I stayed in England after Oxford, married Alyson, my one true love, helped raise three terrific children, and worked in investment management. I became among other things a specialist in emerging market investing. So, it was natural in 1993 that I would visit Vietnam as part of my research into starting a Greater China investment fund. Vietnam was not really open to western investment in 1993 so my vague idea was to include a small number of unquoted investments.

I was by then a so-called managing director of Bankers Trust, a large American investment bank. (American investment banks have dozens of "managing directors.") I believed that anything connected economically with the re-birth of China was likely to attract investors in time.

There are fashions in investing as in anything else. As an investment manager, you hope that the investment ideas you think are timely and attractive will overlap with whatever is the investment flavor of the month so that you can raise lots of money to invest.

I had an additional personal goal. Why shouldn't Bankers Trust and the investors in the fund do something useful for Vietnam? That "something" might also be profitable for the fund over time. I have great respect for Vietnamese energy and ingenuity. And, after all, we had caused the deaths of millions of Vietnamese in the name of what Bankers Trust so perfectly represented—no, not mere greed—capitalism.

Arriving in Tan Son Nhut Airport in Ho Chi Minh City, which for me will always be Saigon, was like landing into a time warp. The airport was the same as it was when we touched down in 1966. The same blast-protected, open-ended shelters for fighter planes were still there, but now housed ancient MIGs. The same terminal buildings, looking very shabby, were in use complete with the old, glaring neon lights inside. Bored-looking officials in worn uniforms with red stars on their shoulder straps stamped our passports in an offhand way.

I'd worried when filling in the visa application. It said, "List all previous visits to the People's Republic of Vietnam." I decided this was not something to fill in with unnecessary accuracy. Anyway, the country I visited as a soldier no longer existed. So I put "not applicable."

My worry was totally unfounded. The Vietnamese were over the war. In Saigon at least, local Communist officials wanted foreign businessmen to visit. Lots of local entrepreneurs were delighted to meet with us to talk openly about their business plans.

By 1993, capitalism was reviving in Saigon. Vietnam had no stock market or quoted securities, but there was an informal market in corporate equities. If a company liked the look of you, it could sell you some of its shares. And if it still liked you later on, it might pay you a dividend or even buy the shares back. Not practical for us but an interesting insight into how capitalism begins; something like Lloyds, the London coffee house, where in 1691 men began informally trading in shipping insurance.

In Saigon, Vietnamese government officials were ready to encourage us, but there was no legally feasible way of making even private placement investments in 1993, given the total lack of legal property rights and the general use of useless, wonky Russian Communist accounting.

I was traveling with Scott McKinley, a multi-talented Bankers Trust sidekick, who was both a Mormon and an accounting star and who spoke Cantonese and Mandarin. I hoped that McKinley would run the China fund.

By sheer accident, we quickly found a bite-sized bank in Saigon that wanted an American co-owner like Bankers Trust. The bank was run by a remarkable old man, Nguyen Xuan Oanh.

An elderly, thin, somewhat detached personality, Dr. Nguyen had a PhD in economics from Harvard, had worked for the International Monetary Fund, and was briefly the acting prime minister of South Vietnam just as the country lost the war.

Despite his age, Dr. Nguyen was very business-like and wouldn't be drawn into telling us anything about his past, though we spent most of a day with him. I assumed that he had survived by humoring both sides during the last phase of the war. How he had performed this feat of juggling with his life was still not something he was willing to share with outsiders.

But he was informative about his bank, which had a full forex license, western-standard accounts and was owned and sponsored by the Saigon branch of the Vietnamese Communist Party. The local politburo was happy to join hands with a capitalist majority partner.

McKinley and I thought that buying into a bank with such backing was likely to ensure plenty of local business and the ability to navigate the bureaucracy. The bank badly needed banking contacts outside Vietnam, which we had in buckets. This was a promising deal.

Unfortunately, after a few irritating phone calls to Bankers Trust HQ, McKinley and I realized that Bankers Trust would never stop bombarding its existing clients—aka suckers—with complex and deceptive—aka crap—derivatives long enough to negotiate the purchase of a small traditional bank in what was still technically a Communist country.

This already profitable small bank would have been a spectacularly rewarding investment. But Bankers Trust—"the bank you love to hate"—collapsed a few years later and was bought by Deutschebank so did it matter?

McKinley and I decided just to try to understand what was happening in Vietnam.

On our last morning in Saigon, I arranged to rent a car with a driver. I wanted to go out to Di An to see what, if anything, was left of our camp. I assumed that the area would have reverted to rice farming.

After some confused discussion with the driver, using the hotel's desk clerk as interpreter, we set out in what I thought was the right direction. Nothing looked familiar, though. I started to bore McKinley with a monolog about wild days and nights in Saigon and about the war.

Occasionally, the driver stopped to consult a map. Suddenly, and without warning, the driver did a U-turn and roared off in a new direction. He said nothing.

After quite a while, we pulled up to what was clearly a government office. I felt like a complete fool and plenty alarmed. Obviously, the driver had realized from my babble that I was an ex-soldier. He thought that I had come back to spy! I'd heard of people being arrested for such suspicions in Communist countries. The driver probably spoke English all along. I'd be fitted up as a war criminal. Color me Agent Orange!

In fact, the "government office" was the headquarters of a bustling young rental car company. The driver got lost, so he went back to base. A pleasant middle-aged woman in the office spoke French. Yes, she knew where Di An was. She smiled at me and explained this to the driver.

We set off again, slowly navigating through a dense mix of bicycles, mopeds, three-wheeled putt-putts, heavy Russian trucks, and a few old American army trucks. The road, which had been high-crowned red dirt, was now more or less paved. Children, dogs, and old people meandered along the crumbling edges of the road, inviting sudden death.

But where was the countryside? We went on and on along a wide street lined on both sides with Asian "shop houses"—open-fronted shop below, family dwelling area above. Even more people on foot and animals mingled with the traffic. Finally, the driver said we were at Di An.

I had to laugh. The population of Saigon had exploded. We were in a suburb that had grown radially out from the city along the highway the American army engineers had built. I realized that the bridge we had crossed miles back was the one that marked the outer boundary of Saigon in my day, complete then with ARVN MPs, pill boxes, and machine gun posts. Now I recognized nothing.

By this time the driver tried to tell us something. He smiled. He wanted to show us some fun, we gathered. I told him briskly that I didn't want to purchase the services of his sister, even if she was a sixteen-year-old virgin. Luckily, he didn't understand.

McKinley recommended that we just find out what the driver had in mind before going back. And McKinley was right; the driver took us to a fine park that was full of young couples out for the day. We had to borrow the entry fee from the driver, since we had no local money.

There we sat for several hours, enjoying what Di An had morphed into, listening to boys playing the guitar for girls, and sipping fragrant tea. I enjoyed the thought that I might be sitting on the exact spot where Jerry Kahle and I had once lain fearfully in a shallow hole, waiting in the dark for the Viet Cong with a loaded M-60 machine gun at the ready.

The new Di An was infinitely nicer without Viet Cong or GIs or hookers or concertina wire or minefields.

The following day, we went on to Hanoi.

In 1993, Hanoi was still in the grips of Communist orthodoxy. No banks were for sale and officials were less than glad to see us. So we looked at where John McCain had been imprisoned—the Hanoi Hilton—and did a lot of walking, enjoying the splendid old colonial French buildings. Hanoi was going in the same economic direction as Saigon, we decided, regardless of official policy. We saw that any real estate investment in Hanoi would be rewarding but found no way of making such investments.

In Hanoi, McKinley and I visited two retired Mormon couples from Salt Lake City who were performing a second, middle-aged Mormon mission. These four gutsy people were trying to unscramble the medical damage caused when the Russians suddenly stopped the flow of cheap medical supplies, as well as all sorts of subsidized raw materials, to Vietnam after the Soviet Union collapsed.

With a dictionary, the Mormons translated X-ray machine manuals from Russian into English and relabeled medicines into English. They wrote begging letters to U.S. medical companies and lived all the while like Vietnamese. Their diet was fish heads and rice, and they lived in one walk-up, non-air-conditioned flat in a social housing project.

We asked them what we could do to help. "Feed us" was the answer. So we took them to the wonderful Metropole Hotel for a blowout French meal, compliments of Bankers Trust.

Somewhere in my expense claims from that trip is buried an expensive meal, labeled "local investment research." As far as I know, this was the only investment Bankers Trust ever made in Vietnam.

Back to America

O ver the years, my acute post-Vietnam disgust with the United States faded. Though I spent my whole business career working in London, my clients were spread all over the world. Many were in the United States. I called on pension fund clients from Armonk, New York, to Pasadena, California. I marketed mutual funds from Florida to Alaska. I talked with ordinary Americans on airplanes and in hotel bars.

Mostly, I liked the people I met on my American marketing tours, though the compulsion felt by blue-rinsed ladies sitting next to me on planes to tell me in horrid detail about their gynecological problems always stunned me. I liked driving through the shambolic vastness of America. Visiting shopping malls was fascinating. Watching what people bought intrigued me. I had always wondered who bought such stuff and now I knew—everyone.

American politics was a fun spectator sport, played by venal windbags with blow-dried hair. I despise most politicians regardless of party, but I liked Ronald Reagan and the way he trashed the moaning, ridiculous Jimmy Carter and revived the spirits of the nation. But I had no serious plan to return to the United States.

When retirement landed on me in 2001, Alyson and I had trouble deciding where to live. Staying in central London was out of the question financially. We had owned a summer house in Provence in the French Luberon, but we had sold it. We went back to Provence in mid-winter to see if we would like living there permanently. Places we had known only in the joyous, crowded summer sun were like a morgue in winter. All our favorite restaurants—an endless pleasure in France—were closed. *Hors de saison* was the theme everywhere.

Finally, we talked to M. Bacon, a French pal who was a good local real estate agent. M. Bacon's office was in the famous old hill town of Bonnieux. Alyson and I went to his office for what we thought would be a preliminary chat about finding a property for our *retraite*.

M. Bacon was delighted to see us as always. It is an Anglophone myth that all the French are difficult; outside of Paris the French are often charming and helpful. He ordered coffees for us from the little café next to his office. We chatted in our usual Franglais. Then he got right to the point.

"'Ow meeny peepul do you t'ink are in Bonnieux today?" he said.

Knowing the town well in the busy summer, I guessed about three thousand.

"More like t'ree 'undred," he told us.

"Mes amis," he said, "I h'advise you not to live here year round."

This shocked us. No real estate agent anywhere has ever advised living, breathing cash clients not even to consider buying a property from him. This was outside the zone of known human possibilities.

M. Bacon told us why.

It was not a comment on my rotten French, he stressed. "Pas de tout," he said. "After all, Madame Thomson speek Francais assez bien. Eet is always possible zat you improve avec practique."

He continued, "I geeve zee same advice to zee francophone Belges."

The Belgians arrived with great enthusiasm, but after one winter they returned to Brussels. Isolation after their summer friends went home and the misery of the mistral winds broke the spirit of retirees. Also, the year round expat retirees saw so much of each other that they soon disliked each other heartily.

"Enjoy le Luberon and Provence only for zee vacances," was his advice. M. Bacon himself was buying a property in Ireland where he planned to spend his own retirement fly fishing. Since his English was as bad as my French, I hope that this plan worked out well for this charming, honest man.

On the same trip to France, we spent time with our lawyer Ron Sokol, another wise man. Of American origin but long resident in France, Ron agreed with M. Bacon but went even further.

"Go back to the United States," said Ron. "It's the only exotic industrial country."

So back to the United States I went, bringing Alyson as soon as the perverse post-9/11 visa process would permit a British wife to enter the land of the free. We bought an old house in rural northwestern Connecticut and prepared to live there happily ever after. But only after a great deal of traveling.

I wanted to share some of the remarkable places I remembered with Alyson. This took some persuasion. Alyson is a keen and adventurous traveler but also tempted by the more restful Edwardian certitudes of Provencal markets and Tuscan hillsides. "Siena, here I come," is her travel cry.

Somehow, though, in 2007 I managed to convince Alyson that, as a freshly minted American citizen, she needed to visit the place that had so changed my life and that of her newly adopted country.

Siena would have to wait. We were off to Vietnam.

Vietnam Reborn

In 2007 I kept a diary during our Vietnam trip. I went to Vietnam with Alyson looking for something, not closure perhaps—I had nothing to close—but an inner clarity and a more detached perspective on the United States. So I recorded what I felt as I felt it. With a few edits and grammatical changes, what follows is that diary:

February 24, 2007, Hotel Caravelle, Saigon

Alyson and I arrived in Saigon on February 24, 2007, fourteen years after my last visit as a bigshot in a U.S. bank and forty-one years after my arrival as a lowly U.S. soldier. This time Vietnam was at peace and thriving. Unfortunately, though, I had to pay for this trip, unlike the previous two.

The Caravelle Hotel in Ho Chi Minh City, currently still the official name for Saigon, is the perfect place to stay at the beginning of a trip to Vietnam. Since I last visited Saigon in 1993, the Caravelle has more than doubled in size and been completely rebuilt to five star standard. It is right in the heart of the city on Lam Son Square, the center of activity since French colonial times. Dong Khoi

Street runs along one side of the Caravelle, down to the Saigon River. Dong Khoi means Unified Uprising, not an odd name for a street in a still technically Communist country.

Not so long ago, when Saigon was still officially Saigon and the capital of a now vanished country, Dong Khoi Street was called Tu Do Street. Tu Do means Freedom. And freedom was what I as a young GI associated with Saigon and with Tu Do Street—freedom and wild night possibilities.

Before the French were kicked out in 1954, Tu Do Street, then Rue Cantinat, was a street of elegant shops. But the Tu Do Street I remember had hookers in every doorway, crowded bars, and pizzerias with thick wire mesh over the front windows to thwart passing grenade hurlers on motor bikes.

Some names haven't changed in the neighborhood around the Caravelle. The Continental Hotel is still across the square from the Caravelle. It looked the same to me as it did in 1966 or in 1993; sleeping in the sun just waiting for Graham Greene to plonk himself down for a drink on the hotel terrace. Or as it appeared on screen when Catherine Deneuve turned down the marriage proposition of the head of the French Deuxieme Bureau or secret service chief in Indochine. *Or as a backdrop for Michael Caine's drooping eyelids in the recent remake of Green's* The Quiet American.

After Alyson and I checked in with our group from Stanford Alumni Travel, I did a jetlagged wander around the Caravelle. Our room was in the new building. The room and the building and the welcoming staff were of a high standard, but I wanted to see something else.

I ambled down a corridor into the old Caravelle building. I took the elevator as far up as it would go, then walked up a flight of stairs and onto the roof terrace. Most of the roof was covered over now, though the sides were open and there was a bar and a dance floor. The new part of the Caravelle towered over the old roof terrace. I walked around the terrace looking out at Saigon. None of the views were familiar, though I'd spent hours on this roof terrace in 1966. I needed to come back at night. My memories of the Caravelle roof terrace were night-time memories.

Early the next morning our whole group went by brand new air-conditioned bus to the Cu Chi tunnels. Once past the Saigon suburban overspill that lined the old roads built by the American army engineers, we drove slowly through the kind of scrubby area I remembered well. We called it the boonies. The Vietnam War wasn't a jungle war for me. My Vietnam was not far out of Saigon, flat, hot and featureless, basically an area of straggly villages surrounded by rice paddies.

Today the one- and two-story cement block houses with banana trees in front and pigs and chickens running around look about the same as they always did, though the satellite dishes were a surprise. And there are still many small shops and restaurants, though none with walls or roofs made of metal sheets ingeniously contrived from discarded American beer cans.

February is the dry season, but dry is a relative term in Vietnam. Vietnam is always humid. In February, southern Vietnam is a hot and dusty place of droopy plants and trees longing for the monsoon, overhanging bumpy, narrow roads.

Most of the roads are now paved, unlike the high-crowned red laterite roads our army engineers rammed through the jungle and countryside. Anyway, you notice the road surface less riding in a brand new air-conditioned Japanese bus than I did riding in the back of the classic U.S. Army two-and-one-half ton truck.

Featured in a zillion TV shots and films, the deuce and a half is the ten-wheel olive-drab brute with the canvas covered back that I still saw in use all over Vietnam in 1993. Now these vehicles have vanished at last.

Alyson and I were reunited on the bus not just with six friendly people we had met in China on a previous Stanford tour but also with Eli Haislip. Eli runs a superb travel company based in San Francisco and is an old Asia hand and man of learning who accompanies the tours he arranges.

In addition we had Professor Lyman "Van" Van Slyke, an emeritus professor of Asian history at Stanford. Professor Van had already helped Alyson unload her bag from the carousel at the airport in Saigon, proving that he wasn't along only to lecture. Van mixes with the troops.

Apart from his deep knowledge of why Asia is the way it is today and of what it was like a thousand years ago, Van knows more about the history of golf than anyone I've ever met. And he escaped many decades ago from Minnesota. We escapees from the Midwest respect each other.

To back up Eli and Van, Stanford Alumni Travel provided Lindsay Rubin as our mother hen and escort. Lindsay is cool, funny, and unflappable. And bright and pretty, but then Lindsay is a 2002 Stanford grad. One's expectations are high for girls from Stanford.

Our guide throughout our time in Vietnam was Mr. Cong. Mr. Cong is a dapper figure who often wore trendy round Italian horn-rimmed glasses. A Catholic from South Vietnam, Mr. Cong had been in university in 1975 and so avoided being drafted before the collapse of South Vietnam.

Despite being a Christian and holding pungently cynical opinions, Mr. Cong had been sufficiently apolitical to avoid being sent to a reeducation camp after the war. His English is perfect. Mr. Cong was full of pithy observations and wry jokes. The jokes were reinforced by Mr. Cong's soft voice and deadpan delivery.

One of Mr. Cong's first cracks about Vietnamese politics was that there was nothing left of local Communism but the "ism." "Communism is like a used Johnny Walker bottle. The bottle is now full of nuoc mam—fish sauce—but the label is still the same."

Even religion is tolerated today in Vietnam as long as it is passive. Believers must take the attitude that "Thy Kingdom not yet come." God should stay in heaven for the foreseeable future.

Mr. Cong's impressive fluency was up to word play in English. He observed, "Junk is the stuff we throw away. Stuff is the junk we keep." He also noted that Americans and Europeans had lots of legal problems with Asian exporters because Asians couldn't distinguish between copyright and the right to copy.

Mr. Cong was David Halberstam's translator and guide for Halberstam's trips to Vietnam after the war ended. And, after Halberstam's recent death in an auto crash, Mr. Cong was invited by the Halberstam family to the funeral and was allowed to go. Vietnam has changed.

Our first visit was to the Cu Chi Tunnels. The tunnels had been the hidden home of a major Viet Cong war effort. As a hater of war and military things, Alyson had dreaded visiting the Cu Chi tunnels, but they proved to be more like a movie set than a battle scene.

The tunnels were in the middle of an area of former rubber plantations, but most of the rubber trees were gone. The mixture of secondary tree re-growth and heavy underbrush was as I remembered. Various tunnels and structures were marked as being cookhouses or division headquarters, but much was obviously reconstructed. Earth tunnels in the tropics don't survive many monsoons.

We were encouraged only to go down certain tunnels. The holes were, as Mr. Cong explained, originally dug in size "S" for Vietnamese and not "XXL" for Americans, but some had been enlarged. Generous-sized members of our party scrambled through various tunnels without getting stuck.

Remembering that Vietnam has some of the world's most poisonous snakes and, infinitely worse from my standpoint, huge hairy spiders, clambering down into two-foot-wide unlighted holes in the ground didn't appeal to me. Hell, I used to be paid over three hundred dollars a month tax-free for such efforts.

So I stayed out of the Cu Chi tunnels and wandered around, looking at examples of booby traps made of sharpened bamboo and craters supposedly left by B-52 bombs. Then I heard what sounded like an AK-47 being fired on full automatic. Rat, tat, tat…rat, tat, tat…

Surprise, surprise! It was an AK-47 being fired on full automatic. Some enterprising young Vietnamese has set up a range right in the tunnel complex where you can fire all sorts of old Russian and American automatic weapons. At about a dollar a round, shooting off a few dozen rounds from these old weapons costs less than it cost the U.S. taxpayer when my buddies and I fired hundreds of rounds from such toys in training.

The Cu Chi tunnels are not far from Saigon and not far from Di An and Bien Hoa where the 1st Infantry Division, my division, was based. Thousands of Viet Cong and North Vietnamese regulars passed through Cu Chi, but simple overhead camouflage seems to have kept them from ever being really investigated by us or by our perhaps unenthusiastic Vietnamese allies.

There were French-owned rubber plantations in the area so possibly the vast tunnel complex was in one of the no-go areas that the South Vietnamese tried to avoid for sound commercial reasons, i.e. some French businessman had paid off some ARVN general. (ARVN = Army of the Republic of Vietnam.)

Whatever the reason, not destroying the Cu Chi tunnels during the Vietnam War was unfortunate. They were used as a launching pad for the 1968 Tet Offensive attack on Saigon. Apart from briefly occupying the U.S. Embassy, the Saigon Tet attack was a major military disaster for the Viet Cong. The local Viet Cong cadres in the South were decimated. The rest of the war was fought by troops from North Vietnam.

Seeing the Tet Offensive on TV, though, caught the attention of the great American public and convinced Walter Cronkite and his millions of insightful viewers that the war was lost.

During my 1993 trip to Vietnam, I'd been too involved with business issues to wax pensive about the war. This time was different. There was only one other Vietnam vet on the Stanford trip, but almost all of us on the trip were of that generation of Americans permanently marked by the Vietnam War.

The other Vietnam vet was a quiet, successful, gay Jewish lawyer from San Francisco who clung to his 1960s student past by sporting a Young Einstein Jewfro of now grey, but still luxuriant, frizzy hair.

Saul and I talked a lot on the bus about the experiences we had in 'Nam. Despite his moral reservations about the war, Saul had allowed himself to be drafted. After training, Saul soon found himself in Vietnam and assigned to the 82nd Airborne Division as a machine gunner. A fortuitous injury yanked Saul out of the 82nd prior to any combat and left him in one piece with only wry, quirky stories to tell about Vietnam.

The career outlook for a machine gunner in the 82nd Airborne was problematic.

Saul's military career thus confirmed the worst nightmare of every white suburban mother from Maine to California. In fact, it was rare for unwilling college graduates to find themselves in the infantry, let alone as a parachute-jump-trained volunteer in the 82nd Airborne. The army generally didn't squander draftees who could type, add, and subtract. I suspect that Saul had been much more of a brave volunteer than he now admits.

Back in Saigon that evening, I was already feeling a trifle melancholy when we went up for an after-dinner drink on the luxurious roof terrace of the Caravelle. Chatting with friends in the dusk on the roof, I still recognized nothing on the horizon but memories flooded back. Not all the memories were pleasing, nor was it a pleasure not to be young. I was glad not to be on my own.

———◆———

The day after my roof terrace-induced lapse into the past, we left Saigon after visiting Diem's Presidential Palace, the History Museum, the wonderfully French art deco Bureau de Poste and the Cathedral.

President Diem is now forgotten, but this tiny, determined man had more than a minor impact on history.

Diem came to power after the Geneva Peace Accord in 1954. A devout Catholic and brilliant academic, Diem had attended the same high school as Ho Chi Minh and General Giap, the victor at Dien Bien Phu. Catholics in 1954 were only some 8 percent of the population of South Vietnam, but they were a highly coherent group. Most Catholics were from the North and fled south after the Peace Accord. They had supported the French and were anti-Communist.

The Geneva Peace Accord agreed that nationwide elections would be held in 1955, but Diem rejected this agreement. With American support, just as we had supported the French during the French Indochina War, Diem proclaimed the Republic of Vietnam with himself as president.

This was later held up as evidence that the United States created a corrupt Catholic dictatorship in a Buddhist country, but it isn't clear that Diem initially planned to be a dictator or that fair nationwide elections were ever possible.

After the Peace Accord, North Vietnam immediately started hauling small landlords before people's tribunals in the Stalinist tradition. Communist cadres used terror and assassinations to control great areas of the countryside north and south. And, quite apart from the Catholics, more than million non-Catholic refugees fled the North to escape Communism. Giving Diem a chance was not an unreasonable or undemocratic thing to do.

Alas, Diem wasn't up to the challenge and relied on his corrupt relatives to enforce his policies. Guerrilla war accelerated while Diem's generals in Saigon spent their energies on plotting and stealing.

Eventually, the American diplomatic advisors in Saigon persuaded President Kennedy to allow the overthrow of Diem. Diem was forced to flee his palace when the inevitable coup took place. A day later, November 2, 1963, Diem was murdered by some of his senior officers in the back of an armored personnel carrier immediately after surrendering. Diem thus had his rendezvous with history only days before Kennedy had his rendezvous with Lee Harvey Oswald.

In Vietnam, the political result of the death of Diem was no better than the mess that followed Jimmy Carter's not resisting the overthrow of the Shah of Iran. (Kennedy, of course, was not around to deal with the consequences of his decision.)

Ordinary Vietnamese never fought for the ever-changing post-Diem governments in Saigon with any more enthusiasm than they had fought for Diem. By the end of 1963, fifteen thousand American military advisers were in South Vietnam, so North Vietnam decided to accelerate the War.

Johnson and Nixon will always carry the blame for Vietnam in the mind of the American public, but in my opinion Kennedy was responsible; he escalated the war by sending thousands of advisors to Vietnam, and he permitted the overthrow of Diem.

Soldiers in Vietnam used to say, "This is only a little war but it's the only war we got." Diem was only a little dictator, but he was the only one we had. At least he had some sort of vision for his country.

The Presidential Palace is a sad and shabby reminder of past American betrayals, a place of tattered curtains and grubby memories. A bunker in the basement is full of antique American radio gear. In this bunker Diem learned of his fate, due to American duplicity.

Or was it due to an unusual burst of American realism? Anyway, Afghanistan shows that we still have no knack for managing puppet leaders or for controlling their corruption.

The History Museum brought home the points Professor Van Slyke made in his talks about the cultural evolution of Vietnam. "Nam" means south and "Viet" is the region south of Canton or modern Guangzhou. Ethnically, the Vietnamese are a Chinese subgroup who moved south.

(The Chinese diaspora throughout South-East Asia still continues. Mr. Cong observed that, "a Thai hates all Chinese, except his father." Mr. Cong also noted that many of the "Vietnamese" boat people were actually ethnic Chinese.)

The Vietnamese were always warlike and soon polished off their Cham rivals who blocked their expansion to the south. The Cham, who had perfected growing two crops of wet rice a year, called double cropping, also warred with the Khmer Empire of Angkor Wat. The Cham seem to have been better at agriculture than at war. They vanished but left some wonderful, disturbing sculpture.

In double cropping, rice seeds were planted in seed beds, and then transplanted, so that farmers had in effect a growing year of 410 days. Empires could be erected on the resulting rice surpluses. The need to cultivate rice communally also lent itself to centralized control and easy tax collection.

By the tenth century AD, the Vietnamese had created an independent kingdom in the north of Vietnam. They acknowledged the Chinese Emperor in a tributary relationship with the aim of securing their northern frontier with China.

The Vietnamese always had a difficult relationship with their big brother to the north. Wars and skirmishes were always the norm. As recently as 1979, the Chinese decided that the Vietnamese, having beaten the Americans, were behaving in an uppity manner and needed a lesson. So the Chinese staged a small invasion. The Vietnamese quickly trounced the Chinese and killed thousands of Chinese soldiers.

The Vietnamese people think of their original home as the Red River delta near Hanoi. Over time the Vietnamese constantly moved farther south. Vietnam is shaped like two rice baskets connected by a pole.

The southern rice basket has Saigon as the capital and the Mekong River Delta as the most fertile land in Asia. The settlement of the south wasn't complete until the eighteenth century. If you were landless or lawless, you went south. Saigon itself was founded as recently as 1698 when the Emperor in Hue sent an envoy to establish the city and to separate the south from Cambodia.

Many tribal peoples inhabited the mountainous areas of Vietnam. The Vietnamese are a lowland people who live along the coastal plains. Like the dominant Han Chinese in China, Vietnamese attitudes toward these mountain tribal groups smacked historically of racism. There is a Vietnamese word for these mountain peoples that could be translated using our own forbidden "n" word. Accordingly, most of the tribal groups supported first the French and then the Americans. The French called them montagnards.

February 26, 2007; Morin Hotel, Hue

The Morin is a charming old French hotel, full of photos of long ago French travelers and their 1920's French cars. We ate in the hotel on our first night in Hue and, as everywhere in Vietnam, the food was excellent.

One of the few totally happy results of the French interaction with the Vietnamese was the fusion of two of the world's great foodie cultures. This means that you can munch a perfect baguette with imported Normandy butter for breakfast and have the world's best spring rolls—nem—at every other meal. Or have such treats as banh xeo—an omelet-like crepe. Or fabulous seafood. Or noodles. Or complicated salads for the intestinally brave.

The next morning we went on walkabout in Hue. I hadn't been to Hue before and didn't realize that it had not simply been the imperial capital but was a scaled-down replica of the Forbidden City in Beijing.

The Hue Citadel on the Perfumed River was the fortress protecting the Forbidden City. The much photographed citadel was the scene of ferocious fighting during the Tet Offensive in 1968 but has been largely restored. Bullet marks in the stone walls indicate where the fighting was most intense. Viewed from across the Perfumed River, the citadel looks low, dark, military, and menacing, a bit like an old Civil War print of the CSS Merrimac.

Behind the citadel is the Forbidden City. Sadly, this was largely destroyed by the French in 1946. For once, Americans had nothing to do with this cultural barbarism. The Forbidden City is being slowly restored, but at this time there isn't much to see.

Before the French rule, Vietnam had a similar political structure to China's with an emperor, Confucian rule by mandarins who were chosen by public examination, oppressive landlords, and miserable, over-taxed peasants. But the historical parallels with China are not exact. Christianity hit Vietnam much earlier and much more effectively. A French Jesuit created a Romanized alphabet for Vietnam in 1627, and the French were dabbling in Vietnamese politics before the French Revolution.

North and South Vietnam were split politically at times in the past, and the emperor had different degrees of influence at different times. Many of the emperors seem to have been fairly useless or had poor political judgment.

The Emperor Tu Duc, for example, ascended to the throne in 1847 with the objective of eliminating Christianity in Vietnam. To advance this objective, Tu Duc decreed that native Catholics should be branded on the left cheek with the characters ta dao, meaning infidel.

This was not a wise move, nor was executing French missionary priests. After a complex series of provocations and maneuvers, the French captured Saigon in 1861. The following year Tu Duc had to grant a treaty of concessions to the French. Tu Duc was an unlucky man in a number of ways. Despite having 103 wives, he had no children. Tu Duc was impeccably sterile.

In 1887 the French created the Indochinese Union of Cochin China, Annam, Tonkin, and Cambodia. Cochin China is the area around Saigon and the Delta; Annam is the middle including Hue; and Tonkin is the north and Hanoi. By 1893 the French also controlled Laos.

But fate or yin and yang were already in hot pursuit of the French. In 1890, Ho Chi Minh was born near Hue. Though an admirer of French culture (and a sometime cook and left bank intellectual in Paris), Ho's life work was the successful destruction of French rule in Asia.

The next day we drove to Danang, formerly known as Tourane. Our bus went through rugged, beautiful country, mostly skirting the mountains and going along the coast. In the morning we stopped at the tombs of Tu Duc and of Khai Dinh, a playboy emperor of the 1920s.

Along the road, Mr. Cong pointed out to us the elaborately restored "spirit houses" where family records are kept. Ancestor worship and the extended family have proven more resilient than Communism. On the first day of Tet, a good Vietnamese son is expected to visit his father's tomb. Mr. Cong, a Catholic, noted that only thirty percent of Vietnamese are Buddhists but one hundred percent are ancestor worshipers.

I also noticed that the one-meter gauge, north-south railway is running again, though how useful it is to have a narrow gauge railway as the main north-south line is questionable.

The French were not good colonialists anywhere and were particularly brutal and inept in Vietnam. Apart from the dinky railway, the French developed little in the way of infrastructure or industry or educational institutions.

British colonies of any size were expected to be self-financing and commercially successful. In Egypt and in India there were large stock exchanges before the First World War. The British introduced legal systems, accounting, and created local universities. The British built proper railways and massive dams and bridges. True, the British were out to make money— "trade follows the flag"—and they were sometimes racist, but they left a solid infrastructure behind.

Vietnam is rich in minerals and has wonderful soil. It has splendid harbors and energetic people with a Confucian attitude towards learning. The French did little with this potential, though they did create a major prison system complete with Polo Condore or Con Son Island, the local Devil's Island. The French built a few bridges and brought a few bright or pliable Vietnamese to France to be acculturated. But that was it.

The railway runs along the old Route One, the Street without Joy, which our bus drove on. Much evidence of the French and American wars is visible: pillboxes, concrete emplacements, and so on. We went over the spectacular "Sea of Clouds" pass. Nervous travelers should sit on the mountain-side of the bus.

Going up the steep pass, we saw western bicyclists. The humid heat outside our air-conditioned bus was fierce. Mr. Cong said that when he first saw westerners on bikes on Route One, he wondered what crime they had committed at home. The heat and the heavy truck traffic make Route One unappealing as a biking venue.

At the top of the pass are a series of pillboxes and a low fort. Crouching inside one of the pillboxes in the nightly fog, waiting for a Viet Cong sapper to lob a grenade through the firing slit, must have been the essence of terror.

Having only known the cities and the flat rice growing areas of South Vietnam, I hadn't realized the horror of fighting up in the hills. Seeing the hills and the long valleys leading up into them from the coastal plains made me wonder why I had ever believed that the Vietnam War was winnable. Though there is little physical resemblance, I had the same feeling of military hopelessness when I visited the beaches at Gallipoli and looked up at the heights.

I brooded on these matters.

Alyson urged me not to notice things like pillboxes and not to talk about the war; there were wonderful views and stunning plants to look at everywhere. While we were in Vietnam, the frangipani had no leaves, but the first flowers were appearing. Hibiscuses were everywhere, as were lilies and orchids.

Vietnamese dietary habits mean there is far less to see in the way of bird and animal life.

As with the Chinese, vegetarianism isn't big with the Vietnamese. Snakes, dogs, rats, and monkeys should move smartly if they wish to avoid appearing on menus. Mr. Cong told us that he likes fried water beetles and crickets. And fish heads—most particularly fish heads. Not only is our food too bland for Mr. Cong; it lacks bones. Mr. Cong would like to write a cookbook, to be titled The Joy of Fish Heads.

Vietnam is a young country of eighty million people. The population has more than doubled since the war and is still rapidly growing. More than half the population is under twenty-five. The war is ancient history for them; Americans are of great interest to the young Vietnamese and not just as sources of tourist income. Everyone wants to practice English.

Alyson is right. Young Americans should go to Vietnam, completely forget the war and enjoy a spectacular country.

For those of us who are somewhat older, whether American or Vietnamese, forgetting may never be easy. Many fine American books have been written about the war, particularly Stanley Karnow's magisterial Vietnam.

Those wanting to understand what the Vietnamese felt should read Bao Ninh's The Sorrow of War, *a novel of extraordinary power and grief, that in a deep way echoes* All Quiet on the Western Front.

During the Vietnam War, Professor Van Slyke led a faculty antiwar protest movement at Stanford. We talked a great deal about what the war had meant to different Asian peoples as well as to Americans. It was a great plus to have this wise and warm man on the trip, quite apart from learning so much from his wonderful informal talks about Asian history.

March 1, 2007; Furama Resort, China Beach, Danang

This low, elegant beach resort is a good example of how easy it is to ignore the war in modern Vietnam. The resort is right on the beach where the Marines landed in 1965, but there is no sign whatsoever of a military presence. Instead there is one of the longest and most spectacular beaches you will ever see. The sea, however, is rough, and there is almost always a dangerous offshore Pacific current. Flags on the beach warn swimmers of the currents.

When swimming, the cross-current off China Beach demands constant caution. I had some good body surfing close to shore, and then swam laps in a vast freshwater black infinity pool.

Unfortunately, our time at this really beautiful and luxurious resort was marred by Alyson developing the worst allergic reaction I have ever seen. First, she was covered with vast geographic hives, complete with a raised map of Africa on her backside. Then, she became pale and weak and her mouth and eyelids began to swell.

Always brave, Alyson was calm, but I was terrified. Alyson is never ill and isn't allergic to anything. What if she had trouble breathing, I thought?

A key advantage of going with Stanford was that Eli and Lindsay were on the case at once and could call Stanford for advice. "Happy Rubbernecking Tours

Inc." do not have people like Eli or Lindsay. Eli had loads of past medical crisis experience to draw on and was highly reassuring, though he told us later that he had been greatly concerned. The resort's resident doctor, a young, elegant Vietnamese woman, arrived pronto and gave Alyson prednisone and pain killers.

March 2, 2007; Metropole Hotel, Hanoi

The next morning Alyson was no better, but we flew to Hanoi anyway. After reaching the hotel, Eli arranged for us to go to International SOS, a chain of Australian-based private clinics that are in most major Asian cities. I can recommend International SOS highly.

We had a bit of a wait, but the clinic was well organized, had modern equipment, and was clean. We saw Dr. Soraya Berrreghis-Mazery, a Frenchwoman long resident in Hanoi. She said that the Vietnamese doctor's treatment had been correct but the dosages too low. At that, Alyson was given a massive cortisone injection and serious anti-histamines.

Dr. Berrreghis-Mazery also said that she saw lots of allergies like Alyson's, that it was almost never possible precisely to identify the cause, though it was often shellfish, and that Alyson would need to carry an ephedrine pen in the future.

Alyson improved rapidly. We were able to join the group on a cyclo tour of Hanoi that afternoon. We were pedaled slowly through various old neighborhoods where all the shops on a given street catered to a single trade like metal working or tailoring.

Unlike say, Venezuelans, the Vietnamese have a strong tradition of making things from metal and a flair for mechanical tinkering. I'd noticed in 1993 how the Vietnamese were keeping our old American Army trucks running. I'd seen men and boys by the side of the road, squatting, filing pieces of raw steel into truck parts, using only files, calibers for measuring, and emery cloth.

As the cyclos slowly moved past the shop houses, we noticed large lathes and drill presses crammed into tiny shop fronts. Young boys handed older men complicated metal pieces for machining. Teenaged apprentices sat in front on the pavement taking apart compressors.

The weather was overcast while we were in Hanoi, so the heat was bearable. I walked a lot. Rain made me buy an imitation Nike baseball hat from a street vendor for a dollar. Mr. Cong informed me later that this was precisely twice what I should have paid. Hanoi is generally a good deal cooler than Saigon year round. Hanoi is lower in points than the Red River and is protected by raised dikes. Han Oi means "inside river."

I love the Metropole Hotel in Hanoi. It never closed under Communism and is like a grand old ocean liner with wonderful Franco-Vietnamese fusion food and antique Louis Vuitton steamer trunks on display in the marble-tiled lobby. Miranda, our globe-trotting daughter, took a Vietnamese cooking course at the Metropole.

That evening we went to see the water puppets, a five-hundred-year-old art form. The large puppets float on a pond at the front of the theater. They are moved by long poles under the water. The puppets act out village boy meets village girl stories to a musical accompaniment. I enjoyed the performance, though some of our party, generally an open-minded lot, found it tedious. The traditional music played on old instruments was the greatest charm of the water puppet show for me.

The next day, our group made the customary visit to Ho's Mausoleum. Even though Ho had been freshened up recently by the same Russian embalming team that maintains Lenin, I refused to wait in line in the sun for more than an hour to see him. Not out of some American pique, but because it was fiercely hot and more agreeable to stand in the shade, guard the cameras—Ho like Lenin is camera shy—and talk with Eli and Professor Van Slyke.

I had also seen enough capitalist changes in Hanoi since my visit in 1993 to be sure that Uncle Ho would be very, very unhappy about them, so there was no need to gloat over his actual goat-bearded corpse.

Much is made of Ho's role as the George Washington of Vietnam. He was indeed the father of his country in many ways, but Ho only wished to be the father of a workers' and peasants' Communist state, whatever the price the country had to pay in blood. Ho was a true believer.

So sing halleluiah! Ho's Vietnam has disappeared; Vietnam has lost its Communist faith. The Vietnamese people are saved.

Alyson, who queued, reported that Uncle Ho was in fine form, right down to his wispy beard.

That night we walked with most of the group to the Hanoi Opera House, across from the Metropole. The Opera House is a little jewel of a French theater that seats about three hundred with tiers of boxes rising above the original carved wooden orchestra seats where we were sitting. The music was mostly Mozart and well performed, but I was most taken by the pretty young female violinists.

Our group went on to Laos and Cambodia. We witnessed much of interest in those beautiful countries that had paid a heavy price for having been part of French Indochine and hence part of the battleground of our war.

But that is another tale.

Goodbye Vietnam

Visiting Vietnam, even the Cu Chi Tunnels, is not like visiting Antietam or Verdun (and if you don't know what those places represent, shame on you). The country is beautiful; there are few marks of war and the people, arguably the best looking on earth, are intelligent, friendly, and interesting. But there is another level, another dimension, to life in Vietnam. The country you see was paid for in blood.

Hanoi is not really about opera or folk art performances. Basically, Hanoi is about politics. Hanoi will always be to Saigon as Washington is to LA.

To understand the price ordinary Vietnamese paid for a Communist victory, visit the Fine Arts Museum in Hanoi. Despite the name, this is a museum of Vietnamese history and culture.

In a gallery containing examples of Vietnamese living quarters, there is one recreated room showing a truly Spartan lifestyle. The label on this exhibit read: "1975–1986 was a dramatic period and a profound lesson about the laws of social development."

This is a profound understatement.

During that period after the end of the war, an individual without party connections was rationed to five meters of cloth per annum. The sandals worn by most people were made from old American tires and called "Ho Chi Minh Nikes." Rice was also strictly rationed because of the failure of collective farming. Hunger was routine. People sat on wooden crates and looked into their empty rice bowls for entertainment because chairs and TV were only for cadres.

And this was the life of the politically acceptable. Hundreds of thousands of the politically tainted were put through reeducation camps. Many died in these camps. Millions had died in the war. There were reminders everywhere of those who were gone.

For years, Vietnam went nowhere spiritually or economically. It was one of the poorest countries on earth.

Over time, younger Vietnamese came to realize that such a life was not endurable. The older party leaders were sidelined. The younger ones cozied up to capitalism, just as in China.

Since 1993, Vietnam has gone through *doi moi* or economic openness. The boom that started in Saigon has spread to Hanoi. Much of the Hanoi Hilton prison, where John McCain was held, has been torn down for a real estate development. Corruption is rampant and is known as "lubricating oil." There is a thriving stock exchange and over two hundred listed companies. GDP per capita has more than doubled since 1993. Many women have started tiny businesses.

Officially, Vietnam is a "market economy with a socialist orientation." Just like Norway or The People's Republic of Vermont.

The population of Vietnam is among the youngest on earth. They appear optimistic and have good reason to be. Writing and music and art have revived. Vietnam is rich in resources and well placed geographically. A promising future lies before it.

The future of the United States is less clear. American veterans now in their sixties can remember not just another Vietnam but another United States—a country that seemed on the verge of shaking off a constricting society and creating a freer and more exciting one.

After wrenching change, a new American society emerged, but it is not the hopeful and vibrant one that some expected; it is fractured and unhealthy. Vietnam poisoned some of America's hopes and dreams. Did America fail in Vietnam? Yes, we failed ourselves.

We gave way to a contemptible and ongoing love affair with failure and self-contempt that still pollutes our greatest universities and our politics.

But, in an odd and indirect way, we did not fail the Vietnamese. The impact of western reality and the overwhelming effort of the war ruined the dream of Communism. Ultimately, the Vietnamese defeated their own demons and may be on the verge of creating a good society.

Eat your heart out, Ho Chi Minh.

Made in United States
Troutdale, OR
05/18/2024

19964667R00174